Synagogue Song

ALSO THESE WORKS WERE
COMPILED BY JONATHAN L. FRIEDMANN
AND PUBLISHED BY MCFARLAND

---

*Music, Theology and Worship:
Selected Writings, 1841–1896* (2011)

*The Value of Sacred Music: An Anthology
of Essential Writings, 1801–1918* (2009)

*Music in Jewish Thought: Selected
Writings, 1890–1920* (2009)

Synagogue Song

An Introduction to Concepts, Theories and Customs

Jonathan L. Friedmann

McFarland & Company, Inc., Publishers
Jefferson, North Carolina, and London

LIBRARY OF CONGRESS CATALOGUING-IN-PUBLICATION DATA

Friedmann, Jonathan L., 1980–
    Synagogue song : an introduction to concepts, theories and customs / Jonathan L. Friedmann.
       p.   cm.
    Includes bibliographical references and index.

    ISBN 978-0-7864-7061-7
    softcover : acid free paper ∞

    1. Synagogue music — History and criticism. I. Title.
ML3195.F74 2012
782.3'6—dc23   2012005929

BRITISH LIBRARY CATALOGUING DATA ARE AVAILABLE

© 2012 Jonathan L. Friedmann. All rights reserved

No part of this book may be reproduced or transmitted in any form or by any means, electronic or mechanical, including photocopying or recording, or by any information storage and retrieval system, without permission in writing from the publisher.

Front cover image © 2012 Shutterstock

Manufactured in the United States of America

McFarland & Company, Inc., Publishers
  Box 611, Jefferson, North Carolina 28640
    www.mcfarlandpub.com

Table of Contents

Preface 1

Introduction 3

I. Foundations, Functions and Figures 9

What Is Sacred Music? 9
Music and Civilization 10
A Most Ancient Ritual 12
Musical Supervisors 13
Community and Liturgy 15
Sacred Time, Sacred Sound 16
Practical Functions of
 Synagogue Music 18
A Resonant World 19
Singing Metaphysics 20
Sanctification 22
Music as Language 23
Beauty in Sacred Song 24
Some Thoughts on "Traditional"
 Synagogue Music 26
Creating a Synagogue Musical
 Tradition 27
The Development of Jewish
 Music Traditions 29

Judging Synagogue Song 31
The Problems of Meaning 32
Conformity and Survival 34
Charismatic Tunes 36
Jewish Youth and Musical
 Change 38
Nusach Variations 39
Sacred Classics 41
Sing a New Song 43
Musical Layers 45
A *Shir Koddesh* 47
Instruments of Worship 48
Richard Dawkins and
 Synagogue Song 50
Darwin, Heschel, Music,
 and Marriage 53
Liturgical Hits 55
The Legacy of Jack Gottlieb 57

II. Spirituality, Emotions and Identity 59

Religion, Emotion and Music 59
The Divine Lover of Music 61
To Edify and Glorify 63
Six Songs in the Hebrew Bible 64
Music, Prayer and Concentration 66
An Instrument Divine 67
Singing Is Believing 69
From Heart to Heart 70
Moods, Modes and Musical Meaning 72
Mystery and Melody 73
Singing, Health and Prayer 74
Heart and Mind 76
Serving God with Joy 77
Niggunim and Augustine 79
Holy Noises 80
Songs Without Words 82
Hymns of Praise 83
Stereotyping Synagogue Sounds 84
Singing for Joy 86
Being the Music 87
Absolute Music, Absolute Worship 89
Fight Songs and Fighting Words 90
Musical Taste, Musical Fact 92
Ethnicity in Jewish Music 93
Historicism and Futurism 95
Music and the *Mitzvah* of Nostalgia 96
Musical *Minhag* 98
Identity and Memory 101
Performing Identity 103
Diversity and Balance 104

III. Holidays and Liturgy 107

Shabbat Singing 107
Music and the Moods of Shabbat 108
Opening Songs on Shabbat 109
Vayekhulu and the Renewal of Time 111
Reinterpretation Through Song 112
Thanksgiving Every Week 114
The Modern Origins of an "Ancient" Tune 115
Springtime and the Song of Songs 117
Song of Redemption 118
Sound of the Sea 120
Akdamut and the Power of Song 121
Songs of Renewal 123
Moses, Music and Eurocentrism 125
The Curious Case of *Kol Nidrei* 127
The Sound of Sincerity 128
Rejoicing in Torah 130
Songs of Victory and Light 131
The *Maoz Tzur* Melody: Sacred or Sinful? 132
Making Noise 134
Music, Midrash and *Megillah* 135

Tension and Release   137
Aleinu: Its Storied Past and Sacred Melodies   138
Adon Olam: Master of the World   141
The Myth of *Ein Keloheinu*   142
The Religious Roots of *Hava Nagila*   144

IV. Cantors, Choirs and Congregations   147

The Cantor at the Center of the World   147
Singing and Prophecy   148
Cantors and Levites   149
More Than a Voice   151
The Cantorial Ideal   152
The Cantor's Prayer   154
Cantors, Rabbis, Hitters and Pitchers   155
The Choir in Jewish History   157
The Music of Heaven on Earth   159
Unity, Participation and the Choral Experience   160
From Choir to Congregation   161
Why Congregations Sing   163
A Blended Sound   165
The Limits of Congregational Singing   167
Good and Friendly Music   168

Appendix: Jewish Music Research   171
Bibliography   183
Index   189

Preface

It seems that music has always and everywhere been a fixture of Jewish religious life. There is no shortage of musical references in the biblical account, which appear in celebrated contexts like the Red Sea crossing and King Solomon's coronation, and the everyday settings of work and family gatherings. We are reminded throughout the Book of Psalms of the importance of chanting hymns and singing prayerful songs, an idea that traveled into the Talmud's recommendation that prayers be offered "in a pleasant voice" (BT *Hullin* 91b). In our own time, music plays a central role in virtually every Jewish occasion, from worship and weddings, to funerals and memorial services.

Though the specific sounds are shaped by a myriad of geographical, denominational, and historical influences, Jewish worship songs of all types exhibit four main functions: communing with the divine, imparting key concepts and ideals, giving voice to personal and collective emotions, and strengthening bonds to community and heritage. More than any other ritual element, liturgical song is the lifeblood of the Jewish faith, and a primary mode through which Jewish identity and affiliation are articulated and sustained.

This book is designed as an introduction to theoretical approaches to the study of Jewish sacred music. Through one hundred brief and focused examinations on a range of topics, it explores reasons for — and not merely the existence of — Jewish prayer song. Though the essays are interrelated in terms of subject matter and theoretical approach, each imparts a unique, self-contained lesson. And while the chapters offer diverse perspectives and cover wide ground, a number of intentionally reoccurring themes emerge, most prominently the diversity of Jewish music, the interaction of music and identity, music's emotional and spiritual impact, the text-tone relationship, and the manner in which the prayers are sung (cantorial, choral, accompanied, *a cappella*, etc.). The goal is that these digestible distillations of complex and sometimes challenging topics will invite readers to a fuller appreciation of theories, concepts, and customs in the fertile field of synagogue song, and a grasp of underlying rationale for the ubiquitous presence of musical tones in Jewish worship.

Several individuals helped shape the content of this book, whether directly or indirectly, wittingly or unwittingly. Each essay began with a spark of insight, which gradually developed into a refined argument as I reflected upon and applied the resulting thesis to a given setting or circumstance. These flashes often arose during my thinking or reading on the subject, or while listening to or performing a certain piece. Other times, they grew out of formal and informal discussions with colleagues, teachers, students, and friends. Because the chapters that follow were written over an extended period, it is difficult to recall each person who stimulated, encouraged, or challenged me along the way. Nevertheless, I wish to thank those who come immediately to mind, as this book would not be what it is without their input, big or small. Those who helped guide my thinking include: cantors Perryne Anker, Jay Frailich, Don Gurney, Nathan Lam, and William Sharlin; rabbis Meredith Cahn, Mordecai Finley, and Haim Ovadia; my pulpit partners, rabbis Hershel Brooks, Yocheved Mintz, and Elaine Schnee; professors Joel Gereboff, Tamar Frankiel, Michael Isaacson, Kathleen Rochester, Jon R. Stone, Carlos R. Piar, Brad Stetson, Marvin A. Sweeney, and Herrie van Rooy; and editors David W. Epstein, Roni Kripper, and Robert Mirisch. Special gratitude is owed as well to my loving wife, Elvia, whose keen eye and honest feedback have been vital to the development of this volume.

Introduction

I began writing this book sometime in 2008. Having recently made the transition from a graduate program in the sociology of religion to the seminary setting of cantorial school, I eagerly set out to locate and absorb as much literature as I could find dealing with socio-theoretical, philosophical, and theological aspects of the synagogue musical experience. As a theoretically minded practitioner of synagogue song, my primary interests were in origins and functions—that is, explanations for the union of text and music in Jewish worship. And as an educator equally drawn to the minutia of the relevant disciplines and committed to reaching the widest audience possible, I made a point of presenting my findings in a way that was substantive enough to appeal to the expert, yet accessible enough to attract the lay reader.

From the outset, this project was met with an obstacle that complicated my search for pertinent inquiries and challenged me to arrive at my own conclusions: Jewish scholars rarely attempt socio-religious or theological explorations of worship song. These areas have received much fuller and more abundant consideration from writers on church song; so much so that pre-modern research into Judaically related music was predominantly penned by Christian authorities, the perspectives of whom tend to be too dogmatic for easy application to Jewish thought. And though a number of useful surveys and regional histories have been published over the past several decades, both in book and article form, material confronting the basic question of why Jewish liturgy is more often sung than spoken remains scarce. Motivated by this gap in scholarship, I decided to compose one hundred short essays employing religious theories, ethnomusicological tools, theological concepts, sociological observations, and other academic devices to explain in fresh and creative ways the fundamental relationship of music and prayer in Jewish religious life.

Before a reader embarks on this journey, it is worthwhile to consider a few points regarding the paucity of theoretical investigations in the field. This shortage of material can be attributed to several converging factors. First, there is an emphasis on text study over aesthetics in Jewish religious circles that has existed since at least the rabbinic period. With the rise of *Wissenschaft des Judentums* in the nineteenth century, Judaism's logocentrism was carried into the critical-scientific investigation of Jewish history and literature. And so, while the historical development, stylistic features, and linguistic nuances of sacred texts were regarded as deserving of study, the music with which these texts were presented was given little (if any) attention outside of a handful of writings. Related to this is a second, more general perception of music's secondary role. While humans are conditioned to process the symbolic system of language and rely on words in virtually all facets of life — whether the words are thought or articulated in some way — the abstract symbolism of music, while communicative, is notoriously subjective and difficult to pin down or describe. This has led to an unspoken consensus that music is more apt for experience than examination. Third, the analysis of music is a skill historically limited to a small group of specialists. In the Jewish world, the evolution from oral transmission to written transcription of synagogue song was rarely known prior to 1800. And despite the laity's familiarity with a plethora of tunes and chanted motifs, deeper knowledge of origins, accretions, and technical aspects is for the most part limited to professionals. Fourth, the specialized nature of Jewish musicology, while certainly intriguing, has placed the bulk of studies out of popular reach. What is available to lay readers can be boiled down to a handful of worthy historical overviews.

This is not to say that research into synagogue music is in any way disappointing. On the contrary, my attraction to the field and desire to contribute to it are inspired by the insightful contributions of others and the many doors their work has opened. The high level of talent and acumen displayed by this small group of experts has been evident since the inception of the field, which came with the Jews' larger embrace of modernity in the nineteenth century. As mentioned, the majority of scholars of that period devoted their attention to text study; but a handful turned their focus to music as part of the wider acceptance of historical concepts and methods, cultural and ritual analysis, and other areas of Western scholarship. In the main, these early contributors took a broad view of the subject, producing sweeping historical surveys along with ethnographic works that included far-reaching claims about the unity of the world's Jewish music—a romantic notion that has since given way to the sober recognition that Jewish music is as diverse as the people who perform it. Since the nineteenth century, the study of Jewish musical output has blossomed into a fertile enterprise. Yet, while seemingly all subcultures, movements, and regional forms have received at least some degree of attention—a fact made apparent in this book's appendix—the music of the Jews remains an underappreciated subcategory within the academic study of Judaism.

As noted, particularly lacking is the appraisal of synagogue song through the tools of religious theory. Over the past few years my efforts to shine greater light on the theoretical side of Jewish music has taken me into three distinct directions. The first was an edited anthology, *20th Century Synagogue Music: Essential Readings* (Isaac Nathan, 2010), which includes nineteen brief articles originally published between 1904 and 1988. Each is a seminal essay written or presented by an influential twentieth-century scholar and/or practitioner of Jewish music and that, more importantly, touches on a key theoretical area of synagogue song: music's relation to divinity, the social functions of worship music, the concept of tradition, the position of the cantor, or future directions. Addressing these subjects from a variety of personal and disciplinary approaches, the writers share a keen understanding of the invaluable role music plays in shaping and defining Jewish religious practice and identity. Favoring an insider's perspective, the book brings together essays from individuals with a vested interest in synagogue music—cantors, composers, conductors, and Jewish musicologists—yet avoids articles too bogged down by technical detail to have wide appeal. Among the esteemed authors included are Jacob Beimel, A. W. Binder, Irene Heskes, Samuel Rosenbaum, Sholom Secunda, and Eric Werner.

The second project, *Quotations on Jewish Sacred Music* (Hamilton, 2011), was likewise compiled in response to what I view as a need for Jewish music education and appreciation. It consists of more than 700 quotations—mostly one to three sentences—culled from sources ranging from rabbinic texts and scholarly books and articles, to lectures and letters written by historians, musicologists, cantors, rabbis, composers, conductors, educators, sociologists, anthropologists, Bible scholars, poets, novelists, and social critics. The quotations are divided into five chapters: the first addresses the sundry nature of synagogue music; the second offers words on the role of music in Jewish spirituality and prayer; the third gives insights into the history, requirements, functions, and impact of the cantor; the fourth examines the development and purposes of cantillation, the chanting of biblical texts; and the fifth explores the nature and significance of *nusach ha-tefillah*, modal systems of liturgical chant. The main objective for collecting these opinions and observations was to create a user-friendly research book for scholars, students, and clergy, and, more crucially, to present copious evidence of music's vital place in Jewish religious life, and dispel the common perception of music as mere adornment to sacred texts.

Synagogue Song is my third effort to promote an awareness of theories, concepts, and customs of Jewish sacred music. Like the previous books, it is designed to reach a wide readership, from the uninitiated to the seasoned professional. In order to achieve this, I have employed an inviting tone and, to the best of my ability, strived to blend sophistication with clarity. Some of the angles taken and arguments proposed are by nature intricate, and some deal with topics that might on their surface seem of little interest to non-specialists. But it is a purpose of this volume to expose readers of all levels to these important discussions, and show that their relevance extends beyond insular circles of clergy and synagogue musicians. Because Jewish ceremonies are so saturated with music, all who partake in them can benefit from a better grasp of the issues covered in these pages.

However, in contrast to the two earlier books, the present effort is wholly original. In addition to consisting of my own words (as opposed to an edited compilation), its chapters are meant to add depth to or fill specific gaps in the available theoretical literature. To do so, I have utilized pertinent information from Jewish musicological books and articles, as well as from a slew of interdisciplinary sources, like anthropology and neuroscience. In some cases, this process took me into unusual and unexpected places, as with my evaluation of (mis)conceptions of synagogue song through the writings of Richard Dawkins. But, no matter how abstract a theoretical avenue might at first appear, it is used to clarify, not obscure, the issue at hand.

Despite the creative and sometimes "radical" ideas employed, this book is, in the end, an introduction to the theoretical study of Jewish sacred music. This designation owes to three main characteristics. The first is scope. Many and assorted topics are covered within the four sections of the book. In "Foundations, Functions, and Figures," I delve into the origins and major uses of synagogue song, and turn the spotlight on a few thinkers and composers whose contributions are instructive for understanding this music. The next section, "Spirituality, Emotions, and Identity," explores how and why Jewish prayer melodies stir profound associations, draw congregants together, and create a sense of a transcendent connection. "Holidays and Liturgy" presents case studies in familiar prayers and prayer melodies, and investigates the musical component of a number of central holidays—all with an eye toward discovering the purpose of these musical settings and practices, and assessing the relationship of text and sound. The final section, "Cantors, Choirs, and Congregations," takes an analytical view of the varied ways prayer-songs are performed.

Second, this book is an introduction because, rather than carrying a sustained argument throughout, it is comprised of one hundred lessons in miniature. These essays are self-contained excursions into particular subjects, designed to be both readily intelligible and intellectually sophisticated. Each chapter presents the background, propositions, examination, and implications in one thousand words or less, and each can be read alone, in a grouping, or along with all the others.

The third way this book is an introduction is that its chapters are not intended as the final word, though they are thorough within their limited size. The questions posed, arguments made, and phenomena explored could be expanded to fill larger essays—or in some cases entire volumes—but their aim is to highlight important themes rather than exhaust them. Indeed, this book would fulfill its highest end if it were to inspire further research using tools and concepts I have laid out.

Before concluding, it should be noted that no book on a subject as regionally, denominationally, and aesthetically varied as synagogue song can hope to be truly comprehensive. The sheer volume of rites, customs, personalities, trends, genres, movements, migrations, patterns of assimilation, and so forth makes the field so wide as to exceed the scope of any single volume, introductory or otherwise. Realizing this overwhelming complexity, this book takes a selective approach. Some issues are given more space than others, and there are, inevitably, certain topics that did not fit my agenda. Additionally, because I am a practitioner of synagogue song, many of the examples cited come from my own personal experiences. Although the ideas proposed can be applied to an array of regional, cultural, and historical settings, I write from the perspective of a cantor serving twenty-first century American liberal synagogues. Admittedly, this comes with certain, if unintended, biases toward Ashkenazi sounds, non–Orthodox customs, and concerns that may on the surface appear most relevant to liberal services. Nonetheless, the chapters presented should resonate widely and encourage deeper reflection on and appreciation of synagogue song.

I

Foundations, Functions and Figures

What Is Sacred Music?

The term "sacred music" is somewhat misleading. Unlike jazz music or country music, sacred music does not refer to a specific style. There are, in fact, a number of sacred services written in jazz, country, and other ostensibly "secular" idioms. And lest one think that certain types of music are only found in the church or synagogue, one needs only listen to the recordings of Gregorian, a group that performs Gregorian chant-inspired versions of modern pop and rock songs. Generally speaking, sacred music is designed for use in worship settings, and usually accompanies texts derived from or based on Scripture and liturgy. But many songs marketed for radio play also have strong religious themes. An obvious example is the music of Hassidic reggae singer Matisyahu, whose lyrics are filled with references to Psalms, Kabbalah, rabbinic teachings, and other Jewish sources. All of this suggests that songs of various genres can be called sacred, as long as their content and/or function is religiously directed. Of course, some musical genres have become associated with worship by convention. A large portion of Sephardic synagogue music is essentially the same as Ottoman high court music. Twentieth-century America witnessed the emergence of liturgical music written in the style of 1960s protest songs. Even the core musical elements of the High Holy Days are derived in part from ballads and street songs of medieval Germany. And while it can be argued that a song's sacredness should be based on its ability to bring people closer to God, this, too, is a subjective trait. One person may be spiritually moved by a simple, repetitive chant, while another is touched by the strains of a dissonant, twentieth first-century choral piece. In short, there is no single tone or rhythm that is inherently more sacred than another.

Rabbi Abraham Joshua Heschel offered his thoughts on this matter, arguing that music should never be viewed as holy. Heschel pointed out that Jews "revere sacred Scripture, sacred words," but have no holy music: "[God] is concealed in the biblical words, and our prayers are an attempt to disclose to ourselves what is concealed in those words."[1] In this view, Music is, at best, an indirect conduit to God: it can help us connect to Jewish texts, which in turn help us connect to God. Yet, although his opinion is well grounded theologically, it conflicts with the experience of those who have felt God's presence in music without words, or with words lacking overt religious content.

So, what is *sacred* in sacred music? The answer to this question is that it is the wrong question. "Sacred" is not an adjective describing an aspect of the music itself, but a broad description of its function. Virtually all styles of music have been used in this capacity, and their suitability for worship is, in the end, a matter of taste. It is not necessary (or really possible) to apply objective standards to sacred music. What is important is that the music helps cultivate a prayerful mood, no matter what it sounds like.

1. Abraham Joshua Heschel, *The Insecurity of Freedom* (New York: Macmillan, 1963), 250.

Music and Civilization

The use of music as entertainment is a late and relatively rare phenomenon in human history. Rather than an end in itself, music most often serves as an aid to other, non-musical, objectives and events. Musical tones accompany ceremonies, rituals, and celebrations throughout the world. Songs and chants are frequently used to transmit messages, stories, values, and ideals. Music's many utilitarian genres include work songs, lullabies, military marches, and national anthems. These observations point to the fact that music is much more than a peripheral concern. Since ancient times, music has been a constant and indispensable part of human life. Allusion to this is even made in *Parshat Bereshit*, the opening chapters of the Torah.

The first reference to music in the Bible appears in a compressed passage in Genesis listing the descendants of Cain and the growth of human civilization (Gen. 4:17–22). As in many ancient cultures, the Bible links the invention of music with a mythological personage. His name is Jubal, "the father of all those who play the lyre and pipe" (v. 21).

This short verse is the only place Jubal appears in the biblical text; we have no other accounts of his personality or the music that he made. However, this paucity of information does not necessarily negate Jubal's status or significance. On the contrary, it may be an indication that music — and perhaps the Jubal legend — was so well known in Israelite culture that further descriptions were not needed. As musicologist Alfred Sendrey explained, "The biblical authors took it for granted that the people were thoroughly familiar with musical matters, so that they considered it unnecessary to indulge in long descriptions and minute details."[1]

Jubal's importance is also gleaned from the context in which he is found. In the same passage, we read that his brother, Jabal, was the first to raise cattle (v. 20), and his half-brother, Tubal-Cain, "forged all implements of copper and iron" (v. 22). Mention of music's invention alongside the origins of cattle raising and tool forging reveals an early recognition of the vital role of music in society. Indeed, the Torah seems to imply that herding, metal forging, and music making are the three fundamental professions upon which humanity depends.

Music in ancient Israel was almost entirely of a practical kind, or *Gebrauchsmusik*. It served a variety of daily purposes, like education and divine worship. And, from those days to the present, the collective memories, oral histories, wisdom, and sacred stories of the Jewish people have been contained and passed on in musical tones. Thus, while Jabal can be seen as the ancestor of food production and Tubal-Cain as the ancestor of technology, Jubal is in many ways the ancestor of knowledge.

It is tempting to group music among life's superfluous or auxiliary elements. But doing so ignores the role of melody in conveying ideas and information, facilitating social bonding and cohesion, and a host of other functions. Historically and cross-culturally, music resides at the center rather than the fringes of human experience. This is why we find music placed prominently in the stories of Creation. Without Jubal, the Torah teaches, civilization would be incomplete.

1. Alfred Sendrey, *Music in Ancient Israel* (New York: Philosophical Library, 1969), 60.

A Most Ancient Ritual

Rituals are a link to the past. Lighting Shabbat candles, spinning a dreydl, reciting blessings, eating hamantaschen — these things connect Jews to their ancestors and to the seemingly eternal cycle of the Jewish calendar. Day after day, week after week, year after year, Jews engage in purposely-repetitious activities in order to maintain and feel part of Jewish continuity and collective identity. Because rituals are prescribed and perpetual, they give the impression that they have always and everywhere been a part of Jewish life. It is, perhaps, tempting to envision King David wearing a *kippah* or the rabbis of the Talmud eating bagels and lox before morning Torah study. But, of course, these customs — and indeed all Jewish rituals — developed over centuries and in accordance with specific and changing tastes, ideologies, cultural influences, social and economic conditions, existential needs, and so forth.

This is true even of holidays mentioned in the Bible. In general, these observances began as nature festivals marking a change in season and the harvesting of crops. As time progressed and civilization advanced, these festivals accumulated spiritual significance, and old ceremonies were given new symbolic meanings. A prime example is Passover, which originally marked the coming of spring, but over the ages morphed into an occasion for the retelling of the Exodus and all of the foods, pillows, and other paraphernalia it now requires. But throughout all of these transformations and accretions one thing has remained constant: song.

The Bible's first mention of communal worship is also its first description of what can be called congregational singing. When Moses, Miriam, and the Israelites escaped Pharaoh's forces and crossed the

Red Sea, their response was to sing praise to God. This spontaneous prayer-song, evidently sung as a call and response, set a pattern for virtually all Jewish celebrations and ceremonies that would follow. Various biblical verses associate song with ritualistic occasions, including weddings (Jer. 7:34), funerals (Job 30:31), banquets (Isa. 5:12), and religious festivals (2 Chr. 30:21). In the Jerusalem Temple, singing and instruments were a constant accompaniment to the sacrificial rite. As these practices evolved over the centuries into the liturgical traditions we have today, the musical component persevered. This does not mean to suggest that the actual melodies were preserved: we do not know what music sounded like in biblical times, and the majority of melodies sung today are derived from the nineteenth century and later. Rather, it is the activity of singing that has survived countless other changes to Jewish ritual.

It can thus be said that singing is the oldest form of communal ritual. Before the first challah was ever baked, there was devotional song. Before the first prayer book was ever printed, Jews communicated with the divine through musical tones. Indeed, before there was a Torah, the Israelites sang to God. So, whenever a congregation sings a prayer, and no matter how recent the melody, it is engaging in a most ancient form of religious expression. It is, in a very real way, carrying on a practice that began at the shores of the Red Sea.

Musical Supervisors

Work songs have long served an important purpose in manual labor. Music provides rhythmic support and accentuation to daily work, helping to coordinate the efforts, relieve the tedium, and ease the burden of laborers. From archaic times to the present, songs have accompanied herding, ploughing, harvesting, sailing, building, and a variety of other tasks. Musician and researcher Ted Gioia notes the prevalence of work songs in the three major types of labor: agricultural, pastoral, and industrial[1]; and others cite the use of music in domestic, office, and retail jobs.

The Bible mentions song in connection with well digging (Num. 21:17–18), farming (Isa. 16:10), and construction (Job 38:6–7). It is also likely that the Israelites sang during their toils in Egypt, and that building projects in Judah and Israel were aided by music. This latter point may, in fact, be hinted at in 2 Chronicles 34:12–13, which states that the Levites supervised Temple repairs during the eighteenth year of King Josiah's reign.

These verses do not make explicit reference to work songs, but simply relate that Levites were appointed as overseers of artisans, masons, and "all who worked at each and every task" (v. 13). Most commentators read this as an expansion of the Levitical role, which, up to that point, was primarily centered on the sanctuary and the singing and playing of ceremonial music. As such, the Levites would have been expected to watch over and direct scores of laborers whose skills fell outside their realm of expertise. However, the text is careful to identify the Levites as "master musicians" (v. 12), which may suggest that their supervisory function was as musicians rather than foremen.

It is not difficult to imagine the Levites setting up choirs and orchestras to provide musical accompaniment for the Temple workers. Just as their music supported the choreography and gave a rhythm to the sacrificial ritual, it would have helped pace the work and synchronize the movements of the presumably hundreds of laborers. Such music would have taken the workers' minds off of the monotonous and arduous chopping, piling, loading, hammering, cutting, breaking, lifting, digging, etc., or perhaps even provided religious motivation for them to carry on. After all, as restorers of the Temple, they were engaged in a sacred duty.

Another reason 2 Chronicles 34:12–13 may be a subtle reference to Levitical work songs is because the Bible is generally vague when it comes to describing music or musical performances. Life in ancient Israel was apparently so saturated with music that the biblical authors deemed it unnecessary to delve into such details. Many musical references are brief or incidental to larger storylines, and in some cases the use of music is only implied from context. Viewed as a whole, these citations reveal a civilization in which singing and instrumental playing were part of virtually all aspects of life. In such a setting, it seems natural that music would have been played to assist the Temple workers.

1. Ted Gioia, *Work Songs* (Durham, NC: Duke University Press, 2006).

Community and Liturgy

The centrality of prayer in Jewish religious life is evidenced by the complex, multi-layered, and highly structured nature of the liturgy. Over centuries, liturgical texts developed to meet the changing socio-religious concerns and needs of the world's Jewish communities. The prayer book contains selections from the Bible, rabbinic writings from the Talmudic and Geonic periods (third to eleventh centuries), and a variety of prayers, poems, and meditations from subsequent generations. Wide-ranging spiritual and theological interpretations, shifting conceptual emphases, ideological biases, and the voices of myriad authors found their way into the liturgy. At their core, these prayers are meant to draw attention to the divine presence in the world and stipulate the moods and themes of specific sacred times.

The fixed forms of Jewish prayer reflect an early rabbinic recognition that spontaneous prayer alone, no matter how eloquent or sincere, ultimately falls short of fulfilling humanity's obligation to address the divine. If prayer arose exclusively as a natural response to important moments in one's life, good or bad, then it would follow that "ordinary" life does not call for gratitude or praise. On the other hand, if one were to recognize divinity in all things, he or she might become consumed by an impractical desire to pray all day. The sages therefore established the ritual of thrice-daily prayer, which fulfills one's obligation to pray regularly as well as the personal need to praise, petition, and thank the Almighty in response to the events of life.

Jewish liturgy is also community-oriented: most prayers are scribed in the first person plural form and address issues of corporate concern. Certain sections of the liturgical service are omitted in the absence of a *minyan*, a quorum of ten adult Jews. For example, if fewer than ten are present, the *Kaddish* is not recited, and the designated portions of the Torah and *Haftarah* are not chanted (*Megillah* 4:3). Maimonides gave divine justification for the communal character of Jewish prayer: "Congregational prayer is always heard by the Lord.... Hence, a person should assimilate himself with the congregation, and never recite his prayers in private when he is able to attend a congregation" (*Hilchot Tefillah* 8:1). This position is reflected in the custom that if an individual must pray alone, he or she should try to pray at the same time as the congregation and use the same liturgy, excluding only those prayers that require a *minyan*.

These two characteristics of the liturgy, fixity and emphasis on community, account largely for the pervasive use of singing in Jewish worship services. Because Jewish prayer is highly ritualized, following a set order determined by the time of day and date on the calendar, it relies chiefly on interpretation to ensure its ongoing vitality. Just as the Torah has its dynamic counterpart in the *midrashic* (interpretive) literature, the static words of prayer are given "new life" through musical exploration. These interpretive traditions not only provide the Torah and prayer book with a sense of freshness, but have also contributed to the very survival of the fixed texts.

Music likewise amplifies the communal character of Jewish worship. Much more than words alone, music promotes a sense of unity within a group. The shared experience of music works to consolidate the intellectual and emotional energies of the community, fostering or enhancing a sense of affiliation and unity. Heschel wrote that the cantor's singing can "convert a plurality of praying individuals into a unity of worship."[1] And when a congregation sings together, individual voices blend in a unified sound, creating an audible representation of the group itself.

The musical nature of Jewish services is rooted in more than merely *hiddur mitzvah*— the beautification of a commandment. Perhaps more directly than any other medium, music connects worshipers to the words of prayer and to one another. Thus, the singing of liturgy serves the crucial dual function of defending against the potential monotony of language and uniting the congregation in common purpose and sentiments.

1. Abraham Joshua Heschel, *The Insecurity of Freedom* (New York: Macmillan, 1963), 243.

Sacred Time, Sacred Sound

One of the main functions of ritual music is to facilitate collective experiences. Music closely tied to specific occasions, texts, or concepts can transform a group of individuals into a community imbued with a shared mythic consciousness. In virtually all of the world's religious traditions, the sounds of song and chant demarcate sacred from secular time and space, and substantially comprise the emotional underpinnings of worship. Through the direct pathway of human emotions, ritual music can stimulate a deep sense of unity among worshipers, and facilitate or enhance communication between humanity and the divine. Taken together, these relationships—horizontal between individuals and vertical between the community and God—form the foundation of religious life itself, and validate the prominent role of music within it.

In the synagogue, communal emotions are often aroused by changes in the musical presentation of the liturgy. Modal and melodic variations serve to distinguish morning from evening services, weekdays from Shabbat, festivals from holy days, and so on. Much more than plain reading, the singing of liturgy works to fuse group focus, fastening the worshipers' attention on a particular service or section of liturgy, and evoking common associations through the shared experience of familiar sounds. For an individual aware of the musical nuances of the liturgical year, and in communities where musical choices are determined by the sacred calendar, music serves as an emotionally charged symbol of the sacred moment.

This collective transformation is readily achieved through seasonal leitmotifs: melodies and melodic fragments that embody and recall specific times on the Jewish calendar. Examples include the so-called *Mi-Sinai* motifs of Rosh Hashanah and Yom Kippur and the various holiday songs that have come down through the generations. Such melodies are, in essence, mnemonic devices, storing and prompting distinct feelings and memories.

These leitmotifs are typically used for several texts during a given festival or holiday. This practice is meant to stir up sentiments linked to a time or place, and immediately bring to mind the personal and communal significance of the day. In congregations of the Western Ashkenazi rite, this is displayed in the adaptation of holiday melodies to *Mi Chamocha* (Who is like You), a prayer found in evening and morning services throughout the year. On Hanukkah, for instance, the representative theme for *Mi Chamocha* is taken from *Maoz Tzur*, which commemorates the triumph of the Maccabees. On Passover, the melody is derived from *Addir Hu*, which longs for the re-establishment of the Jerusalem temple "speedily and in our day." Shavuot finds *Mi Chamocha* sung to *Akdamut*, an Aramaic poem sung prior to that festival's Torah reading, and on Sukkot it adopts the melody used for the shaking of the *lulav*.

These variations demonstrate the power of a familiar melody, even when detached from its original text, to instantly create musical associations. Upon hearing these seasonal leitmotifs, the listener is not only reminded of what occasion it is, but also of the various personal and communal memories, relationships, sentiments, and sensual experiences associated with the day.

Practical Functions of Synagogue Music

Throughout human history, singing has been a primary medium for retaining and passing on culture and oral traditions. Ancient Greek authors used chant in memorizing and performing their works, and wandering poet-musicians of West Africa, known as *griots*, are living repositories of history. In a similar way, chanting has for millennia been central to the transmission and reception of biblical texts. Through melodic presentation, the Bible's historical narratives, moral and ethical teachings, religious concepts, wisdom and laws are instilled in the minds of listeners. All of this points to an important phenomenon: words set to music are more easily remembered than those that are only read or spoken.

This is seen in synagogue worship. Jewish liturgy is generally sung rather than recited, and most Jews who attend services develop an affinity for a setting or two of a given prayer. This is not simply a matter of preference, though there are many personal reasons for an individual to prefer one tune to another. On a practical level, a familiar melody helps one to recall the prayer it accompanies. This is true for both short verses, like *Bar'chu*, and longer texts, like *Adon Olam*. And since Hebrew is not the spoken language of most Jews, such memorization is especially important.

Worshipers who repeatedly sing a prayer-song usually have little trouble remembering the text in its entirety — a phenomenon that stands in contrast to the "gist memories" recalled after hearing a sermon or speech. This is because songs utilize musical and linguistic devises that compress messages, such as rhyme, alliteration, rhythmic patterns, recurring melodic phrases, and repeated choruses.

Learning prayers through song also encourages worshipers to take ownership of the liturgical ritual. The better one is acquainted with prayer-texts, the more he or she feels a full participant in the service. This is a main reason why synagogues typically stick to a limited repertoire of congregational tunes. These melodies, sung one service to the next, make it possible for the entire congregation to become well versed in the liturgy.

There are, then, two primary functions of familiar synagogue songs: facilitating the absorption of texts, and enabling ownership of the prayer experience. Like most people, most synagogues have favorite melodies. These cherished tunes, sung on a regular basis, invite participation and, in turn, deepen the congregation's engagement in religious life. Familiar prayer settings are therefore essential tools for shaping and intensifying Jewish religious identity.

A Resonant World

All known cultures have singing, associate singing with the supernatural, and accompany religious activities with song. These general observations, confirmed by volumes of anthropological research, demonstrate the ubiquity of two aspects of the human experience: music and religion. We are distinguished from other animals not only by our reasoning capacity (Homo Sapiens), but also our instinct for music (Homo Musicus) and our yearning for a transcendent force in the universe (Homo Religiosus). Since the dawn of humanity, people have sought to establish divine contact through music-infused rituals. And, more often than not, these rituals have taken place in especially resonant settings, where prayers are amplified and sounds are echoed back to the worshipers—a mysterious reverberation analogous to the voice of the holy.

The idea of sacred acoustics has ancient roots. The acoustic properties of several archaeological sites suggest that religious rituals were performed in caverns and rooms with the liveliest sound. Paleolithic paintings, for instance, are generally clustered on the most resonant cave walls, suggesting that they were used in conjunction with ritualistic chant. Neolithic stone configurations, like Avebury and Stonehenge, were similarly composed of echoing rocks. As society advanced, the association of vibrant sounds with the holy found its way into sacred architecture, where reverberating sanctuaries convey a sort of back-and-forth between humanity and God. Prayer-songs originate from the worshipers' lips, but their echo is a transcendent, disembodied sound akin to a voice from heaven.

A hint of this holy resonance is found in Isaiah 44:23, where the prophet proclaims: "Shout for joy, O mountains, O forests with all your trees!" Here as elsewhere in the Hebrew Bible, shouting for joy is a synonym for songs of praise. Of course, rocks and trees are incapable of producing these exalted sounds on their own; musical praise is a creation unique to the Homo Sapien-Musicus-Religiosis. Yet, this verse may very well be a reference to human songs echoing through the wilderness, creating the impression of nature singing along.

It is safe to assume that the Israelites recognized mountains and forests as acoustically rich environments, and that they were, like people before and since, awed by the apparently miraculous vibrations they generate. These reverberations undoubtedly informed the builders of the Jerusalem Temple, who designed halls to accommodate choirs and orchestras that made joyful noises to God. And it is possible that Isaiah, a prophet well acquainted with the Temple and its ritual, saw parallels between the Temple's vibrant walls and ceilings and the echoes of nature — two settings where God's presence was particularly palpable.

In our own day, worshipers continue to congregate in resonant places — both natural and constructed — to sing prayers to God. We remain a species innately attracted to the mysterious effect of lively acoustics, and the Ultimate Mystery they convey to us. It can even be said that, historically and cross-culturally, the striving to locate and build active sonic spaces for worship is as much a part of religious devotion as prayer-song itself.

Singing Metaphysics

Heinrich Heine (1797–1856) famously remarked that Jews pray archaeology and sing metaphysics.[1] In his evaluation, prayer-texts are relics both because they are comprised of ancient verses — many of which date back to the Bible — and because their perpetual usage can, for some, make them come off as bland, trite, or platitudinous. This effect is exacerbated when the structured liturgical language, poetic though it may be, is recited in the ordinary tones of speech. According to Heine, it is only when statutory prayers are delivered in song that they reach beyond the mundane level of redundancy and begin to convey the divinity and splendor the authors hoped to capture in words.

If Heine's appraisal of Jewish prayer seems overly harsh, it is probable that he said it with a sarcastic wink. Heine was well known for his sharp wit, as James K. Hosmer, a nineteenth-century professor of German literature, recounted: "The Germans have been accused of wanting greatly in wit and humor, but certain it is that this German Jew more than any man probably of the present century in the civilized world possessed these gifts."[2] And, despite Hosmer's reference, Heine did not wish to flaunt his Jewish identity, but rather, like others of his generation, accepted baptism as a ticket to cultured society. Viewed in this light, his unfavorable opinion was probably a jocular comment uttered in part to assert his distance from the "old religion." As a master wordsmith, it is hard to picture Heine being so dismissive of the prayer book's literary merit, regardless of how burdened it is with repetitious (and superstitious) ideas.

But, even if we do not take Heine's assessment entirely seriously, his classification of text as archaeological and music as metaphysical does eloquently address the perceived link between music and transcendence. There is a long tradition of reading and re-reading Jewish sacred texts to find new insights and discover hidden layers of meaning. Yet, it is also a general rule that truths and principles tend to lose their potency when they are endlessly repeated in plain reading. One time-tested remedy for this potentially dull routine is the infusion of melody, which, again as a general rule, is less likely to tire the ear after many repetitions. Music has long been used to revive stale doctrines, deepen connections to ancient wisdom, and draw people to concepts that might otherwise be shrugged off as obscure, outmoded, or obsolete. In this profound sense, singing not only masks the potential dryness of words, it helps inspire worshipers to desired feelings of affirmation and wonderment.

This brings us to the arena of metaphysics. Though the term has various connotations, it is, in its classical sense, a branch of philosophy concerned with the fundamental nature of being and the world. Applying this definition to Heine's view of Jewish singing, it can be understood that through the act of offering prayerful songs, Jews catch a glimpse of the ultimate reality. Or, to put it in even more romantic terms, singing forces worshipers to suspend their cynicism, and propels them into a deeper experience of themselves, the universe, and the Eternal.

1. Joseph Leiser, *American Judaism: A Historical Survey* (Westport, CT: Greenwood, 1979), 260.
2. Henry Baruch Sachs, *Heine in America* (Philadelphia: University of Pennsylvania, 1916), 48.

Sanctification

Kedushah, the Hebrew word for holy, implies separateness. Holy things or actions are set apart from the ordinary; they rise above the standards of everyday experience. Objects like the *mezuzah* and *tallit* are considered holy because they serve spiritual purposes. The Torah is holy because it contains the mythology, values, and wisdom of the Jewish people. God's words, "you shall be holy because I am holy" (11:45), signals a level of ethical behavior exceeding that of "regular" existence. And much of Jewish law gives holiness to acts that would otherwise be mere necessities, like eating or waking up.

Jewish custom also maintains that the words of prayer be distinguished from mundane discourse. Expressing oneself in language is not a remarkable feat; it is a defining feature of human life. But ritual prayer, in addition to having God-directed words, achieves a degree of sacredness through its mode of presentation. Jewish prayer is typically in Hebrew (or, in some cases, Aramaic) and is sung or chanted rather than recited. For ages, these qualities have assured that worshipers remain mindful of the sanctity of the act of praying.

Hebrew is called *Lashon Kodesh*—"The Holy Tongue." This term is first used in the Mishnah to distinguish Hebrew from "secular languages" (*Sotah* 7:2–4). One reason for this designation is that Hebrew is the exalted language of Torah and prophecy. It therefore has an air of authenticity, connecting Jews to their sacred history and to God. While local languages are effective in normal communication, Judaism maintains that human-divine communication is best performed in Hebrew.

Jewish prayer is also sung. Like Hebrew, singing is an elevated form of expression: it provides words with heightened purpose and profundity. In Judaism as in numerous other traditions, singing is considered the most appropriate way of addressing the divine. When set to song or melodic chant, the words of petition and praise rise above the monotony of everyday speech. This phenomenon is captured in the rabbis' astute remark: "Where there is song, there shall be prayer" (*Devarim Rabba* 80:2).

The architects of Jewish worship realized that it is not enough for the subjects and themes of prayer to be sacred; the way in which prayerful words are expressed must also be extraordinary. This is a primary reason why prayer is written in the "holy tongue" of Hebrew and presented in the sacred sound of musical tones. Through these converging elements, the words of prayer are made holy.

Music as Language

When asked how many languages he speaks, klezmer violinist Yale Strom usually answers four: English, Yiddish, Swedish, and Music.[1] Like a spoken language, music has a certain — if somewhat subjective — expressive power. The clarity of a musical message varies depending on a number of factors, including the quality and sincerity of a performance, the piece's simplicity or complexity, and the level and type of connections listeners make. In Strom's experience, playing klezmer tunes in places as disparate as Mississippi, Moldova, and Mexico City, music has served as a bridge of understanding and mutual respect. Though in many cases his audience is not intimate with the nuances, innuendos, and allusions wrapped up in the klezmer sound, the performance nevertheless communicates something profound. And since all societies are musical to a greater or lesser extent, it is easy for listeners to appreciate, relate to, and be moved by his violin playing, no matter how foreign it may sound. For this reason, Strom aptly calls music the "Esperanto of the world."

Esperanto is an auxiliary language that was devised by Russian-Jewish eye doctor L. L. Zamenhof in 1887. This politically neutral linguistic system was designed to foster peace and unity between people who speak different regional and/or national languages. Despite gaining some dedicated proponents, a few speakers, and a spattering of academic support, no country has adopted Esperanto as its secondary language, and it is now viewed more as a curiosity than a feasible path to world peace. However, as Strom suggests, the main objective of this constructed language — creating harmony between people — is readily accomplished through musical dialogue.

Recognition of music's ability to forge common ground has, among other things, inspired interfaith concerts around the globe. Performers and audience members representing the spectrum of world religions come together to share in each other's music, and allow the transcendent language of tones to cut through often-contentious disagreements over theology, practice, and politics. While the texts sung might not be comprehended and the musical subtleties not fully grasped, these concerts demonstrate the common humanity that lies beneath the external trappings of religion, ethnicity, and culture.

This leads us to the subject of synagogue song. If music can unite people of divergent backgrounds, shouldn't it have an even greater effect within its community of origin? Indeed, this is borne out each time a congregation gathers to sing familiar liturgical songs — music that has, through repeated usage, accumulated collective memories, emotions, and associations that act as solidarity points around which congregants focus their hearts and minds. Such music is analogous to language in more than just the general sense of promoting understanding between two parties: it is a native tongue that carries specific information and speaks directly to the congregation.

Musical language communicates on two important levels. It conveys particular meanings to the group that produces it, and transmits general messages to humanity at large. In both instances, music can bridge divides, impart ideas, and stir shared sentiments. And it is in this way that music, more than Esperanto itself, can be called the "Esperanto of the world."

1. Yale Strom, *Dave Tarras: The King of Klezmer* (Kfar Sava: OR-TAV, 2010), 9.

Beauty in Sacred Song

"If men take great pains to compose beautiful music for profane songs," wrote Italian Renaissance composer Giovanni Palestrina (c. 1525–1594), "they should devote at least as much thought to sacred song, nay, even more than to mere worldly matters."[1] As a major figure in the development of church music, Palestrina insisted that only the most exalted musical offerings be used in divine worship. He argued that God, the designer of the universe and endower of artistic abilities, deserves appropriately elevated music in response to His presence. Though composers may work tirelessly to create beautiful secular music, even greater attention should be given when devising music for sacred purposes.

The demand that composers exert their highest talents in writing sacred music is certainly a worthy religious ideal. The more beautiful the music, the more effective it is in attracting, moving, and inspiring a congregation. However, contrary to what Palestrina seems to have claimed, the most enlightened or thoughtful music is not always the most beautiful or well suited for devotional settings. Jewish liturgical works by Arnold Schoenberg, for example, while sophisticated and highly expressive, are too abstract for synagogue use. On the other hand, pieces by contemporary songwriters like Craig Taubman, which are far less complex, have proven an effective means of connecting people to the spirit of worship.

Sacred songs may also exhibit different kinds of beauty. Depending on the text for which it is used, the music may exude serene beauty, joyful beauty, contrite beauty, and so on. The genre of a prayer-song likewise determines the standards by which its aesthetic properties should be judged. For instance, a melody sung by children may express the beauty of innocence, while a simple congregational tune may exude the beauty of community. In general, the intention behind this music is practical — i.e., that it be easily sung and remembered — and thus the extra care in construction Palestrina desired is not always evident. These songs are not necessarily more intrinsically pleasing or interesting than music of the secular realm; but the setting and manner in which they are performed imbue them with distinct shades of beauty.

Still, Palestrina's words are instructive to all who compose or perform sacred songs. Such music, regardless of style, should accurately communicate the message of the text and strive to elicit specific responses. Performers should likewise be mindful in interpreting the music, and devote their energies to raising it to its highest aesthetic potential. Though beauty is ultimately a subjective and variable quality, it should nevertheless be held up as a primary goal of worship music.

1. Josiah Fisk, ed., *Composers on Music: Eight Centuries of Writing* (Boston: Northeastern University Press, 1997), 8.

Some Thoughts on "Traditional" Synagogue Music

The term "traditional" is frequently attached to synagogue songs. In some cases, it is applied to tunes that have been passed on from one generation to the next, as in oral tradition, and may come with regional modifiers, like traditional French Sephardic melody. More often, however, the term is given to songs meeting a variety of loose qualifications. Common examples include songs from one's childhood, melodies sung regularly at a given synagogue, and tunes exhibiting an "authentic" sound, however defined. Music thrown under the banner of traditional may be hundreds of years old or written in the past decade, and may have been transmitted from anonymous sources or invented by known composers. At times, traditional seems little more than a glorified word for familiar. And, just as what is familiar to an individual or group may not be familiar to another, there are no objective standards for determining what constitutes traditional synagogue music. Virtually any melody a congregation sings on a consistent basis may eventually be labeled traditional, regardless of its age or origins.

Composer and conductor Chemjo Vinaver (1900–1973) summed up the problem of musical tradition in his 1948 address to the Cantors Assembly: "The term 'traditional' itself, has been so extended and interpreted, in the past and even more so in the present time, that it has become almost unintelligible. It embraces, in fact, a number of traditions, some few of which are genuine, and many of which, unfortunately, are spurious and unworthy of the name."[1] This statement recognizes not only the wide range of music that may potentially be called traditional, but also that much of this music is not "genuine" in the sense of originating within Jewish communities or deriving exclusively from Jewish practice. Jews have always and everywhere adapted musical elements from host cultures, and numerous songs featuring these local accretions have been designated traditional.

Among the traditions Vinaver identified as "spurious" is the music of Louis Lewandowski (1821–1894), which was celebrated in his native Germany and is still sung in modern services despite bearing a strong resemblance to German marches and Lutheran hymns. Moreover, Lewandowski's music represented a "new tradition" (a seeming contradiction of terms), arising and gaining popularity as large numbers of

Western European Jews moved away from orthodoxy and insulation in favor of cultural-religious reformation and acculturation.

New traditions have similarly emerged in other settings, putting to question the notion that traditions are necessarily long established. For instance, American synagogues witnessed the rise of camp and folk rock music during the latter years of the twentieth century, certain melodies of which have come to be embraced as traditional. Though this music is contemporary and exhibits secular/non–Jewish influences, it is nevertheless accepted and repeatedly sung (at least in some synagogues), and thus for many has gained the status of tradition.

While a song deemed traditional has increased emotional or sentimental appeal, such a designation is fraught with ambiguity. This is evidenced each time a request is made for "the traditional" tune of a prayer, ignoring that several settings from diverse locales have at one time or another held that title. It is therefore advisable to take a more humble approach to categorizing synagogue songs. Instead of calling a melody traditional, one is better off saying "a well-known tune," "one of the popular settings," or "the version we're accustomed to." That way, the problematic term can be avoided altogether.

1. Chemjo Vinaver, "Synagogue Music — Traditional," in Jonathan L. Friedmann, ed., *20th Century Synagogue Music: Essential Readings* (Woodland Hills, CA: Isaac Nathan, 2010), 39.

Creating a Synagogue Musical Tradition

Each synagogue has its own musical tradition, usually consisting of an amalgam of tunes spanning in origin from medieval Europe to contemporary America. These liturgical songs represent the "mixed bag" of Jewish musical heritage. They vary in style and genre, may or may not conform to parameters of *nusach ha-tefillah* (modal chant), and display different levels of musical sophistication. Children's songs, church-like hymns, Hassidic melodies, and other song types can potentially become part of a synagogue's musical tradition. And once these songs are "canonized," they gain a sense of fixity and an aura of genuineness.

Melodies included in this cherished corpus need not be time-honored or generally known. Rather, they achieve traditional status through prolonged and repeated use within a congregation. In many cases, these tunes are so highly guarded that it is almost impossible (or at least unwise) to introduce alternative settings. Indeed, congregants often refer to a favored tune as "*the* melody," even though melodies for some prayers number in the hundreds.

A significant aspect of these tunes is their perceived timelessness. Through continued usage, a liturgical song tends to be stripped of its status as a human creation. The composer's identity is almost invariably forgotten, and the music becomes inseparable from the text for which it was written. This is equally true for ancient melodies passed on through the oral tradition, which have no identifiable authors, and popular tunes composed in modern times. For example, the pervasive setting of *Shalom Aleichem* did not, as many would have it, originate on Mount Sinai, but was composed in 1918 by New York rabbi Israel Goldfarb. And the most widely sung version of *Oseh Shalom* was not transmitted to us from our ancestors, but was written in 1969 by Israeli songwriter Nurit Hirsch.

Synagogue musical traditions are generally quite limited. As mentioned, numerous tunes may exist for a given piece of Jewish liturgy, yet most congregations become attached to only one or two. Clergy or lay leaders may direct this selection process, or it may come about naturally through the forces of taste and time. According to theologian Edward Schillebeeckx, the latter process is historically more common.[1] He explained that new music typically enters religious services on an ephemeral (temporary) circle. If the music is not rejected outright, it may pass into a conjectural (more stable) circle, and from there eventually be incorporated into a structural (mainstream) circle. This natural selection process accounts for the survival and continued singing of a handful of melodies from disparate periods and places, as well as the "new traditions" that emerge within a generation.

It is a mistake to assume that the music we now hold dear has always existed. All melodies considered traditional were new at one time. As a general rule, the music that "sticks" is that which is singable, catchy, and suitable for the text. But, like the term tradition itself, these qualities are, in the end, subjective. It is, then, better to judge a song based on what it does for a congregation, rather than what it is.

---

1. Edward Schillebeeckx, *Jesus: An Experiment in Christology* (New York: Seabury, 1979), 577.

The Development of Jewish Music Traditions

It is natural to assume that the music we are used to singing in the synagogue has always existed. The repetition of melodies on specific occasions helps to convey the idea that these days exist on a continuous stream. Shabbat, for example, is a weekly reenactment of the biblical account, in which God, on the seventh day, "ceased from all the work of creation that He had done" (Gen. 2:2). In this sense, each Shabbat is really the same day — transcending the boundaries of ordinary time — and the repeated use of Shabbat melodies brings us back into this sacred flow. Through this process as well, the tunes themselves gain an eternal quality.

But, in truth, all familiar synagogue songs were new at one point, and, more often than not, they enter the mainstream not by way of official selection, but only *after* they were already accepted by the people. In fact, it is not uncommon for religious authorities to initially object to musical changes instigated by the laity, only to embrace these changes when their hold on the people becomes too strong. Communal leaders of past centuries condemned the intrusion of foreign musical elements into the synagogue, such as opera and church hymns, on the grounds of *chukkat ha-goy*—imitation of the gentile. Yet a number of pieces in these styles were eventually deemed "traditional." In more recent times, the music of Debbie Friedman, which was at first criticized in cantorial circles, has found its way into most liberal American synagogues.

In light of this, it is interesting to note that eleven biblical psalms are attributed to the Korachites (Pss. 42, 44–49, 84–85, 87–88). The Korachites were a class of priestly singers entrenched in the musical establishment of Jerusalem's First Temple. That their liturgical works are included in the Psalter is an indication that the music and poetry they produced was generally accepted within the highly structured Temple system. In other words, their songs were conventional. This is significant, as their patriarch, Korach, was killed centuries earlier for rebelling against the established tradition.

During the course of Israel's wandering in the desert, Korach organized a community revolt against Moses' authority (Num. 16:1–18:32). With the backing of chieftains, other men of repute, and scores of followers, Korach declared to Moses and Aaron: "You have gone too far! For all the community are holy, all of them, and the Lord is in their midst. Why then do you raise yourselves above the Lord's congregation?" This was a populist movement, arguing against the notion that only the priests were sanctified to perform religious rituals. Ordinary people, Korach maintained, also had a right to operate within the ceremonial realm. Perhaps not unlike the democratic synagogues of today, where laypeople often lead services and congregational singing is the norm, Korach and his supporters desired a more intimate relationship with the ritual. In punishment for this defiance, the earth opened up and swallowed many of the rebels, including Korach, and the chieftains were consumed by fire. Communal stability, the story tells us, was too fragile to tolerate this anti-establishment push.

Music is not mentioned in this episode, but, given the Korachites' musical proclivities, it is not unreasonable to suggest that their forefather was a musician as well. Historically and cross-culturally, music is typically a family trade, passed on from one generation to the next. And, given what we know of the powerful role of singing in creating a participatory service, Korach may have introduced congregational song as a way of stirring and uniting his followers.

Korach's revolt and its aftermath have much in common with the way musical innovations are sometimes handled in the synagogue. If we imagine Moses as the head of a powerful ritual committee and Korach as an unconventional though popular songwriter, we can understand both why Korach and his followers were dealt with so harshly, and how Korach's descendants became keepers of the musical mainstream. As mentioned, musical changes are often met with condemnation from religious authorities. By their very nature, these new sounds threaten the solidity and continuity of communal ritual. But, over time, these changes can seep into worship services and eventually become part of standard practice. No matter how much strength the leadership exerts, if the people want the music, it is exceedingly difficult to bar it from devotional expression. So, even as Korach and his supporters were killed for challenging the set ways of ritual, his music lived on with his sons and the populace. Despite the efforts of those in charge — or, more correctly, *because* of the efforts of the people — the Korachites were able to take this once-controversial music into the rigid Temple system. What was at first revolutionary became conventional.

Judging Synagogue Song

What kind of music is appropriate for prayer? This question is often tossed around in discussions on worship in the modern synagogue, where dwindling attendance and a desire to stay relevant has given rise to a "whatever gets people through the door" permissiveness. In response to this unprecedented musical diversity, some have contemplated whether ground rules should be established for assessing the appropriateness of this or that given setting. After all, they argue, the holiness of the service should be matched with equally elevated sounds, and a melody should not be chosen merely because it pleases the congregation. Yet, while this perceived need to set standards for liturgical song seems a concern unique to the present day, it is probably as old as the service itself.

Synagogue song has never been an uncontaminated or completely indigenous art form. Whether it is the cantillation of a Moroccan *minyan* or the inclusive sing-alongs of a Renewal congregation, Jewish music is everywhere the product of its environment, informed by outside influences and shaped by the shifting preferences of time and place. To paraphrase the poet John Donne, no melody is an island. And so, quite naturally, objections to foreign influences have cropped up throughout Jewish history. Twelfth-century rabbi Yehudah Ha-Chasid, for instance, cautioned that "If a Jew likes a poem that was composed by a monk as a church hymn, he should not translate it into Hebrew to be used as praise to God,"[1] while Moses Isserles included this ruling in his sixteenth-century commentary on the *Shulhan Arukh:* "A *sheliach tzibbur* [cantor] who sings melodies that the gentiles use in their worship should be prevented from doing so, and if he refuses to comply and persists in doing so, he is to be removed from his position."[2]

Whereas in ages past musical borrowing may have been a subtle or selective process, liberal synagogues of today consciously and eagerly draw their musical literature from varied sources. As such, many have refrained from excluding music simply on the grounds of origin, and instead attempt to make musical choices using the criterion of suitability. In this view, if a tune clashes with or does not adequately capture the message of a prayer, it should be rejected. This is a difficult standard to uphold, not only because texts can convey multiple ideas and elicit more than one emotion, but because certain melodies "speak" to some congregants and not to others.

This suitability argument is nothing new. Herbert Spencer (1820–1903), the English philosopher, biologist, sociologist, and political theorist, put it this way: "they ... sin against science by using musical phrases that have no natural relation to the ideas expressed, even where these are emotional. [The melodies] are bad because they are untrue."[3] Spencer's statement typifies the notion that assessing a tune's appropriateness for a text is somehow "scientific." However, while it is easy to oppose singing a dire petition to a gleeful melody, this measurement is not always so obvious. To take just one example, *nusach ha-tefillah*, the highly guarded system of chanted motifs, does not generally change to accommodate the emotions or meaning of the words, but rather shifts according to the time of day and date on the calendar, regardless of what the text has to say. Yet traditionalists who adhere to the strictures of *nusach* are not offended by this apparent "sin against science."

No matter how hard one tries to apply objective standards to worship music, determinations about a setting's fittingness ultimately stem from a web of subjective factors, like comfort, exposure, preference, and catchiness. In light of this, perhaps the best answer to the question of what kind of music is appropriate for prayer is that it depends on whom you ask.

1. Yehudah Ha-Chasid, *Sefer Chasidim*, quoted in Jonathan L. Friedmann, ed., *Quotations on Jewish Sacred Music* (Lanham, MD: Hamilton, 2011), 1.
2. Moses Isserles, Commentary on the *Shulhan Arukh*, quoted in Jonathan L. Friedmann, ed., *Quotations on Jewish Sacred Music* (Lanham, MD: Hamilton, 2011), 1.
3. Herbert Spencer, *Education: Intellectual, Moral and Physical* (New York: D. Appleton and Co., 1864).

The Problems of Meaning

A quick glance at the mission statements and self-descriptions of modern American synagogues reveals a regularly recurring term: "meaningful." It usually comes in statements like "we conduct meaningful services," "join our meaningful community," "we make the holidays meaningful," or "come have meaningful experiences." Synagogues typically use the term to distinguish themselves from others, as if to say, "don't go to there; come here where you'll find meaning." The problem with such thinking is that all synagogues believe they offer meaningful ceremonies and programs. Again, this is attested to by the frequency with which the term appears in their promotional material. And there is another problem: meaningful merely connotes having meaning; it tells us nothing of definite features and eludes objective criteria. It is not the same as claiming that a service will be fun, relaxing, or even terrifying — adjectives that specify sensations and intent. Though the word might be used to signify that something deep or transformative occurs at the synagogue, such an experience is personal. Different people take meaning from different things. One might identify Jewish yoga as a source of meaning, while another might find playing bingo or eating bagels and lox to be a meaningful activity. It is, then, perhaps presumptuous for an institution to guarantee that its offerings will have an intense impact on all who attend.

There is also a larger issue that bears attention. Meaning, even when it is generally agreed to — as in "the Passover *seder* is a meaningful ritual" — is by nature transient: holidays, customs, and other areas of religion are constantly subject to modification and re-interpretation in order to ensure that they remain meaningful. So, not only does the perception of what constitutes meaning vary from person to person (or group to group), but specific things deemed intrinsically meaningful can in fact lose their meaning. This has particular relevance for prayer-song.

Much of what constitutes contemporary synagogue music grew out of a desire for meaning, or, perhaps more accurately, out of a rejection of old music that was perceived as lacking meaning. For the first half of the twentieth century, hymns and other nineteenth-century European forms dominated the music culture of liberal synagogues. In the 1960s and 70s, youth who attended Jewish summer camps were exposed to a new kind of liturgical and paraliturgical music that blended Jewish identity with popular trends emanating from the counter-culture movement. This style of worship song was a breath of fresh air for the younger generation, who felt the music of their parents and grandparents clashed with their own self-image. Before long, the folk-rock style they celebrated entered the synagogue and replaced many of the older tunes. Music that resonated with the older crowd was tossed aside in favor of songs the youngsters considered meaningful.

Today, most liberal synagogues are filled with this folk-rock music. Those whose musical tastes were shaped in the 1970s are now rabbis, cantors, educators, and temple board members in charge of selecting worship music. And many who create melodies for Jewish services continue to write in this style of forty years ago. However, while the genre has entered the mainstream, it is becoming just as fossilized as the music it replaced. As the baby-boomers grow older, their children and grandchildren will likely rebel against this type of music, which was once new and refreshing but is now increasingly trite. Whatever meaning it had or still has will at some point fade away and another form regarded as meaningful will take its place.

This musical example demonstrates the ephemeral nature of meaning. Aside from being thoroughly subjective, differing from one individual to the next, those things labeled meaningful do not usually retain that quality forever. Though the term is often used to attract membership or to indicate that a ritual element, like song, has some intrinsic significance or power (whatever it may be), there is an obvious irony: "meaningful" is, in the end, an essentially meaningless term.

Conformity and Survival

It is a rarely discussed reality of Jewish life that synagogues, like other businesses vying for a share of the marketplace, compete with one another for patrons and funds. In their effort to bring people through the doors, synagogues regularly put on concerts, host visiting speakers, purchase ads in the newspaper, and engage in other types of outreach. This organizational competition is, of course, most intense in cities boasting large Jewish populations. But even in areas with few Jews, services struggle for attendance against the pull of more universal attractions, like television, shopping malls, and children's sports.

It is, then, not surprising that congregations often rush to emphasize their uniqueness in hopes of gaining membership. One might claim to be the most *haimish shul* in town, while another might bill itself as the most compassionate, spiritual, or family oriented. Yet, though this urge to stand out is certainly understandable, the survival of any institution, religious or otherwise, requires isomorphism: the process by which organizations come to resemble one another in substance and form.

It is a paradox of marketing that an organization's desire to create a distinctive product is usually not as crucial as its willingness to adopt conventions held by similar organizations. As sociologist of religion

Robert Wuthnow points out, "one way to ensure at least a minimum share of the resources available in any environment is to make one's organization indistinguishable from all the others."[1] Wuthnow uses the analogy of breakfast cereals to illustrate the point. Nearly all major cereal brands package their products in rectangular boxes of about the same size and weight, use similar ingredients, and stay within a general range of nutritional content. This consistency establishes an even playing field, in which each box has a chance at capturing the customer's coin.

In like manner, if we were to examine Friday night services in American liberal synagogues we would find that they typically begin around the same time, run about the same duration, and finish with predictable offerings at the *oneg* table. The services are generally led by a team of rabbi and cantor (or soloist), alternate between singing and recitation, include sermons and announcements, and share common (if unstated) guidelines for dress, decorum, and conduct. Wuthnow gives two reasons why this isomorphism is so important: it helps identify an organization as part of a set or system, and signals compliance with larger norms in the institutional environment. For synagogue services, adherence to widely accepted content and patterns gives potential members the dual impression of authenticity and familiarity. In other words, the service is attractive because it is normal.

Isomorphism is also evident in melody choice. The dominance of congregational singing in liberal synagogues has given rise to a number of widely known tunes. And while most congregants can tolerate occasional departures from these accepted melodies, it behooves a synagogue to use familiar settings as the core of its musical repertoire. Sticking to tried-and-true tunes not only fosters a welcoming environment for people seeking to add their voices to prayer, it also helps solidify the legitimacy of the service. Conventional music, like other established elements of the synagogue, gives participants the impression that they are involved in something "real." In contrast, new melodies, no matter how artistically desirable, can upset the regulars and turn off prospective members. In this sense, isomorphism operates on a basic premise: people like what they know.

It is worth noting, too, that the inclination to conform often results in once-innovative ideas becoming standard fare. If these new practices prove successful in their place of origin, they are likely to spread to other synagogues. This accounts for the ubiquity of guitar accompaniment and the increasingly pervasive use of bands on Friday nights (usually once a month)— both of which began as creative twentieth-century additions to Jewish worship, but have become ordinary, mainstream components of American synagogue song.

As these examples show, a "play it safe" approach is essential to a synagogue's growth and survival. To be sure, there are thriving congregations on the experimental end of the spectrum, but these tend to be smaller, *havurah*-style groups with limited general appeal. And though most large synagogues stand out in some way, their success owes mainly to their embrace of norms and appeasement of expectations. In short, it is vital that a synagogue service looks, feels, and sounds like a synagogue service.

1. Robert Wuthnow, *Producing the Sacred: An Essay on Public Religion* (Urbana and Chicago: University of Illinois Press, 1994), 31.

Charismatic Tunes

Whether scribed by a known composer or gradually developed through an anonymous folk process, music always has its first performance, during which it may be embraced, rejected, or simply ignored. Of course, this first hearing does not always determine a work's ultimate fate. There are numerous instances of pieces with lackluster premieres that went on to become iconic; and it is not uncommon for music to hover in a state of uncertainty before finding ideal conditions under which to soar: the right performer(s), the right audience, the right venue, and so on. But, regardless of their unique sounds and circumstances, one quality unites all popular pieces: charisma.

Certain melodies, like certain people, have a compelling, almost irresistible charm. Within the expansive and endlessly varied realm of vocal music, for instance, there exists a select class of tunes that draw in devoted followers, either on a "cult" or "mass" level. In some cases, it can be difficult to separate the charismatic tune from its charismatic creator, since the personalities and images of performers are oftentimes as recognizable as the music they make. Yet, even the songs of universally admired musicians like Louis Armstrong and Elvis Presley can take on a life of their own, independent of the performer's identity—a fact evidenced in fake book offerings and wedding band set lists. In addition, like charismatic religious or political leaders whose rise to prominence poses a threat to the established authority, charismatic tunes often conflict with or innovate upon the norms of the given genre, arousing tensions between infatuated fans and adherents of conventional sounds. And, similar to the charismatic leader whose worldview or system of governance becomes entrenched, outlasting his/her own lifespan, once-novel charismatic tunes frequently become standard fair.

This latter phenomenon has special relevance for synagogue song. The library of popular liturgical settings is filled with tunes that once garnered excitement and controversy but are now situated within the ordinary musical structure. Sociologist Max Weber called this shift from tantalizing appeal to dependable attraction the routinization of charisma: a gradual transformation of charismatic leadership (or some other charismatic element) into an established form of authority.[1] Weber used this term to describe religions or sects that started around a magnetic individual and eventually grew into large, multi-faceted, and bureaucratized institutions. This applies, for example, to Christianity in general, which expanded from a modest charismatic cult to a massive socio-religious system, as well as the normative, mainline Christian denominations, most of which originated as break-off groups led by captivating personalities. This transition also took place with the music of Shlomo Carlebach, Debbie Friedman, and others, whose styles initially attracted small and enthusiastic followings and upset defenders of the "old school," but have since become ubiquitous in congregations far and wide.

Related to this process is the charisma of office, a term Weber attached to the automatic reverence given to certain positions in society, regardless of the identity of the officeholders. To use a biblical illustration, this is the difference between the institutionalized charisma of a priest born into a position of respect and the "pure" charisma of the anointed prophet. Similarly, numerous synagogue tunes have a strong, built-in attraction, often existing apart from and beyond the texts for which they were intended. These melodies are analogous to the charismatic office in at least two ways: like the office, they are held in high esteem and command worshipers' attention; and like the person who occupies such a position, it often matters little which text is set to the charismatic tune. Examples of this include the singing of *Mi Chamocha* to the Sephardic folk melody *Cuando El Rey Nimrod* and the setting of *Kevodo Malei Olam* in the Shabbat *Musaf Kedushah* to the tune of Yosef Hadar's *Erev Shel Shoshanim*.

It is not the purpose of this essay to identify the ingredients that make a melody charismatic, especially since the seemingly magical pull of a given piece — like the quasi-mystical allure of certain leaders — seems to defy all scientific measurements. But, whatever factors contribute to a melody's charm, it is clear that, when it becomes sufficiently widespread and well worn, the excitement that once surrounded it gives way to a more subdued kind of appeal, similar to the routinized charisma of institutions and their various offices. And, importantly, it is largely through this evolution that standard repertoires of synagogue song are formed.

1. Max Weber, *The Theory of Social and Economic Organization*, ed. Talcott Parsons (New York: Simon and Schuster, 1997), 363–372.

Jewish Youth and Musical Change

Jewish continuity is a powerful concept. For the Orthodox, it entails no less than a belief in the verbatim transmission of the Torah — both written and oral — from Moses to subsequent generations. Jews of all types affirm the importance of teaching Jewish ways and wisdom to their children, and defining elements of the Jewish religion — the calendar, sacred writings, and customs — have to a greater or lesser extent been faithfully passed on through the years.

Yet, this continuity of thought and behavior is not an absolute force. Jews have always been affected by the conditions under which they have lived. And, just as these conditions can change within a generation or from one generation to the next, Judaism also experiences changes — subtle or otherwise. Sometimes, the movement of change runs counter to the ideal of passing information from parent to child, or teacher to student. This is certainly true of musical innovations, which occasionally stem from the youth.

Aspects of Jewish musical heritage have been preserved through the years, including biblical cantillation and numerous folk tunes. But, Jewish music has also undergone transformations initiated by young people. Two examples from different times and places demonstrate this bottom-up influence: the hymns of Germany and the camp songs of America.

The Reform movement in nineteenth-century Germany aimed to make Judaism compatible with modern principles of autonomy, universalism, and historical-philosophical thought. It challenged traditional beliefs, introduced liberal theology, and adapted or eliminated customs according to the norms of the general society. The encroachment of church hymns into synagogue services would thus seem a natural development; but it was actually spurred on in large measure by Jewish youth, who considered Christian-style worship an attractive alternative to "outmoded" Jewish practices. In great numbers, young Jews drifted away from their heritage, and became increasingly immersed in the larger Christian environment. As a result, rabbis considered it good policy to embrace Christian musical forms, along with other customs of church worship, in order to lure these young men and women back into the synagogue.

A similar phenomenon occurred in the American Reform movement during the latter years of the twentieth century. Young people who attended National Federation of Jewish Youth summer camps began experimenting with campfire songs in their worship services. By the 1970s, songwriters like Jeff Klepper and Dan Freelander were providing these campers with easy-to-sing folk-rock settings of liturgical and liturgically based texts in Hebrew and English. When the youth returned home after their summer sessions, they were no longer content to sing the songs of their parents. Instead, they wished to replicate the camp experience inside the synagogue walls. Many congregations complied, seeing it as a way to retain and even increase youth involvement in Jewish life. Before long, synagogues were hiring guitar-playing cantors and rabbis who could lead this new repertoire.

Although Judaism favors the passage of knowledge and ritual from the older generation to the younger, youth also exert influence on Jewish practice and aesthetics. This is evidenced in Jewish music, which bears an imprint of the tastes and trends of young people. Such youth-driven changes do not, however, necessarily challenge Judaism's survival, but encourage the participation of generations that might have otherwise strayed from Jewish life.

Nusach Variations

The practice of thrice-daily communal prayer produced distinctive musical modes in the Ashkenazi world, known collectively as *nusach ha-tefillah*. Rather than a set of tunes, where melody dominates and words are subject to strict rhythmic and tonal constraints, *nusach* is text-driven chant, with words directing the flow and contours of the music. Interval options, opening and intermediate phrases, cadences, and other signatures of a mode are used to serve the verses of prayer, however uneven or syllabically dense they may be. And though the modes can be reduced to scales for the sake of categorization, motifs—not isolated notes—comprise the building blocks of *nusach ha-tefillah*.

The chant patterns of Jewish liturgy vary as a service progresses and differ from one service to the next. Scholars usually cite two benefits of these *nusach* variations. One is their ability to announce time. An individual absorbed in a "*nusach* culture," where praying three times a day is the norm, can instantly recognize the day of the week, time of day, season of the year, and date on the calendar just by hearing the liturgical chant. This is especially important, as much of the liturgy remains the same (or receives only slight modification) throughout the course of the year.

The other reason given is that modal patterns can bring out the character of the liturgical section and sacred moment. It is, in fact, largely through the musical mode that a service's atmosphere is set. In general, chanting intensifies as services build toward their climax, and grows in complexity as the calendar moves from weekday to Sabbath to festival to High Holy Day.

There is, however, a third, more fundamental rationale for these modal changes: the human need for musical variety. If each service were chanted in the same mode, and even if that mode were explored in all possible permutations, boredom would quickly set in. Instead of being drawn in by the sound—a central purpose of worship music—participants would become disengaged from the content and experience of the prayers. But the result would not be dullness alone. The constant repetition of melodic phrases often has negative psychological effects, ranging from annoyance to anguish, and their impact usually lasts beyond the actual listening, with melodic snippets continuously looping around in the mind, sometimes for extended periods.

The narrator in Mark Twain's short story, "A Literary Nightmare" (1876), describes being tormented by "jingling rhymes" trapped in his head: "All through breakfast they went waltzing through my brain.... I fought hard for an hour, but it was useless. My head kept humming.... I drifted downtown, and presently discovered that my feet were keeping time to that relentless jingle.... [I] jingled all through the evening, went to bed, rolled, tossed, and jingled all night long."[1] Two days later, the narrator meets with an old friend, a pastor, and accidentally gets him hooked on the jingle. The pastor, in turn, infects his entire congregation with the dangerously catchy tune.

Music of all sorts contains repetitious elements that can promote its burrowing into the mind. Classical pieces and film scores typically employ recurring themes, and popular music from bluegrass to bossa nova is rooted in a back-and-forth between verse and chorus. We are instinctively attracted to this predictability. So, as neurologist Oliver Sacks writes, "we should not be surprised, not complain if the balance sometimes shifts too far and our musical sensitivity becomes a vulnerability."[2]

Yet it is hard to resist griping when incessantly swirling musical snatches, aptly referred to as "earworms," plague our heads. The potentially debilitating effect of these invasive tones is documented in patients with Tourette's syndrome and obsessive-compulsive disorder, who are especially prone to involuntary repetitions of movement and sound. For them, as well as anyone else who has struggled to shake off a seemingly ceaseless tune, the value of musical variation is obvious: without it, music tends to be a source of aggravation instead of enjoyment.

Knowledge of this principle contributed, however consciously or unconsciously, to the calculated changes found in the modal patterns of Jewish liturgy. Not only do these alterations help distinguish one sacred time from another and give a unique flavor to each occasion, they also help to ensure that thrice-daily prayer remains a gratifying institution rather than a distressing routine. The standard strains of *nusach ha-tefillah* therefore provide worship with an agreeable blend of soothing familiarity and refreshing variety.

1. Mark Twain, "A Literary Nightmare," quoted in Oliver Sacks, *Musicophilia: Tales of Music and the Brain* (New York: Vintage, 2008), 46.
2. Sacks, *Musicophilia*, 52.

Sacred Classics

Each week, Jews congregate to enact the ritual repetition of Shabbat. Following a set order of liturgical texts and gestures, they restate formulas of gratitude and praise to God, the creator of the world. Though the lack of variance from one week to the next might suggest a level of staleness, those who come to services regularly tend to favor constancy over change. Even the subtlest alterations can be met with great resistance, as if departing from the familiar somehow sullies the sanctity of the day. Introducing silent devotion, abridging sections of liturgy, or adding raisins to the challah is enough to disturb and disorient many congregants. This is partly because humans are wired for routine: we relate to the world in terms of patterning, and construct coherent, predictable patterns in events and relationships. Added to this, the sacred status of the day raises concerns that a shift from routine — abrupt or otherwise — may in fact be a profanation.

Few changes stir more controversy than the introduction of new prayer melodies. Musical innovations in the synagogue have long encountered fervent objections, at times from rabbinic authorities, but more often from the people in the pews. This is due largely to the factors given above: the instinct for preservation, the comfort of routine, and the perceived holiness of long-established tunes. It is this mindset that led to the establishment of fixed modal chant in traditionalist circles, as well as to the sealing of melodic selections in more liberal congregations. Most synagogues can tolerate a few musical changes from time to time, particularly on special occasions and when it is clear that they are temporary. But, by and large, congregations stick to an intentionally limited collection of prayer-songs.

This self-limited musical range seems to run counter to an important function of synagogue music: the enlivening of static texts. The prayer book is, for the most part, an unchangeable document. It has been historically permissible to add to the liturgy, but not to take anything away. Though the strictness of this policy varies between groups, it has formed a protective shield around what is called *matbeah shel tefillah*—the liturgical core—and has helped to ensure an essential continuity of thought and practice through the ages. Liturgical melodies have not been subject to the same regulations; there is freedom to explore these canonized texts with different sounds. Yet, despite this option, most synagogues cling to "their" melodies, perhaps in order to give the service an additional layer of predictability, or to forge a sonic bridge connecting Sabbaths past, present, and future.

But why do certain melodies become entrenched and keep their luster after seemingly countless repetitions? Part of the answer lies in the nature of music itself. In his classic study, *The Symbolism of Music* (1941), linguist Dwight L. Bolinger noted, "Repetition, or return to the familiar, to the learned, is more striking in music than elsewhere — a very good book may be read twice, a masterpiece of literature three or four times, a poem a dozen times; but in no other art-form could we expect the literally hundreds of repetitions to go on pleasing us."[1] There are many reasons a piece might beg for repeat performances. These include musical qualities, such as harmony, form, and texture, as well as qualities people bring to the music, such as nostalgia, affirmations, and associations. Specific to synagogue songs are additional aspects like suitability for a text, ritual, or devotional moment, and ability to inspire religious sentiments. There is, indeed, an abundance of functions and values that might make a prayer-song worth singing again and again.

Theologian Albert L. Blackwell calls these perpetually repeated melodies "classics." He writes that such works "reward repeated exposure with new disclosure."[2] Using the contrasting examples of Joni Mitchell albums and Brahms symphonies, Blackwell explains, "Rehearing such music, I not only take pleasure in its perfection but also discover things I had not noticed before."[3] In the case of a synagogue classic, it is not only that the music is familiar, comfortable, and accepted, but also that its richness—whether musical or associational—invites new insights each time it is sung. Shabbat tunes of this type are numerous, including Sulzer's *Shema*, Rothblum's *Veshamru*, Helfman's *Hashkiveinu*, folk tunes for *Yism'chu* and *Etz Chayim Hi*, and many others. Instead of growing tiresome after years of regular use, these melodies continue to stimulate and satisfy. It is hard to pinpoint the exact elements that make this endless repetition enjoyable, particularly as the source of the music's appeal varies from person to person. What is certain is that these old familiar tunes somehow manage to retain a sense of freshness.

1. Dwight L. Bolinger, *The Symbolism of Music* (Yellow Springs, OH: Antioch Press, 1941), 27.
2. Albert L. Blackwell, *The Sacred in Music* (Louisville, KY: Westminster John Knox, 1999), 17.
3. Blackwell, *The Sacred in Music*, 17.

Sing a New Song

Anyone who has attended synagogue services knows the integral part singing plays in Jewish worship. Melodies accompany virtually every ritual ceremony, and Jewish prayers are regularly set to musical tones. This seemingly natural relationship of music and prayer has persisted throughout Jewish history. The Book of Psalms, the prayer book of Jerusalem's Second Temple, contains forty-three references to songs or singing. One of the most familiar of these comes from Psalm 96: "Sing to God a new song; sing to God, everyone on earth." More than simply promoting the union of prayer and melody, this verse encourages musical creativity. Every worshiper, it tells us, should direct a new song toward heaven.

This proclamation can be interpreted in three distinct ways. First, the phrase "Sing to God a new song" justifies the creation of new Jewish liturgical music. Most major prayers of the Jewish liturgy have several musical settings. Musicologist Abraham Z. Idelsohn noted in 1929 that there were over 2,000 melodies for *Lecha Dodi* alone.[1] More than 80 Hebrew services and 250 individual liturgical compositions were published in the United States between 1925 and 1955. Jewish recording labels and music publishers generate more new music today than ever before. And cantors in even the most traditional congregations are expected to improvise liturgical chants within the framework of the synagogue modes. New melodies can bring fresh perspectives to the fixed liturgy. They help to ensure the congregation's continued interest in the prayer-text, and in the worship experience more broadly.

Second, this verse can refer to the singer's state of mind, rather than the music itself. If one is completely focused on the activity of singing, as well as the text being sung, there is little risk of old melodies becoming stale. Singing a "new song" in this sense means finding continuous inspiration in a familiar tune. Cantor William Sharlin embodied this attitude during his forty-year career at Leo Baeck Temple in Los Angeles. "Whenever I sang in the synagogue," he recounts, "I was in a state of prayerfulness. This was especially important when I approached *Etz Hayim Hi*, a melody I sang every Shabbat morning. Each time I sang the prayer, I experienced it as something new."[2]

Third, "sing to God, everyone on earth" affirms that prayerful songs from around the world are welcomed offerings to God. Although this verse originated in the Holy Temple, which likely had a stable and singular musical mainstream, it foreshadowed a time when Jews would be scattered across the globe. This dispersion began in the aftermath of the Temple's destruction in 70 C.E. As Jewish communities adapted to various lands, they developed unique customs and practices, including musical traditions. This is illustrated in Idelsohn's ten-volume *Thesaurus of Hebrew Oriental Melodies* (1914–1933),[3] which includes musical transcriptions from Yemenite, Babylonian, Persian, Bukharian, Oriental Sephardic, Moroccan, German, Eastern European, and Hassidic Jewish communities living in Palestine and the Diaspora.

These three interpretations are significant. We should encourage the creation of new melodies for the synagogue, which speak in the musical language of their place and time and bring relevance to the ancient words of prayer. We should also be motivated to breathe new life into old prayer-songs, no matter how many times we have sung them before. And we should be aware that Jewish musical traditions are as numerous and varied as the communities that produce them. In this way, the words "Sing to God a new song; sing to God, everyone on earth" teach us the importance of musical diversity, innovation, and preservation in the synagogue.

1. Abraham Z. Idelsohn, *Jewish Music in Its Historical Development* (New York: Henry Holt and Co., 1929), 116.
2. William Sharlin, "Trust the Process: My Life in Sacred Song," in Jonathan L. Friedmann, ed., *Perspectives on Jewish Music: Secular and Sacred* (Lanham, MD: Lexington, 2009), 114.
3. Abraham Z. Idelsohn, *Thesaurus of Hebrew Oriental Melodies* (Leipzig: Friedrich Hofmeister, 1914–1933).

Musical Layers

Rabbinic biblical exegesis is often grouped under the heading Pardes, an acronym derived from the initials of four levels of interpretation: *Peshat* ("plain"), *Remez* ("hints"), *Derash* ("inquiry"), and *Sod* ("mystery"). *Peshat* involves the contextual reading of a verse, *Remez* deals with the allegorical meaning, *Derash* includes homiletic expositions, and *Sod* delves into mystical insights. As this overview indicates, these layers expose distinct understandings of the biblical story, each deeper than the one before. More generally, the Pardes method demonstrates how static texts can be encountered in a variety of dynamic ways, from simple to mystical.

In a very practical sense, the layered approach to ancient texts helps ensure their continued relevance and interest. Flexibility of elucidation is essential for the reading and rereading of texts—a cognitive exercise whose vitality depends on creative investigation. But can this multi-dimensional appreciation of sacred words also take place in the predominantly experiential setting of liturgical worship? More specifically, can the music to which a prayer is sung be perceived in multiple ways?

An answer to these questions is found in the writings of church music scholar Albert Matson. Buried in the pages of his 1907 book, esoterically titled *Psalmodic Science vs. Psalmodic Sciolism,* is brief mention of four "uses" of sacred music. Like the four components of Pardes, these musical approaches grow in intensity as they move from one to the next: display, drapery, convenient expression, and real devotion.[1]

Display refers to a sacred song's entertainment value, which invites positive—if sometimes superficial—engagement in the prayer ritual. Drapery involves musical embellishments, which draw attention to certain words or phrases. Convenient expression is the translation of a prayer's themes into musical tones. And, lastly, real devotion occurs when music lifts the worshiper into transcendent communion with the divine.

It is not difficult to draw parallels between the four-point systems of Pardes and Matson. The simplicity of *Peshat* corresponds with the straightforwardness of display. *Remez* draws out meanings of the text in a way similar to the embellishments of musical drapery. Just as *Derash* unlocks new applications of ancient words, convenient expression seeks to turn these words into a vibrant experience. And the mysteries unfolded in *Sod* are akin to those discovered when prayer-song is felt as real devotion.

A few additional points should be made regarding the value of Matson's categories. Though they travel from simple to profound, with real devotion as the spiritual ideal, it is not a failure if the music falls short of inspiring mystical union. Each level fulfills an important role in prayer, whether it is to create a delightful atmosphere or illuminate prayerful words. Moreover, these levels are not mutually exclusive: a melody can be simultaneously display and convenient expression, or be perceived as drapery one week and inspire real devotion the next.

---

1. Albert Matson, *Psalmodic Science vs. Psalmodic Sciolism* (San Diego, CA: Press of Frye and Smith, 1907), 71.

A *Shir Koddesh*

The question of what makes a song holy is, on its surface, easy to answer. By definition, a song is music with words, and so a holy song is one with words of a religious nature. In this most basic definition, it matters little what the song actually sounds like: its character is determined by subject matter rather than chord progressions, rhythms, note sequences, or any other strictly musical feature. A freely chanted *Ahavat Olam*, for instance, is no more intrinsically holy than a version that moves to a disco beat; the difference is one of style, not sanctity. Put simply, as long as the song's text derives from the liturgy, Bible, or other religious poetry, it is classified as holy, whether its music is good, bad, or indifferent.

But can a holy song, or *shir koddesh,* be comprised of lyrics that fall outside the obvious realm of sacred literature or later prayers derived from it? More precisely, can it be considered sacred without making explicit reference to God or religion? This topic was addressed in an article by Israeli professor Natan Greenboym. Using synagogue music as his starting point, Greenboym determined three elements found in most identifiably Jewish religious songs: (1) they are sung publicly in the context of a ceremony; (2) their words are delivered on behalf of the community; and (3) God is directly or indirectly referred to in the text.[1]

Before proposing pieces that meet these criteria, it is worthwhile to examine what Greenboym's three-part classification tells us about Jewish prayer-songs in general. Jewish liturgy is largely defined by its communal orientation. Not only do most prayers utilize first person plural language — we, us, our, etc.— but Judaism prefers that prayers be offered in group settings. This is reflected in the belief that whenever and wherever ten Jews are assembled in prayer (a *minyan*), the divine presence dwells among them. Additionally, Jewish sacred music is, quite naturally, focused on God. Flipping through a book of synagogue songs, one is hard-pressed to find pieces that do not make clear reference to the divine, either with a standard blessing — e.g., "*Baruch ata Adonai ...*" — or terms like *Adonai* and *Elohim* interspersed in the text.

According to Greenboym, these fundamental elements of Jewish prayer can be located in songs that are not liturgical *per se,* and that express religious sentiments in a less straightforward way. Representative of this type is the popular Israeli song "*Bashanah Haba'ah*." Like a prayer of hope, it looks forward to "the year that will be," when peace and tranquility will permeate the earth and be felt in activities as mundane as watching birds fly, children play, and grapes ripening on the vine. Though this song uses contemporary Hebrew and makes no explicit mention of God, it has nevertheless found its way into many religious services. This promotion from secular to sacred owes to the song's adaptability for group singing, its universal longings and sentiments, and, most importantly, its almost messianic theme of a future peace. It is not difficult to draw parallels between the song and liturgical selections like *Sim Shalom* and *Oseh Shalom*, and though "Bashanah Haba'ah" is by no means a theological exposition, it at least implies the intervention of the divine Maker of Peace.

Other examples of non-liturgical holy songs include Naomi Shemer's "Yerushalayim Shel Zahav," the folk tune "Hevenu Shalom Aleichem," and the Israeli national anthem "Hatikvah"—each of which is simultaneously secular and saturated with religious concerns. To reiterate, a *shir koddesh*, whether from an established sacred source or lyrics scribed in modern Hebrew, English, or another language, is holy not because of what it sounds like, but because of what it says and where it says it. Specifically, a *shir koddesh* gives voice to communal beliefs and aspirations, is used in public ceremonies, and is infused with an awareness of God, however subtle it may be.

1. Nathan Greenboym, "Yerushalayim Shel Zahav Ke'shir Koddesh," *Mayim Midalav* (1993): 32.

Instruments of Worship

Instrumental music was a vital part of religious worship throughout biblical times. The Song of the Sea, the Bible's first instance of praise singing, was accompanied by women dancing and playing timbrels (Exod. 15:20). King David established Levitical choirs and orchestras for the express purpose of enhancing the mood of sacred services (I Chr. 15:16). Instrument playing was a required feature of holiday celebrations (Num. 10:10), and an outlet for religious emotions (e.g., Ps. 150). The Bible's many musical references reveal an environment in which the sound of instruments was virtually synonymous with worship. But, with the fall of the Temple and rise of rabbinic Judaism, instrumental music was substantially silenced.

Following the destruction of the Second Temple in 70 C.E., rabbinic authorities banned instruments on Shabbat and holidays. This prohibition came gradually, and likely did not reach into all communities. Over time, however, the proscription became the norm, and to this day places limits on the sonic complexion of Orthodox and some Conservative services.

To be sure, this ruling was not arrived at arbitrarily, though the reasons behind it are not particularly strong. The main source for the ban is a *mishnah* in Tractate *Beitzah*, which states, "one may not smack or dance or clap on Shabbat and Yom Tov" (5:2). The Talmud explains that such smacking, clapping, and dancing could cause an instrument to break, and fixing it would be a forbidden form of work (BT *Beitzah* 36b). Rashi echoed this position, noting that if exuberant movements are forbidden because they might lead to fixing an instrument, playing an instrument should be banned for the same reason.

Another source argues that Jews should constantly mourn the Temple's destruction, and thus refrain from any and all music (BT *Gittin* 7a). The scope of this opinion was debated by *halakhic* authorities, some of whom allowed for (dignified) instrumental music at events such as weddings. But the idea of mourning for the Temple persisted as a popular rationale for silencing instruments on Shabbat and holidays.

Neither reason for the prohibition is terribly compelling. If fixing a broken instrument is such a major transgression, then musicians could have been advised to bring a spare or simply sit out if their instruments became unplayable. And using the ban as a sign of mourning seems to contradict the idea of Shabbat as a day when mourning is not permitted. Nevertheless, the rule found its way into the legal codes and remains a defining aspect of traditionalist practice.

It is probable, however, that the law was socially rather than theologically driven. The message behind the legal rationale is clear: the rabbis did not want instruments in sacred services. There are at least three reasons for this position. First, surrounding pagan cultures recognized instruments as attributes of deities, and used them in cultic rituals, including those of an orgiastic nature. These instruments were very similar to those found among the Jews, and so the rabbis likely instituted the ban as a policy of purity and separation.

Cantor-composer Stephen Richards offers a second theory.[1] He notes that Temple worship was hierarchic, with music performed by a select group of trained professionals. In contrast, emerging synagogues were democratic, and favored stylized folk tunes. With the dispersion, there was no longer a need for the art music of the Temple or the instruments it required. The skills for constructing and playing them were eventually forgotten, and the legal ruling was invented as a justification for the instruments' disappearance.

A third possibility is that the proscription stemmed from a general desire to break ties with Temple practices. Though the rabbis had some connection to the Pharisees, and many were themselves *kohanim*, they worked to eliminate vestiges of the old system. This entailed, among other things, the elimination of certain rituals linked to the Temple, such as the sacrificial rite and its handmaiden, instrumental music.

These explanations provide a practical basis for the rabbis' stance against instrumental music on Shabbat and holidays. Like the bulk of *halakha,* these opinions grew out of specific socio-religious needs and experiences. They were likely devised to give theological cover for the social reasons mentioned above. As such, the ruling was made permanent, even as times, places, and situations changed. Jews no longer need to differentiate themselves from orgiastic cults. History has produced many skilled Jewish musicians and instrument makers. The Temple rituals are now a distant and faded memory. But for those who champion Jewish law, the prohibition remains as relevant as the day it was conceived.

1. Stephen Richards, "Music and Prayer in Reform Worship," *Journal of Synagogue Music* 9:1 (1979): 20.

Richard Dawkins and Synagogue Song

Even the most beloved and widely sung melodies were once strange to the ears of congregants. Over time, a portion of this music has become so familiar that it is hard to imagine certain prayers ever existing without it. There are a number of reasons why music becomes attached to liturgical texts, not the least of which are musical qualities like pleasantness and memorability. However, three particularly strong influences on synagogue musical choice are not merely matters of aesthetics, but forces that direct religious life more generally: tradition, authority, and revelation.

Richard Dawkins, the evolutionary biologist and outspoken atheist, lists tradition, authority, and revelation as "three bad reasons for believing anything," since they are derived from factors other than empirical data.[1] Admittedly, it is strange to use Dawkins's analysis to gain a better understanding of synagogue musical decisions; but his observations do explain, at least in part, why people tend to believe that certain melodies are more authentic and/or suitable than others. And, while these may not necessarily be "bad" reasons, as Dawkins suggests, they are rooted in sentiment rather than science.

The first, tradition, refers to beliefs and practices handed down from one generation to the next. For many religious people, this is the most compelling reason to adhere to stories, doctrines, rules, and rituals. Because they were deemed correct and valuable in the past, they carry the weight of truth to the present. According to Dawkins, "The trouble with tradition is that, no matter how long ago a story was made up, it is still exactly as true as the original story was. If you make up a story that isn't true, handing it down over a number of centuries doesn't make it any truer."[2] While this does not have perfect parallel in synagogue music, music that achieves the status of tradition does have the clout of being "the right way." Songs and musical systems that have been passed on through the ages tend to be vehemently adhered to. The music may not be especially beautiful or particularly apt for the text it accompanies, but because it is long established, many consider it a sin to introduce new melodies in its place.

The second element, authority, also holds sway over musical decisions. Religious beliefs and behaviors are often decreed by important individuals and governing bodies. This is seen in the rules and customs of rabbinic Judaism, and is evident in the doctrinal and ritual guidelines of the various denominations. To be sure, all unified groups—religious and otherwise—require that its members agree to a set of shared standards and convictions. But, the issue for Dawkins is that religious authorities are free to dictate dogma and regulations without providing convincing rationale. It is not our purpose here to diminish the intrinsic value of much of these rulings, or to cast all religious authorities in a bad light. What is important to note is that some musical norms are the product of this top-down process, wherein prominent individuals or committees decide that certain melodies are to be used in worship instead of others. This is confirmed in the publishing and dissemination of denominational songbooks. The melodies they contain may not necessarily be the best, and the reasons they were chosen may not always be clear. Yet, no matter how arbitrary the tunes may seem, the fact that they have received a stamp of approval from the powers that be gives them "official" status, and makes them more likely to enter the synagogue mainstream.

A third way religious ideas are received is through revelation. Leaders and prophets of all religions rely on revelation for insights into the supernatural world, divine guidance, and other aspects of the faith. For Dawkins, revelation is simply a hunch: "When religious people just have a feeling inside themselves that something must be true, even though there is no evidence that it is true, they call their feeling 'revelation.'"[3] Regardless of the veracity of these experiences, their force is wholly dependent on the individual's testimony. Concepts and precepts traced to revelation have special significance in religious circles. In the case of synagogue music, the title "*Mi-Sinai*" links a corpus of Festival and High Holy Day tunes to Moses on Sinai, Judaism's central revelatory experience, even though the music originated in medieval Germany. In a less dramatic way, folk tunes can become so widely known that they lose their standing as human creations, and garner a sense of having been revealed in some distant, mystical time and place.

Certain prayer-melodies will always be favored over others. This is partly because ritual and its constituent elements, like music, are by nature repetitive, and communities tend to cling to a modest assortment of tunes for a given service. Yet, this does not necessarily account for why specific music is chosen. Of course, some melodies are selected because they are catchy and suit the general taste of the congregants. This is a natural process directed by general consensus. However, in other instances the powerful forces of tradition, authority, and revelation influence musical choices. Liturgical songs and modal systems situated in these exalted categories are perceived as "correct" and "authentic," and are very difficult to change.

---

1. Richard Dawkins, "Good and Bad Reasons for Believing," in Dale McGowan, ed., *Parenting Beyond Belief: On Raising Ethical Caring Kids Without Religion* (New York: Amacom, 2007), 14.
2. Dawkins, "Good and Bad Reasons for Believing," 15.
3. Dawkins, "Good and Bad Reasons for Believing," 16.

Darwin, Heschel, Music, and Marriage

"Nothing exists in isolation," wrote Protestant theologian Samuel Harris (1814–1899). "Nothing exists by and for itself. Everywhere interaction, intercommunication...."[1] This rule applies not only to things of nature, like galaxies and ecosystems, where everything affects everything else and vice versa. It is also true that no theory, sentiment, or artistic creation arises independent of prior encounters, experiences, and observations. Thus, innovations are properly understood as new links between existing ideas and information, rather than changes that emerge out of thin air. Without doubt, any field can experience groundbreaking advancements, usually coming from gifted individuals who are keenly aware of their environments and skilled at synthesizing material. But, as Kohelet taught us millennia ago, "there is nothing new under the sun" (Eccl. 1:9).

This mixture of openness to inspiration and drawing connections is a hallmark of science and theology, two often-competing branches of knowledge that make grand assertions about our intricate and intertwined world. These disciplines consider a variety of phenomena and draw far-reaching conclusions from a range of evidence, both anecdotal and tested. And it is often the case that profound scientific insights and influential theological claims are prompted by unlikely and seemingly unrelated sources. It is, then, not surprising to find that major concepts in the work of Charles Darwin and Abraham Joshua Heschel were stimulated by the sound of music.

Though these men lived in different times and places, had differing interests, and engaged in disparate fields of inquiry, they did share important things in common—namely that they were non-musicians married to accomplished pianists. Darwin was captivated by his wife Emma's daily piano playing, and took note of its ability to shape his mood. These musical experiences eventually led him to two key evolutionary theories. One is his supposition that "musical notes and rhythm were first acquired by the male or female progenitors of mankind for the sake of charming the opposite sex."[2] This claim was no doubt influenced by his own enthrallment with Emma's playing, and the intense attraction it stimulated. The second theory involves inherited traits, which came partly from Darwin's observation that his ten children possessed varied levels of musical ability. In particular, he surmised that his daughter Annie's aptitude for the piano was passed on from her mother, and subsequently wrote, "If we suppose any habitual action to become inherited — and I think it can be shown that this does sometimes happen — then the resemblance between what originally was a habit and an instinct becomes so close as not to be distinguished."[3]

Heschel's thought was similarly guided by his wife Sylvia's piano playing. Heschel only began writing on theology after he was married, and Sylvia's music inspired him to see religious life in terms of musical metaphors. Viewing God as an "ineffable mystery," Heschel felt that the only mode of expression appropriate for conveying God's presence is the elevated speech of music. As he wrote, "Music is more than just expressiveness. It is rather a reaching out toward a realm that lies beyond the reach of verbal propositions.... While other forces in society combine to dull our mind, music endows us with moments in which the sense of the ineffable becomes alive."[4] He also admired Sylvia's dedication to her instrument, and the many hours she spent practicing and refining her skills. This total involvement was, in Heschel's mind, analogous to Jewish devotion. Like a great concert, the full expression of Judaism requires commitment, discipline, and concentration. "For a mitzvah is like a musical score," Heschel explained, "and its performance is not a mechanical accomplishment but an artistic act."[5]

Four general conclusions can be drawn from the above discussion. First is the aforementioned principle that novel ideas are in essence new connections, sometimes between apparently dissimilar things. The second is how important music is to human existence and how much it can teach us about ourselves. Third is the susceptibility of non-musicians to music's emotional impact—a purity of experience often lost among musicians whose tendency is to analyze and critique the music they hear. Fourth, and perhaps most importantly, is that Darwin and Heschel's writings confirm the old adage: behind every great man is a great woman.

1. Samuel Harris, *The Self-Revelation of God* (New York: Charles Scribner's Sons, 1886), 323.
2. Charles Darwin, *The Descent of Man* (New York: D. Appleton and Co., 1871), 477.
3. Charles Darwin, *On the Origin of Species* (New York: D. Appleton and Co., 1864), 186.
4. Abraham Joshua Heschel, *The Insecurity of Freedom* (New York: Macmillan, 1963), 245.
5. Abraham Joshua Heschel, *God in Search of Man: A Philosophy of Judaism* (New York: Farrar, Straus and Giroux, 1955), 315.

Liturgical Hits

Denis Crowdy, a music professor at Sidney's Macquarie University, posed a penetrating question in his 2006 study of cover bands in Papua New Guinea: "Why are some songs, bands and genres featured more than others in the selection of covers?"[1] This question gets to the heart of a fascinating, though not easily decoded, aspect of songwriting: the anatomy of a hit. Cover bands, especially those in outlying areas like Papua New Guinea, are usually comprised of unknown performers whose success depends entirely on their ability to reproduce songs already liked by the general public. There is little room in their repertoires for "forgotten gems" or "unknown masterpieces"—only the most popular songs of a given genre will do. They may specialize in a decade, group, or style, or have a more eclectic approach, and can be found at venues ranging from wedding receptions to casino lounges. No matter where or which type(s) of music they perform, cover bands are careful to select material that will immediately resonate with their audience.

Professor Crowdy gives four reasons why certain songs are chosen instead of others—characteristics that speak to the larger issue of what makes a hit. These features are: exposure on radio and other media; representation of a particular style; impact of the original performance/recording; and subject matter. To be sure, these broad qualities are not the only ingredients of a popular song and do not account for details of context, such as its connection to a historical event. Nevertheless, they are aspects shared by most popular tunes, and are therefore instructive in explaining—at least on a cursory level—what determines a hit.

Crowdy's observations are not limited to the secular realm. They can be applied to contemporary synagogue music, especially that of singer-songwriter Debbie Friedman (1951–2011). Many of Friedman's melodies became synagogue standards during her nearly forty-year career, including "*Sh'ma/V'ahavta*" (1972), "Not By Might—Not By Power" (1974), "Aleph Bet Song" (1981), "Miriam's Song" (1988), "*Mi Shebeirach*" (1988), and "*T'filat HaDerech*" (1988). A portion of her musical output is so pervasive in liberal synagogues that it is easy to lose track of who wrote it. Through years of usage, these songs have not only become inseparable from the service, but have taken on the character of folk tunes—that is, of being old songs with no known composer. However, rather than demanding constant credit for her melodies, Friedman was thrilled that her music was, in a sense, the property of the people. "I feel that I have been blessed with the gift to create this music," Friedman told the Milken Archive of Jewish Music. "I do not take ownership because I do not feel that it is mine. I am totally committed to working to reach as many people as I can through this music."

Friedman was equally gifted as a songwriter and performer. She enjoyed a busy schedule playing at synagogues, community centers, conventions, retreats, and concert halls, and released twenty albums of original songs. Her passionate voice and accessible songwriting merged to form a sound that inspired countless Jews to reexamine, renew, and reinvigorate their connections to the faith. Because she was so widely known as a performer, a case can be made that cantors, rabbis, and others who sing her music in synagogue are, in a way, functioning as cover bands. And though it may not always be a conscious process, they generally select music from her catalogue using the criteria Crowdy stipulated.

Like most notable songwriters, some of Friedman's melodies are more popular than others. Less readily obvious is why these pieces get more attention. The four reasons Crowdy gives are helpful in this regard. First, the more popular songs have had more exposure, either through inclusion in songbooks and other publications, or by earning the "blessing" of official bodies and trend-setting congregational leaders. Second, the songs are particularly strong representations of folk-rock music, the idiom in which Friedman excelled. Third, their popularity owes to the quality and effect of Friedman's own performance—either live or recorded—including the timbre of her voice, energy exuded, sincerity of expression, and so on. Fourth, the words are especially moving or address subject matter from a fresh point of view, as with her English interpretations of biblical themes and liturgical texts.

Any combination of these elements helps to explain the popularity of Friedman's songs, and it is almost certain that her music will remain a defining part of American Judaism for decades to come. Despite the fact that she wrote in a style that had its heyday almost forty years ago, her songs are still as relevant as ever. Indeed, it is a testament to Friedman's genius that her music is able to transcend time and place, and resonate with Jews young and old.

1. Denis Crowdy, "Tribute Without Attribution: Kopikat, Covers and Copyright in Papua New Guinea," in Shane Homan, ed., *Access All Eras: Tribute Bands and Global Pop Culture* (Berkshire: Open University Press, 2006), 229–240.

The Legacy of Jack Gottlieb

With the recent passing of composer Jack Gottlieb (1930–2011), American Jewish music has lost one of its most inspired, creative, and articulate voices. Not only was Gottlieb among a handful of highly trained composers who have applied their gifts to Judaically related music, he was also an authority on Jewish music history, known especially for his research into Jewish influences on the rise of American popular music. He studied with Aaron Copland, Max Helfman, Irving Fine, and other eminent composers, and from 1958 to 1966 served as Leonard Bernstein's assistant at the New York Philharmonic. Gottlieb described his own music as "basically eclectic," informed equally by Jewish sources and distinctly American harmonies and rhythms.

Gottlieb was in every respect a serious musician and a serious Jew. Unlike many of his colleagues, he was not willing to dumb-down his considerable talents for the sake of creating "accessible" or "singable" synagogue tunes. As a result, much of Gottlieb's musical output falls outside the range of average synagogues. His high artistic standards earned him a reputation as a champion of serious liturgical music, which strives to capture the dignity of prayer and the elegance of the Hebrew language. He was, in fact, a prominent critic of the use of folk-rock idioms in the American synagogue. Instead, he advocated the blending of cantorial art with the most sophisticated elements of jazz, Broadway, and other contemporary American genres.

The call for synagogue music that is at once historically grounded, contemporary, and sophisticated placed Gottlieb squarely between the traditionalists, who cling to a fossilized body of modes and melodies, and the functionalists, who see the appropriation of straightforward and popular styles, like folk-rock, as the best way to appease Jews of varying levels of musical and Judaic expertise.

At present, Gottlieb's position seems the least sustainable of the three. There will always be a significant number of Jews who buck current trends and actively work to retain a "tried and true" synagogue musical culture. This is, of course, the dominant position of all forms of Orthodoxy, but also resonates with those in less rigorous branches who stick to "old favorites" and reject musical change. An even more prominent view belongs to those who consider commercial music familiar to the American ear as the most suitable for modern worship. This attitude is pervasive in liberal denominations, which generally opt for relevance over refinement.

Compared to these approaches, Gottlieb's vision of an elevated contemporary sound places far greater demands on the composer and the congregation. Both parties need sufficient training in order to bring such music to life, and in a society that celebrates convenience and downplays commitment, few congregations seem up to the task. There are, indeed, numerous synagogue songs by Gottlieb and others that have been deemed too complex for the worship setting.

In light of all this, it is possible that Gottlieb's point of view will accompany him to the grave. But it is also possible that, with the wealth of music and writings he has given the Jewish people, his opinions will persist alongside the traditionalist and functionalist views, and have at least a modest impact on the future direction of synagogue song in America.

II

Spirituality, Emotions and Identity

Religion, Emotion and Music

Spirituality can be defined as "religion plus emotion." When one speaks of a spiritual experience, it usually includes intuitive feelings couched in theological or supernatural beliefs. Such phenomena are regarded as utterly separate from and more intense than ordinary emotions, and are often related in weighty word pairings like "spiritual joy," "religious trembling," and "devotional ecstasy." However, because these occurrences are by definition beyond material things and mundane classifications, they are both highly personal and ultimately ineffable. And, though their perceived distinction from other kinds of moods and emotional states can be attributed in part to context — setting, frame of mind, and worldview — spiritual episodes reside in a category seemingly impervious to rational criticisms or explanations.

The "beyondness" of spiritual experiences, and specifically divine encounters, was given treatment in the writings of Protestant theologian Rudolf Otto. All religions, Otto maintained, have their basis in an experience of the holy or numinous — an unmistakable yet indefinable feeling of communion and transcendence consisting simultaneously of fear and trembling (*mysterium tremendum*) and utter fascination (*mysterium fascinans*). These mysterious and non-rational (or supra-rational) components of the religious experience are the subject of *The*

Idea of the Holy (1917), Otto's argument for the objective reality of the "wholly other."

At the core of his thesis is the assertion that the numinous experience, which signals the presence of the sacred, is more fundamental than and exists prior to and independent of any belief or conceptual understanding of the experience. It is, in Otto's words, "perfectly sui generis and irreducible to any other; and therefore, like every absolutely primary and elementary datum, while it admits of being discussed, it cannot be strictly defined."[1]

On the one hand, Otto acknowledged the necessity of rational reflection in interpreting such experiences to the degree that language allows. Because the holy encounter is known by the senses, it does have an intelligible component. On the other hand, he felt that to frame the experience solely in what can be ascertained by sensory faculties would constitute a rejection of the reality that exists beyond it. In such experiences, Otto posited, "to know and to understand are two different things," and can even be "mutually exclusive and contested." This view paints a distinction between the encounter itself (knowing) and later interpretations (understanding). It is through the gradual process of "rationalization and moralization" that numinous experiences gain "progressively rational, moral, and cultural significance," and are sometimes developed into religious systems.

Despite the essentially inexpressible nature of the numinous encounter, Otto did attempt to describe its characteristics, though he admitted in inadequate terms. He explained that it begins with a feeling of "personal nothingness" and submergence before the "awe-inspiring object directly experienced." Elsewhere, he described this feeling as "stupor," which "signifies blank wonder, an astonishment that strikes us dumb, amazement absolute."[2] Almost immediately, this awed state gives way to "shuddering," an overwhelming feeling consisting of dread and unease.

Significantly, Otto compared the sacred experience to "the beauty of a musical composition which no less eludes complete conceptual analysis."[3] Like a symphony, the enormity of the divine encounter occurs instantaneously, allowing little time for one to examine its complexities or decipher particular elements. As he wrote: "Music stands too high for any understanding to reach, and an all-mastering efficacy goes forth from it, of which, however, no man is able to give an account."[4] Music is thus an ideal manner of conveying the sacred experience: it recalls the qualities of marvel and grandeur associated with the divine. The non-rational beauty of music, like the ineffability of the sacred experience, cannot be fully understood within the ordinary parameters of knowledge.

Churches and synagogues have long employed sacred music to induce congregants to moods approximating those aroused in encounters with the holy. In the Western Church, for instance, transcendence is sometimes conveyed in soft passages representing the silent awe felt in the presence of the divine. The modal patterns found in Mizrahi synagogues are likewise designed to move worshipers to specific moods linked to liturgical occasions and themes. In fact, the words mode and mood seem to share a common linguistic root, and modal music of all types is usually tied to certain elementary emotions or affects.

In the worship setting, music that succeeds in capturing a religious mood can inspire devotion and contemplation. Even if one fails to resonate with the message of a prayer, or is distracted from deep worship by worldly concerns, sacred music can stimulate an appropriate emotional state, disarming the rational mind, and inviting an embrace of the sacred moment. For Otto, this is mainly possible because music, like the sacred experience, can stir one to simultaneous feelings of fear and awe. In more general terms, music is used to arouse or intensify a highly emotional, non-rational, and fundamentally inexpressible connection with the divine. This is one reason why the elevated language of tones has for millennia been considered a signal of transcendence.

1. Rudolf Otto, *The Idea of the Holy* (London: Oxford University Press, 1923), 30.
2. Otto, *Idea of the Holy*, 26.
3. Otto, *Idea of the Holy*, 59.
4. Otto, *Idea of the Holy*, 155.

The Divine Lover of Music

The morning service begins with two sets of preliminary prayers. The first, *birchot ha-shachar,* is an assemblage of blessings originally recited during morning routines, such as waking, washing, dressing, and using the restroom. In the liturgical context, these blessings are followed by the more spiritually directed verses of song—*pesukei d'zimra*—

derived from psalms and other biblical sources. A quick glance at this second set reveals an indispensable partnership of music and prayer. It includes numerous musical proclamations, like "make music to God," "come before God with joyous song," and "sing to God a new song." These words capture a central theme in Jewish religious thought: music helps to focus attention on the worship experience.

The most intriguing part of the verses of song is its conclusion: "Blessed is God ... Who chooses melodies of praise." With this statement, we move from music as a means of attaining a worshipful state to an understanding of God as Music Lover. In the words of famed cantor Leib Glantz, "This description of God as a lover of music is based on many manifestations of Jewish religious expression that we find throughout Jewish history, from the days of the Bible through the ceremonial services in both Holy Temples in Jerusalem, up to the early days of the synagogues of the Diaspora."[1]

But what sort of melodies might God prefer? Jewish music is as diverse as the Jews themselves. It exhibits influences from all regions and eras in which the Jews have lived, and spans endless styles and genres from Renaissance to reggae. We should not (and cannot) assume which of these melodies God "chooses." Rather than a purist or harsh critic, it is perhaps best to think of the Maker of all things (including the human capacity for music making) as having eclectic musical taste. "Who chooses melodies of praise" can therefore be read as a general statement, indicating that God favors melodious praise over plain recitation.

Additionally, the idea that God listens to melodies should encourage worshipers to be careful when selecting musical settings for the synagogue. Music has the remarkable ability to convey the mood and message of a prayer, even for those who do not fully understand its language. Skilled composers and songwriters utilize musical tools and techniques to interpret liturgical texts. They can bring out the joyousness of a thanksgiving psalm, the warmth and comfort of a healing text, the plaintiveness of a confessional prayer, and so forth.

The best synagogue songs are not necessarily the most refined or harmonically complex. Instead, they are those deemed most suitable for their given texts. So, while God chooses *that* Jews sing melodies of praise, they must choose wisely *which* melodies they sing.

---

1. Leib Glantz, "The Cantor—A Unique Creation of Jewish Life," in Jerry Glantz, ed., *Leib Glantz: The Man Who Spoke to God* (Tel Aviv: Tel Aviv Institute for Jewish Liturgical Music, 2008), 369.

To Edify and Glorify

Worship music works in two fundamental directions. On the one hand, it transports participants into a shared experience, focusing their energies on the group and the moment of prayer. On the other hand, it establishes a line of communication between humanity and the divine, acting as what Nietzsche called a "telephone of the beyond."[1] Taken together, these relationships—horizontal between individuals and vertical between the community and God—form the basis of religious life itself, and substantially validate the role of music within it.

Music's potential to draw people together and reach toward heaven is the subject of an essay by British scholar and novelist C. S. Lewis (1898–1963).[2] Lewis was not a fan of musical worship, and once remarked that services should have fewer, better, and shorter hymns—especially fewer. Unlike most who have assessed the merits of prayer-song, he was unconvinced that physical and emotional responses to music have any religious relevance, or signify anything greater than "animal" feelings. Yet, because devotional singing is so widely employed, he offered guidelines for creating optimal worship music, rather than advocating its total abolishment (however much he would have preferred the latter). Specifically, he called for music that both edifies the people and glorifies God.

Lewis's concept of edification centers on the belief that discrepancies of taste and musical aptitude within a congregation are not impediments, but opportunities for goodwill, humility, and spiritual growth. For instance, if a cantor introduces a new melody that does not lend itself to immediate participation, or sings a setting that lies outside of a listener's preference or range of exposure, this music should be greeted as a learning opportunity. Not only can it expand musical literacy and shed fresh light on the liturgy, it can also, when heard with appreciative ears, encourage acceptance of fellow congregants for whom the music deeply resonates. Thus, while it is true that worshipers strengthen ties to one another by singing their favorite tunes, this bond can also be fortified through exposure to a new melody and the open-mindedness and appreciation it promotes.

Music that glorifies God is, according to Lewis, "excellent in its own kind; almost as the birds and flowers and the heavens themselves glorify Him."[3] He argued that only our best efforts should be applied to composing, selecting, and singing sacred tunes; banal sounds and superficial performances have no place in the house of worship. With this, Lewis stressed that what is important is not the "high brow" or "low brow" appeal of a piece, but rather its sincerity of composition and execution. The simplest melody can soar to God if sung from the heart, while an intricate masterpiece can fall flat without proper intent. In Lewis's words, "all our offerings, whether of music or martyrdom, are like the intrinsically worthless present of a child which a father values indeed, but values only for the intention."[4]

Lewis's criteria of edification and glorification address the two directions of communication possible in sacred song. Edifying music is for the worshipers, enhancing their prayer experience and, more importantly, their relationship to one another. Glorifying music is for God, lifting prayers toward heaven on the wings of sincerity and devotion. When a prayer-song fulfills this dual aim, it magnifies the horizontal bond between individuals and intensifies the vertical link between the people and God.

1. Gerardus van Der Leeuw, *Sacred and Profane Beauty: The Holy in Art* (New York: Oxford University Press: 2006), 246.
2. C. S. Lewis, "On Church Music," *Journal of Synagogue Music* 8:1 (1978): 27–31.
3. Lewis, "On Church Music," 28.
4. Lewis, "On Church Music," 31.

Six Songs in the Hebrew Bible

In *The World in Six Songs,* neuroscientist and musician Daniel J. Levitin explains how the "musical brain" has helped shape human nature and culture over the past fifty thousand years. According to Levitin, six types of songs—friendship, joy, comfort, knowledge, religion, and love—enabled the bonding necessary for the development of society itself. "Music," he writes, "is not simply a distraction or a pastime, but a core element of our identity as a species, an activity that paved the way for more complex behaviors such as language, large-scale cooperative undertakings, and the passing down of important information from one generation to the next."[1]

It is fascinating to note that the six song types Levitin identifies are found throughout the Hebrew Bible. Songs accompanied all aspects of biblical life, from feasts and festivals to war and mourning. These songs stimulated and enhanced the ancient Jews' sense of identity, solidarity, and cohesion. They captured national sentiments and memories, eased collective pain and sorrow, and gave voice to shared emotions and experiences. In short, they were essential to the development of Jewish civilization.

The Hebrew Bible mentions songs and singing 309 times. Each of these references can be placed into one of Levitin's six categories, though doing so would be impossible in a short essay. Instead, I offer some representative examples.

Songs of friendship promote feelings of camaraderie and social bonding. Biblical songs of this type include Psalm 133, from which *Hinei Ma Tov* is derived: "How good and how pleasant it is that brothers dwell together." Songs of joy are found in disparate biblical books, such as I Kings, "All the people marched behind [Solomon], playing on flutes and making merry...." (1:40), and Job, "They sing to the music of timbrel and lute, and rejoice to the tune of the pipe" (20:12). Comfort songs include the biblical psalms of lament. These psalms were originally sung during fast days and other times of national suffering. They voice personal and collective complaints, ask for God's aid, and express divine praise (e.g., Pss. 3, 12, 60, and 94). Knowledge songs are also prevalent in the Book of Psalms. They transmit central historical and theological information to the community. Psalm 111, for example, delineates central beliefs about God's character and work in the world. The Bible is also filled with religion songs, which were used during worship and other ceremonial rituals. The first account of religious singing in the Bible appears after the Israelites crossed the Red Sea: "Then Moses and the Israelites sang this song to the Lord. They said: I will sing to the Lord, for He has triumphed gloriously..." (Exod. 15:1). And an entire biblical book, the Song of Songs, is a collection of love songs.

The Hebrew Bible chronicles the historical and intellectual development of the earliest periods of Jewish history. With Levitin's study in mind, it should come as no surprise that this development was accompanied by song. As he states: "[Music] has been with humans since we first *became* humans. It has shaped the world through six kinds of songs: friendship, joy, comfort, knowledge, religion, and love."[2]

1. Daniel J. Levitin, *The World in Six Songs: How the Musical Brain Created Human Nature* (New York: Dutton, 2008), 3.
2. Levitin, *The World in Six Songs*, 40.

Music, Prayer and Concentration

The First Book of Samuel begins with the story of Hannah, the favored wife of Elkanah. Unlike Elkanah's other wife, Peninah, Hannah is unable to have children. Peninah uses this to torment Hannah, claiming that God has closed her womb. "This happened year after year," the Bible tells us. "Every time she went up to the House of the Lord, the other would taunt her, so that she wept and would not eat" (1 Sam. 1:7). During an annual pilgrimage to Shiloh, where the Holy Ark was stored, Hannah vows that if she is able to have a son, she will dedicate him to divine service. Her prayer is answered, and she bears Samuel, judge and prophet of Israel.

Hannah's prayer is personal and spontaneous. As the story relates, she "was praying in her heart; only her lips moved, but her voice could not be heard" (1 Sam. 1:12). From this verse, the rabbis derived the principle that true prayer requires sincerity and concentration. The worshiper, they maintained, should strive to be like Hannah, who made her heart attentive to God (BT *Berakhot* 31a). This became known as *kavvanah*: the intention necessary for the performance of religious duties. *Kavvanah* is the ideal devotional state, in which the individual is entirely focused on the words, activity, and object of prayer. As Maimonides put it, "*Kavvanah* means that a man should empty his mind of all other thoughts and regard himself as if he were standing before the Divine Presence" (*Yad, Tefillah* 6:16).

But, Hannah lived in a time before liturgy, when prayers were uttered exclusively in response to the realities of life. Sorrows and joys triggered extemporaneous outpourings of petition and praise; there were no scripts or formulas outlining which words were to be spoken. However, with the emergence of the synagogue service came the need for a set order of prayers determined by the time of day, day of the week, and date on the sacred calendar.

As a communal activity, synagogue ritual necessitates a common literature to guide participants through the themes and sentiments of worship. To this end, most of the prayers are written in collective terms (we, us, our, etc.), and address an array of possible feelings congregants may be having (gratitude, elation, despair, etc.). Of course, the complex liturgical system does allow for some personal, impromptu prayer, especially during silent moments of the service; but it is clear from the intricacy and vastness of the prayer book that the set language of Jewish liturgy is preferred.

While the highly structured service is essential for bringing people together, and for assuring that individuals touch on the many moods of Jewish worship, its fixity can make *kavvanah* difficult to achieve. By definition, liturgy is a prayer routine, and so it is not always engaged in with the same level of intensity as spontaneous devotion. This is one reason why Jewish prayer is so closely linked with music.

As a general rule, the singing of liturgy affects us more deeply than when it is spoken, and if one does not approach a given prayer with complete concentration, the musical setting can bring him or her into a more focused state. Of course, music does not always alleviate the problems inherent in the prayer routine; but it nevertheless helps guide the worshiper into the requisite frame of mind. Twelfth-century rabbi Yehudah Ha-Chasid summed up this function of prayer-song: "If you cannot concentrate when you pray, search for melodies and choose a tune you like. Your heart will then feel what you say, for it is the song that makes your heart respond."

1. Yehudah Ha-Chasid, *Sefer Chasidim*, quoted in Jonathan L. Friedmann, ed., *Quotations on Jewish Sacred Music* (Lanham, MD: Hamilton, 2011), 36.

An Instrument Divine

"Come, let us sing unto God"; "Sing to God a new song"; "It is good to chant hymns to our God." These verses from the Book of Psalms are among the plentiful references to singing in the Hebrew Bible. From those ancient days to the present, and across varied cultures and traditions, humans have sought contact with the divine through song.

The pervasive use of prayer-song has led some to suggest that the human voice is imbued with holiness. The voice has been called "the fine instrument of God's making." All other species of musical instruments—aerophones, idiophones, membranophones, chordophones, and electronic—are fashioned by human hands; but the voice, theologically understood, is an instrument God created specifically for the purpose of prayer and praise. As nineteenth-century poet Thornton Wells wrote,

"No melody is so charming as vocal music. How divine a thing is the human voice!—divine, indeed, literally, since God made it; whereas the sweetest instrument of music that ever soothed the heart of the sorrowful was, after all, but of man's creation."[1]

Even when the rabbis prohibited the use of musical instruments in the synagogue, they encouraged the singing of prayers. The Talmud frequently draws attention to the spiritual efficacy of song. It declares that "Song is obligatory in the ritual of the sanctuary" (BT *Arakin* 11a), and ensures us that "He who sings in this world will sing also in the next" (BT *Sanhedrin* 91b).

Martin Buber relates eloquently the intimate union of soul, voice, and the divine presence: "The soul lays hold of the voice of a man and makes it sing what the soul has experienced in the heights, and the voice does not know what it does. Thus, one *tzaddik* (saintly man) stood in prayer during the High Holy Days and sang new melodies, wonder of wonders, that he had never heard and that no human ear had ever heard, and he did not know at all what he sang and in what ways he sang, for he was bound to the upper world, to the *Shekhinah* (Divine Presence)."[2]

Few recognized the sacredness of the human voice as keenly as Rabbi Nachman of Breslov. He taught, "Music has a tremendous power to draw you to God. Get into the habit of always singing a tune. It will give you a new life and send joy into your soul. Then you will be able to bind yourself to God."[3] He also explained, "It is good to make a habit of inspiring yourself with a melody. There are great concepts included in each holy melody, and they can arouse your heart and draw it toward God."[4]

There are countless other accounts of the religious value of singing, both from written sources and from our own personal experiences. Among its many spiritual benefits, singing can elevate mood, inspire meditation, strengthen bonds between people, and enhance engagement in sacred texts. For these reasons and more, it has been proposed that the voice is an instrument divine.

1. Edwin Davis, ed., *Great Thoughts on Great Truths* (New York: Ward, Lock, and Co., 1882), 423.
2. Irene Heskes, *Passport to Jewish Music: Its History, Traditions, and Culture* (New York: Tara, 1994), 117.
3. Mordechai Staiman, *Niggun: Stories Behind the Chasidic Songs that Inspire Jews* (Northvale, NJ: Jason Aronson, 1994), 34.
4. Staiman, *Niggun*, 34.

Singing Is Believing

It is sometimes difficult to reconcile the ancient words of liturgy with the realities of modern-day life. The prayer book is an assemblage of devotional texts written in distant and distinct times and places. Each prayer expresses a particular view of nature, humanity, and the divine, which does not always resonate with contemporary experience. For many, too, the Hebrew language is a barrier to understanding the Jewish liturgy. And while most prayer books contain translations of the Hebrew (literal and interpretive), these translations often fail to capture the shades of meaning found in the original language.

But both of these problems of prayer — "outdated" elements and difficult words — can be solved when the text is set to suitable music. Music has the remarkable ability to clarify the themes and message of a text (whether or not the language is understood), and to make the words believable. As church music scholar Don E. Saliers explains, "We are asked to say some things that we don't truly think we believe until we sing them or hear them in appropriately complex activities."[1]

Music is able to move us emotionally and spiritually. In the service setting, these qualities of music serve to bolster religious convictions and connections to heritage and community. Through a combination of pitches, timbres, durations, and dynamics, Jews of varying backgrounds and levels of observance are drawn into an intimate experience of worship. This is why Russian-born cantor Pinchos Jassinowsky (1886–1954) wrote, "majestic chants of the synagogue service have been of more powerful effect upon the souls of the listeners than the prayers themselves."[2]

Skilled cantors and composers utilize musical tools to dramatize liturgical texts. Prayers of thanksgiving are given joyous tones and rhythms, melodies for mourning capture the heartbreak of loss, songs of comfort uplift the spirit, and so forth. And, again, all of this can be achieved even when the words themselves are hard to believe or are not fully understood.

Cantor Leib Glantz (1898–1964) exemplified music's capacity to "enliven" sacred texts. He interpreted the meaning of every phrase with his expressive tenor voice, making the liturgy a living experience for the congregation. Idov Cohen, a former member of the Israeli Parliament, described Glantz's gift for drama: "[His] is not only a sweet and resonant voice; one marvels at its rich colors, at its technique, at the contrasts at which Glantz is such a master—from the still, silent tones that penetrate into one's very heart to the ringing fortissimo; whether in quiet lament or pathetic complaint; in richly expressive tones that resemble the blasts of a trumpet or *shofar;* in sounds that recall flutes or violins; in charming trills that are completely unostentatious; in dramatic recitative, and in reading that is half singing and is seldom approached in quality by the actors in our theatres; in rare musical feeling and in all the descriptive, narrative power of a remarkable dramatist."[3]

A liturgical text can achieve a measure of relevance and believability when it is presented in song. One does not have to believe in the literalness of the text to appreciate its underlying message and beauty. One needs only be touched by the music to which the text is sung. It can thus be said that singing is believing.

1. Don E. Saliers, *Music and Theology* (Nashville, TN: Abingdon, 2007), 6.
2. Pinchos Jassinowski, "Hazzanim and Hazzanut," in Jonathan L. Friedmann, comp., *Music in Jewish Thought: Selected Writings, 1890–1920* (Jefferson, NC: McFarland, 2009), 124.
3. Avraham Soltes, "A Lion to Sing His Will," in Jerry Glantz, ed., *Leib Glantz: The Man Who Spoke to God* (Tel Aviv: Tel Aviv Institute of Jewish Liturgical Music, 2008), 45.

From Heart to Heart

Beethoven wrote of his Mass in D, "From the heart it has come, and to the heart it shall penetrate."[1] This statement can be read as a general maxim for music, which speaks directly to the seat of emotions in a language that cannot be replicated in words. Of course, some music affects us more powerfully than others, and Beethoven's Mass is surely more potent than, say, a nursery song. But virtually all music has the potential to move us, whether by simply brightening our mood or by bringing us into more nuanced emotional states, like joyful anticipation. Importantly, too, the type and degree of music's impact is culturally derived. Everyone hears music in their own ears, and appreciation of a piece's subtle contours is largely dependent on upbringing, exposure, and cultural knowledge. If the social or musical training of the auditor differs from that of the composer, the music is unlikely to evoke the intended reaction.

The cultural aspect of music's emotional effect is exhibited in synagogue song. Jewish communities across the globe, from Texas to Tunisia, utilize specific modes and melodies to conjure desired responses. People living within a certain music culture are immediately flooded with sentiments upon hearing familiar sounds, while outsiders might remain unmoved or, more likely, be moved to different feelings. To use just one example, the Ashkenazi *Kol Nidrei* inspires awe and contrition for congregants in that tradition, but does not stir the same feelings among Sephardi, Yemeni, or Moroccan Jews, who have their own melodies for the text.

Yet, while dissimilarities of perception exist between members of different communities, congregants acquainted with a given body of sacred melodies tend to experience the same emotions, differing only in degree. These emotions can be of an abstract kind, set off by a chord progression, succession of intervals, or other musical quality, or stem from associations accrued after years of singing and/or hearing the same tune. Either way, the music fulfills the congregation's need for sounds that emotionalizes the prayer ritual.

According to Idelsohn, satisfying the people's desire for music expressive of Jewish sentiments was a central task of Eastern European cantors. Beyond breathing life into the fixed words of liturgy, the cantor's voice sounded the heritage and hope, sorrows and longings of the community. In Idelsohn's words, "The Jew demanded that the *hazzan* [cantor] through his music, make him forget his actual life, and that he elevate him on the wings of his tunes into a fantastic paradisiacal world, affording him a foretaste of the Messianic time in the heavenly Jerusalem."[2] Playing upon the congregation's musical expectations, the cantor's singing lifted the people into an otherworldly state, where the troubles of daily life were replaced with a mixture of tranquility and elation.

Other Jewish worship settings feature music similarly aimed at producing emotional effects. Whether the music is cantorial, choral, or congregational, accompanied or *a cappella*, it is, to use Beethoven's formulation, a means by which worshipers commune heart to heart, and, ultimately, turn their hearts toward heaven.

---

1. William Henry Hadow, *Studies in Modern Music: Hector Berlioz, Robert Schumann, Richard Wagner* (New York: Macmillan, 1893), 12.

2. Abraham Z. Idelsohn, *Jewish Music in Its Historical Development* (New York: Henry Holt and Co., 1929), 192.

Moods, Modes and Musical Meaning

The field of music therapy emerged after World War II, when doctors and nurses in U.S. Veterans Administration hospitals noticed the positive impact of charity concerts on emotionally and physically traumatized veterans. Hospitals began hiring musicians to perform for patients, and universities instituted music therapy degree programs. Since then, music has been used to help treat mental disorders, sensory impairments, developmental disabilities, aging, and other conditions. Research affirms music's extraordinary ability to reduce stress and anxiety, ease pain and nausea, boost learning and self-esteem, and improve one's outlook on life.

Music's therapeutic effect stems in large part from the close association of musical sounds and human emotions. In the words of musicologist Nicholas Cook, music can "unlock the most hidden contents of [one's] spiritual and emotional being."[1] In any given culture, combinations of tones instantly evoke certain responses. This is particularly true of modal music, which employs ordered sets of intervals to convey distinct moods. A given mode can stir elementary emotions, ranging from fear and anxiety to joy and peacefulness.

The ancient Greek musical system was comprised of seven primary modes, each of which was used for a particular type of occasion. The Dorian mode, for example, was utilized at solemn assemblies, while the Phrygian mode inspired soldiers. In the West, listeners generally associate negative emotions with the minor mode and positive emotions with the major. This is displayed in the brightened mood achieved when a minor chord resolves to major, and the somberness that comes when a major chord shifts to minor.

In the Ashkenazi musical tradition, there are three dominant synagogue modes. The first, *Adonai Malach* (God reigns), is a bright-sounding major mode with lowered seventh and tenth scale degrees. It is often used for the chanting of laudatory prayers, like most of the *Kabbalat Shabbat* psalms. The second mode is *Magein Avot* (Shield of the Ancestors), which is similar to minor and has a distinct pastoral quality. It is utilized throughout the Friday evening service, as illustrated in Max Helfman's well-known setting of *Hashkiveinu*. Third is *Ahavah Rabbah* (With Great Love), the Jewish mode of supplication. Considered the most "Jewish sounding" of the synagogue modes, it features a minor second and major third, forming an augmented interval between the second and third degrees of the scale. Among other prayer-songs, the *Ahavah Rabbah* mode is found in the Ashkenazi folk setting of *Avinu Malkeinu*.

Cantor Joseph A. Levine suggests that the synagogue modes were designed to move worshipers to specific emotional states.[2] In his analysis, *Adonai Malach* leads to righteousness, *Magein Avot* inspires learning, and *Ahavah Rabbah* stimulates contrition. Viewed in this way, the modes serve a similar function as music in therapeutic contexts. Just as therapists use music to trigger sensations, synagogue modes can bring worshipers into emotional states that would otherwise be difficult to attain. The sounds of liturgical chant can move people to higher ideals, deeper contemplation, greater tranquility, and even "peak" experiences. The modal chant of the synagogue can thus be understood as a form of music therapy, woven into the fabric of Jewish religious life.

1. Nicholas Cook, *A Guide to Musical Analysis* (New York: Oxford University Press, 1987), 1.
2. Joseph A. Levine, *Synagogue Song in America* (Crown Point, IN: White Cliffs, 1989), 79–106.

Mystery and Melody

Rabbi David Cohen (1887–1972), a student and colleague of Rav Kook, argued that Judaism is at its core a "spiritual-acoustic" religion. Sound, he asserted, is the least visible or tactile of perceived phenomena, and thus the most closely aligned with the divine realm. Sound surrounds and envelops us, whether or not we are focused on its source, and can shape our state of mind. In contrast to sight, sound is invisible; yet it has the capacity to move us more profoundly than what we see. For this reason, Cohen concluded: "Sound and light are the two angels of thought which accompany man everywhere" but "hearing is greater than seeing."[1]

The mysterious power of sound is captured in the biblical narrative. It states that God was revealed at Sinai through voice, not vision. "The Lord spoke to you out of the fire; you heard the sound of words but perceived no shape — nothing but a voice" (Deut. 4:12). This mode of revelation is central to Jewish theology. If God were a vision at Sinai, worshipers would have surely created icons to represent what they saw. These representations would have been limited in both size and design, reflecting the artist's perception and ability to convey it instead of the vastness or "beyondness" of the divine. Because such depictions are finite, while God is believed to be infinite, the Bible categorizes idolatry as a major sin. Sound, on the other hand, has qualities of limitlessness. It is abstract, having no physical shape or form, and is thus difficult to confine or even describe. Moreover, since God is heard and not seen, the natural human response is to obey (i.e., follow the voice who commands) rather than merely depict.

This link between sound and the holy is carried into the worship setting, where sound is synonymous with melodic chant. A prayer set to music conveys a sense of otherness absent when the words are plainly recited. While the reading of a prayer is primarily an intellectual activity, singing engages us on cognitive, sensory, and emotional levels. As Saliers writes, "music remains within the domain of the senses while pointing to a potential unity of the intellect, the emotions, and our openness to the mystery of being in the world."[2] The mystery of God—the central object of prayer—is made apparent in musical tones.

Music's ability to imbue sacred moments with a degree of mystery owes to the mysterious attributes of music itself. In a television interview, Pierre Boulez cited an author who wrote that a piece of music is first a mystery, becomes clear through study, and, with the performance, becomes a mystery once again.[3] In like manner, the contents of prayer, which can sometimes seem repetitive or even stale, are made appropriately mysterious through musical sound. The divine voice is, at least analogously, experienced through prayer-song.

1. Chaim Lifschitz, "David Cohen," *Encyclopedia Judaica*, vol. 5 (2006): 13.
2. Don E. Saliers, *Music and Theology* (Nashville, TN: Abingdon Press, 2007), 64.
3. Marcel Cobussen, *Thresholds: Rethinking Spirituality Through Music* (Burlington, VT: Ashgate, 2008), 128.

Singing, Health and Prayer

Religious services are among the few occasions when adults are expected to sing with each other. As a society, we have become consumers rather than producers of music. Whereas laborers in the field or factory used to sing songs to ease the boredom of monotonous work, today they are more likely to listen to recorded music. Music programs in schools across the country are being cut, and students are often told to abandon their musical ambitions in favor of more "economically viable" pursuits. This stands in sharp contrast to the esteemed place music held for previous generations of American Jews. As comedian George Burns wrote, "Immigrant parents believed that knowing how to sing or play an instrument was a sign of respectability, and a lot of them made big sacrifices to pay for an instrument and lessons."[1]

In recent years, a number of scientific studies have linked music production to improved health. Graham Welch, a professor at the University of London, found that people who sing are in many ways healthier than those who do not. Singing requires deeper breathing than other forms of exercise, opening up the respiratory tubes and sinuses, and increasing aerobic capacity. This results in greater oxygen intake, which benefits the heart and circulation, and decreases muscle tension. Other research has shown a connection between singing and lowered heart rate, decreased blood pressure, and reduced stress. And music critic Richard Morrison has written on the special benefits of choral singing for seniors. "Singing is the best possible exercise for the lungs," he writes, "whatever your age. But singing in a choir is far more than that. It sharpens up coordination, instills a feeling of comradeship, and breaks down the barriers that lead to feelings of loneliness and isolation."[2]

These studies confirm what Jewish worshipers have known for centuries: singing elevates the mind, body, and spirit. One of the reasons Jewish prayers are typically sung or chanted is because the act of singing, apart from the words being sung, promotes mental and physical wellness. People often leave services feeling rejuvenated, largely because they have engaged in an hour or two of active listening and music making — health-promoting exercises rarely experienced elsewhere. Moreover, certain prayers, like the *Mi Shebeirach* for the sick, are sung with the purpose of bringing comfort to people who are ailing and those who care for them.

The relationship of music and prayer is as old as Judaism itself. The Book of Psalms contains numerous verses that advocate praising God in song. Aside from capturing the belief that God delights in the singing of His chosen people, these verses reveal an understanding of the powerful impact singing has on a congregation. Like contemporary worshipers, the ancient Jews knew the positive effects of singing. These emotional, physical, and psychological benefits likely contributed to the idea that singing to the heavens can bring forth earthly rewards of improved health and happiness. In this way, science and Judaism have come to the same conclusion: we feel good when we sing.

1. George Burns, *All My Best Friends* (New York: G. K. Hall, 1991), 15.
2. Richard Morrison, "Join a Choir and Stave Off the Onset of Old Age," *BBC Music Magazine* (June 2008): 23.

Heart and Mind

Synagogue music is often said to have a dramatizing or vitalizing influence on the words of prayer. A liturgical piece typically grabs us on an emotional level, causing us to experience a certain mood or feeling. The attentive listener will then search for the source of this emotional effect, examining — at least on a cursory level — the various components of the piece (mode, dynamics, tempo, etc.), as well as the memories and associations it may be stirring. Ultimately, too, the sentiments aroused can inspire deeper contemplation on the themes and ideas housed in the text.

Aaron Copland was intrigued by this capacity of music to stimulate the heart and mind. He articulated a humanistic view of music, in which both an appreciation of formal structure and susceptibility to expressiveness have a place. He recognized that emotion alone is not enough to sustain our interest in music. This is especially true of the literate or "gifted" listener, whose mind is also active classifying sounds and determining musical styles. But Copland argued that without its emotional component, there would be little need for music at all.

No matter our degree of expertise, music involves each of us on the "primal and almost brutish level" of emotions. "On that level," Copland explained, "whatever the music may be, we experience basic reactions such as tension and release, density and transparency, a smooth or angry surface, the music's swellings and subsidings, its pushing forward or hanging back, its length, its speed, its thunders and whisperings — and a thousand other psychologically based reflections of our physical life of movement and gesture, and our inner, subconscious mental life. That is fundamentally the way we all hear music."[1]

This initial wave of emotion can be produced by genres as different as chamber music and progressive rock. Yet, while music of almost any kind can have an emotional pull and lead to subsequent intellectual reflection, this function is arguably most crucial in the worship setting, where music is meant to engage participants in the content of prayer. This is certainly the case in formal liturgical systems, such as Judaism, which contain an assortment of theological and spiritual concepts, references to history and heritage, and guidelines for thought and action. Without musical accompaniment, the full effect of these intricate prayers is rarely achieved, and worship itself risks becoming a distant or even impenetrable enterprise.

Because the prayer book travels through so many religious notions and goals—sometimes in rapid succession—it is not always immediately accessible. In contrast, music's impact is instantaneous, occurring prior to and independent of reflection or analysis. This is significant, as musically induced sentiments often serve as a pathway to more complex intellectual activity. In the service setting, this means that music can (and often does) act as a conduit to thoughtful prayer. Put simply, music penetrates the heart, which then activates the mind.

1. Aaron Copland, *Music and Imagination* (Cambridge: Harvard University Press, 1953), 14.

Serving God with Joy

Hassidism's rapid spread through Eastern Europe in the eighteenth century was met with some fervent opposition. Many feared that this new charismatic movement was another in a line of failed messianic campaigns that had dashed the hopes of innumerable Jews. The elaborate, often supernatural, claims of Hassidic rebbes and *tzadikim* were viewed as dangerously reminiscent of the excesses of Sabbatai Zevi and Jakub Frank, and their popularity threatened the authority of scholarly rabbinic leaders. The Vilna Gaon, foremost rabbi of the anti–Hassidic Misnagdim ("Opponents"), labeled the movement heretical because of its belief in God's immanence in all things, no matter how profane, and its unrestricted dissemination of Kabbalah. In the area of religious practice, the Misnagdim were most disturbed by the Hassidic penchant for spontaneous singing, dancing, and clapping—all of which ran counter to the subdued worship favored in conventional interpretations of *halakhah* (Jewish law).

However valid these objections may have been, it is not difficult to understand Hassidism's populist appeal. On the one hand, it offered an accessible way of bringing God's presence into daily life. In contrast to the formal study and intellectually oriented worship of the mainstream, Hassidism promoted the idea that holiness could be found in all activities. On the other hand, it provided much-needed spiritual elevation for a population struggling with declining economic conditions, anti-Semitic policies, outright attacks, and other existential concerns.

Central to this optimistic worldview is the appraisal of joy as a fundamental religious virtue. Hassidism maintains that it is impossible to serve or pray to God in sorrow; only through joy can one establish sincere and unimpeded contact with the divine. For this reason, ecstatic music has always been central to Hassidic devotion. Through joyful song and the dancing and clapping it stimulates, sadness is temporarily wiped away, and wholehearted worship is made possible.

Psalm 100:2 was adopted as a summation of this philosophy: "serve God with joy." The Hebrew of this verse, *ivdu et Hashem b'simcha*, received special attention from Ezekiel of Kuzmir (1812–1856), the first rebbe of the Modzitz dynasty. He asked, "Why does the word *et* appear here? Wherever it appears, it indicates that something additional is implied. What can be additional [to God] here?" Read literally, these words form the clumsy phrase "serve *to* God with joy." The rebbe offered an explanation: "The word *et* consists of the letters *alef* and *tav* [the first and last letters of the Hebrew alphabet], that is, a person must *always* be joyful, no matter what happens in life, from beginning to end, one should be in a state of joy."[1]

The next verse of the psalm reads, "Come into God's presence with singing" (Ps. 100:3), drawing a direct link between song and joy — a connection found throughout the Hebrew Bible. Taken with Eliezer of Kuzmir's patently Hassidic interpretation, the psalm verses become an idealistic decree: serve God constantly with joyful singing. To be sure, this is not a practical way of living: singing all day can interfere with other tasks, a full life includes a spectrum of emotions, and music is capable of arousing many feelings. Still, approaching God in a state of joy is a worthy goal, and one that is best achieved through song.

---

1. Shmuel Barzilai, *Chassidic Ecstasy in Music* (New York: Peter Lang, 2009), 31.

Niggunim and Augustine

Musical expression has always held a prominent place in Hassidic ritual. Emerging in Eastern Europe about 1750, Hassidism began as a revivalist movement rooted in earlier traditions of mystic Kabbalah and medieval pietism. Music was integral to the movement's goals of attaining joy in God's service and forging a "complete merger" of the human soul with the divine. Its founder, Baal Shem Tov, taught that the soul could not soar without melody.[1] Another Hassidic master imagined, "There are castles in the upper spheres which open only to song."[2] This high appraisal of music stemmed from a recognition that words, no matter how exalted, were insufficient in cultivating ecstatic feelings of religious devotion. Song alone, they claimed, could achieve this purpose.

The most significant Hassidic musical innovation is the *niggun:* a wordless melody sung to encourage and magnify joy in the presence of God. A *niggun* is endless, not limited by verses of text, allowing the singer's emotions to pour forth without concern for language. These tunes, usually sung in short, stammering "nonsense" syllables, give voice to sentiments far too intense to be uttered in words. Historically, Hassidic communities would gather during holidays and other special occasions to sing their own *niggunim,* usually composed by their rebbe or leader. The value of these tunes is derived from their spiritual efficacy rather than their artistic merits. They were not intended for any audience, nor did they strive for external beauty; only by means of participation could their exuberant force be realized.

Though the merging of joy, devotion, and wordless song is a concept original to Hassidic theology, it does have striking parallel in the writings of Augustine (354–430), the Latin Church Father who lived over a thousand years before Hassidism was conceived. This does not mean to suggest that the *Hassidic niggun* was in any way inspired by Augustine's thought. Still, it is worth noting that Augustine and the Hassidim came to similar conclusions regarding the effectiveness of wordless tunes in communicating an all-consuming sense of divine joy.

In his commentary on Psalm 33:3, Augustine asked: "What does singing in jubilation signify? It is to realize that words cannot communicate the song of the heart." He argued that this inner-song is best expressed through what he called *jubilus:* a spontaneous, wordless, musical outpouring of one's spirit before God. "In this way," he wrote, "the heart rejoices without words and the boundless expanse of rapture is not circumscribed by syllables."[3]

Augustine's position is nearly identical to that of Hassidic leader Rabbi Shnuer Zalman of Liadi (1747–1813), who summed up the impetus behind *niggunim:* "Melody is the speech of the soul, but words interrupt the stream of emotion."[4] Although these men lived in vastly different times and places, and espoused beliefs that were in many ways incompatible, they both recognized the limitations of language and the power of wordless songs to harness and amplify the joy felt in God's presence. Underlying the *niggun* and *jubilus* is a common belief that when it comes to the emotional side of religious experience, music speaks louder than words.

1. Jonathan L. Friedmann, ed., *Quotations on Jewish Sacred Music* (Lanham, MD: Hamilton, 2011), 37.
2. Friedmann, *Quotations on Jewish Sacred Music*, 47.
3. *St. Augustine on the Psalms* (New York: Newman, 1961), 2:111–112.
4. Friedmann, *Quotations on Jewish Sacred Music*, 37.

Holy Noises

Central to Hassidism is the belief that flickers of the divine presence exist within each individual, and that these holy sparks can be ignited through devotion and discipline to illuminate one's very existence. Unlike most mystical traditions, Hassidism promotes full engagement in worldly things, and so these glimmers of divinity can be manifested in all tasks, no matter how seemingly mundane. Dancing, swimming, walking, sitting, playing, and all manner of activities can be transformed into sacred moments. Additionally, these sparks are not confined to the human realm, but are present in all things, from buildings to food. Indeed, it is considered an exalted duty to recognize and amplify this latent holiness.

Out of this understanding arose *niggunim:* wordless melodies sung to achieve a desired frame of mind and/or emotional state. *Niggunim* vary greatly in style, form, and mood. They may be slow or fast, meditative or jubilant, and may build in volume and tempo as the singing progresses. Nonsense syllables like "bim-bam-bam" and "ai-dai-dai" are sung in place of words, and the singing is typically colored by vocal inflections akin to those found in cantorial music. Most centrally, though some of these tunes are ascribed to specific rebbes or musicians, most are adaptations from non-Jewish sources, like Cossack dances and Central European waltzes.

Transforming profane melodies into *niggunim* is viewed as a way of bringing out their holy sparks, and of returning them to God — the source of all melodies. This process of purification and redemption consists of four steps: recognizing the sacredness dormant in the song; spending time with the melody; discarding the secular lyrics; and singing the remodeled tune with proper intention. Not only does this yield new melodies for worship, it also fulfills an important *mitzvah:* converting something from profanity to the service of God. A well-known story of the *niggun* process involves Shneur Zalman of Lyadi (1745–1813), the first Chabad rebbe, and a street musician. During a stroll one afternoon, the rebbe came across an organ grinder singing a beautiful song. He tossed some coins in the musician's hat, and requested that he sing the song over and over. The rebbe listened intently, following every phrase and reflecting on every tone. After a while, he began singing the tune, replacing its words with repeated vocables and infusing it with fervor and joy. Upon hearing the rebbe's performance, the organ grinder forgot the song, for it had been cleansed and refashioned for sacred use.

Another famous account comes from Russia. It was 1812 and the French army was on its way across the Russian border. A rebbe heard them advancing in the distance to "Napoleon's March," which he understood as a signal from God to flee. In commemoration of this miraculous forewarning, the rebbe designated "Napoleon's March" as a *niggun* to be sung at the *Neilah* service of Yom Kippur, where it came to symbolize the Jewish people's deliverance from evil.

Redemption of the holy sparks—or, better, holy noises—dormant in secular tunes is part of the larger Hassidic project of uncovering the divine essence in all things. Just as there is a glimmer of sanctity in each person, object, and activity, every tone contains a sacred kernel. Thus, by turning temporal tunes into spiritual *niggunim*, Hassidism provides a model for the broader retrieval of holiness in the mundane.

Songs Without Words

Felix Mendelssohn (1809–1847) was fond of writing short, lyrical pieces for piano. He called these compositions "Songs Without Words," as they were, like settings of verses, meant to impart definite ideas and feelings. These "songs," which number over fifty, were part of Mendelssohn's larger philosophy of musical expression. He believed that tones communicate more precisely than texts, and that music's highest purpose is to articulate thoughts and sentiments that language cannot adequately relate. As he wrote to his friend Marc-André Souchay, who sought to put lyrics to some of these pieces, "single words ... seem to me vague, indefinite, and very open to misunderstanding in comparison with real music, the music that fills one's heart with a thousand things finer than any language. What any music I care for means to me is not an indefinite feeling which one might render definite by translating it into words, but something perfectly clear."[1]

Mendelssohn went on to write of the difficultly of putting emotions into language, and of the range of meaning each word or sentence can have depending on who is saying it, how it is said, who is listening, and so on. Much of this vagueness is rooted in the fact that language is a secondary, external representation of something that already has complete inner meaning. Thus, any attempt at translating concrete, pre-linguistic sentiments into words is by nature imperfect and open to (mis)interpretation. However, according to Mendelssohn, music is less likely to give the wrong impression, since it communicates on the primary level of feelings and "can express the same meaning, or suggest the same emotion, to one as to the other." Though there are exceptions to this rule, it is hard to disagree with the thrust of Mendelssohn's argument: because music operates on an emotional plane, without need of an intellectual filter, its message is received more clearly and directly than one comprised of words.

A similar awareness underlies another body of wordless melodies: *niggunim*. Like Mendelssohn's "songs" for piano, *niggunim* are not songs in the classical sense of words set to music. Rather, they are free-flowing melodies, usually sung with syllabic patterns. In their original Hassidic context, *niggunim* are sung at gatherings outside of the synagogue, though they have crept into services as a supplement to the liturgy. Following Mendelssohn's remarks, these repetitive tunes are a form of pure expression, used to either intensify or transform one's spiritual state. And because they are entirely functional, musicologists tend to place them outside the parameters of aesthetic appraisal; whatever beauty they possess derives from their energy and efficacy, not their musical features *per se*.

Significantly, too, *niggunim* can be repeated endlessly, allowing the singer to pour out the innermost contents of his or her soul without the hindrance of intellectual concepts or self-conscious regard for musical form. As Mendelssohn might say, they are unambiguous statements of definite feelings that words can only attempt to express.

1. Felix Mendelssohn-Bartholdy, *Selected Letters of Mendelssohn* (New York: S. Sonnenschein and Co., 1894), 124.

Hymns of Praise

The phrase "Sing unto the Lord" occurs seventeen times in the Hebrew Bible. In each instance, it conveys a sense of urgency, as if the one proclaiming it cannot help but sing praises to God, and invite others to do the same. The impulse to sing joyous songs to deities is common to most faiths, both ancient and modern. Such songs are generally classified as hymns, a term best defined by Augustine: "Hymns are praises of God with song; hymns are songs containing the praise of God. If there be praise, and it is not of God, it is not a hymn; if there be praise, and praise of God, and it is not sung, it is not a hymn. If it is to be a hymn, therefore, it must have three things: praise, and that of God, and song" (*In psalmum* 72.1).

Augustine recognized the essential partnership of text and music in praising the divine. Because God transcends human vocabulary, and because moments for extolling God tend to be highly emotional, we instinctively set praise to music, the language beyond words. As Augustine explained, hymn singing is "the voice of a soul poured out in joy and expressing..." (*In psalmum* 99.4).

Hymns are especially prominent in the Book of Psalms. Bible scholar Hermann Gunkel (1862–1904) identified twenty-three psalms as hymns, and fifteen psalms contain the term *Hallelujah*, "Praise God."

For the most part, these hymns give specific motives or occasions for praising God. Psalm 8, for instance, celebrates the works of creation, while Psalm 114 recalls the miracles of the Exodus. Psalm 117, the shortest hymn in the Psalter, summons all nations to honor the love and fidelity God has shown to Israel: "Praise the Lord, all you nations; extol Him, all you peoples, for great is His steadfast love toward us; the faithfulness of the Lord endures forever. *Hallelujah.*"

According to 1 Chronicles 16:4–7, David appointed Levites with the specific task of singing praises before the Ark. This practice carried over into Jewish liturgy, where hymn psalms comprise the *Pesukei D'Zimra* (Verses of Song) of the daily morning service (Pss. 145–150), the *Hallel* (Praise) chanted on holidays (Pss. 113–118), and other liturgical segments. Jewish services also feature hymns of later vintage, such as *Adon Olam* (Eternal Lord), *Ein Keloheinu* (There is None Like Our God), and *Yigdal* (Magnify [O Living God])— all of which satisfy Augustine's threefold criteria of being praises, praises of God, and songs.

Singing hymns is among the oldest and most universal religious acts. Whether spontaneous outbursts or structured liturgical pieces, these songs are a natural and integral part of the human-divine relationship. Just as joy and gratitude inspire words exalting God, the emotions accompanying such words find most suitable expression in musical tones.

Stereotyping Synagogue Sounds

Most worship melodies are used to accompany devotional words, whether of a liturgical or some other kind. Not only is this music guided by the phrases and contours of the textual verses, it also works to clarify the prayer's concepts and themes. And in the relatively few instances where worship music of a non-textual nature is performed, such as an organ prelude or wordless chant, it is usually designed to prepare for or transition between sections of text. No matter how appealing the music may be on its own merits, its foremost aim is to draw attention to holy words, a task most often achieved through the channel of emotions.

Without doubt, the link between music, prayer, and emotions defies simple generalizations. Each of these elements is immensely complex, exhibiting a range of possibilities and shades of expression, subtle and otherwise. Additionally, whether they are sung or heard in solitude, a small group, or a large congregation, prayer songs are, like everything else in life, experienced through the lens of personal perception. As such, it would be a stretch to claim that all who are exposed to a given prayer song will perceive it the same way.

This subjectivity notwithstanding, there is some benefit in placing musical sounds into broad categories, if only to help the process of creating and selecting music that matches the general thrust of a text. A useful classification of this sort comes from Hassidism, a Jewish system that fully integrates music into religious practice. Though it is comprised of a diversity of styles and sources, Hassidic song is boxed into two overarching types: *devekut* and *rikkud*. *Devekut* tunes are typically slow, flowing melodies intended to evoke a meditative mood. Their name is derived from Deuteronomy 13:4 — "And cleave unto Him" — a reference to their desired outcome of communing with God. *Rikkud* songs, on the other hand, are simple, upbeat, and highly rhythmic. They are commonly sung while dancing, and are devised to propel participants into a frenzied state.

While these dual categories of introspection and ecstasy are not all encompassing, they are wide enough to cover a spectrum of musical possibilities. When taken out of their Hassidic context and applied to synagogue music in general, it is not difficult to begin placing music of a nuanced variety within these larger divisions. For instance, the atoning melodies of Yom Kippur, gentle settings of *Yih'yu L'ratzon* and *Sim Shalom*, and most contemporary healing songs can be labeled *devekut*, as they seek quiet contact with the divine. Examples of energetic *rikkud* songs would include many of the so-called "*ruach* songs," rousing renditions of *Mi Chamocha* and *Yism'chu*, and tunes that accompany the parading of the Torah scrolls.

Admittedly, this exercise, like the Hassidic classifications themselves, sweeps over whatever subtleties the music may express: pensive adoration, confident longing, hopeful joy, etc. But this does not negate the potential value of the approach. By stereotyping sounds as contemplative/introverted or exuberant/extroverted and locating similarly stereotyped themes within a prayer text, we can identify or compose settings that best suit the words. Simply stated, if a prayer is reflective it should be ascribed a *devekut* melody, and if it is joyous it should be given a *rikkud* tune. With such a method, we can help ensure that the music, and thus the prayer it accompanies, achieves its greatest impact.

Singing for Joy

Confucius reportedly said, "Music produces a kind of pleasure which human nature cannot do without."[1] Musical tones can transform moods from darkness to light, and heighten positive emotions already felt. We are uplifted by cheerful melodies, revitalized by happy tunes, and often whistle or sing in response to good feelings. For Jews ancient and modern, the association of music and joy is manifested in songs of praise. Jewish experience has shown that it is not enough to simply speak or read words of elation and gratitude; these emphatic statements require musical accompaniment. Moments of great delight are best communicated in the uniquely pleasing sounds of music, a reality described in Psalm 98: "Make a joyful noise to God, all the earth, break into joyous songs of praise" (v. 4.)

Psalm 98 also demonstrates the human tendency to project our moods on our surroundings. Originally composed following a military victory, the psalm extols God for displaying "His triumph in the sight of the nations" (v. 2). The author, consumed with jubilation, invites all of humanity to join him in singing divine praise. He even imagines things of nature — trees, hills, rivers, etc. — forming a chorus to honor their maker: "Let the sea and all within it thunder, the world and its inhabitants; let the rivers clap hands, the mountains sing joyously together at the presence of God..." (vv. 7–8).

As such, Psalm 98 illustrates two natural impulses: translating joy into song, and viewing the world as a reflection of our own emotional states. We often see the world through the lens of our emotions, and when they are felt intensely, it is hard to conceive (or tolerate) anything around us feeling otherwise. This holds true for both negative emotions, like sorrow, and positive emotions, like glee. This phenomenon is captured in a song made popular by Louis Armstrong: "When you're smiling, the whole world smiles with you."

So, while images of nature singing songs of praise are doubtless metaphorical, it is possible to influence the mood of others through song. This is proven each time a group sings together. Because music is such an emotional medium, and because group energy is so palpable, the feelings induced or amplified through collective songs are hard to resist. This accounts partly for the popularity and effectiveness of sing-along songs in worship settings. Through congregational singing, a group of individuals can be transported into a singular — or at least very similar — state of mind. This is especially true when worshipers join each other in songs of joy, like those proclaiming Shabbat peace or expressing thanksgiving to God.

It is not difficult to picture the author of Psalm 98 stimulating others to join him in singing praise. Whether or not this group of singers actually included animals, rocks, and vegetation is of little significance. What is important is what the psalm reveals about our need for and attraction to joyous songs.

1. Larry Chang, ed., *Wisdom for the Soul: Five Millennia of Prescriptions for Spiritual Healing* (Washington, DC: Gnosophia, 2006), 516.

Being the Music

Abraham Joshua Heschel devoted several pages of his philosophical treatise, *God in Search of Man*, to describing the proper attitude for performing *mitzvot*. According to Heschel, the fulfillment of a religious obligation is much more than a routine; it is "an act of valuation or *appreciation* of being commanded, of living in a covenant, of the opportunity to act in agreement with God."[1] This approach requires the whole person: one must be fully engaged in the task at hand, and mindful of its divine focus. Significantly, Heschel likened *mitzvot* to musical production. For the musician, "It is not enough to play the notes; one must *be* what he plays." And for the Jew, simply doing a *mitzvah* is not sufficient; "one must *live* what he *does*."[2]

This analogy reveals Heschel's keen understanding of the nature of music. Though he was not a musician himself, he saw the musician's total involvement — and even ecstasy — in a piece of music as a model for how one should approach a sacred duty.

This comparison is apt as music, like much of religious behavior, is usually scripted and/or performed in a prescribed way. Yet, even though the guidelines are laid out, both devotional acts and musical presentations demand more than rote rendering. Sincerity, passion, love, and commitment are essential ingredients for successful and satisfying performances. In musical terms, it is difficult to have an inspiring concert when the musicians themselves are not inspired. And in terms of religious behavior, the spiritual efficacy or gratification of an act, whether it is reciting a blessing or visiting the sick, depends on the degree of one's participation. The more intense one's involvement, the more fulfilling the experience will be.

To further this musical analogy, it is worthwhile to look at Aaron Copland's description of the music-making process. First, the composer shapes and organizes musical materials in a way that is intelligible and meaningful. Second, the music is reinterpreted — or better, recreated — by a performer or group of performers. Third, the music reaches the ear of the listener, who relives the "completed revelation of the composer's thought."[3] The individual's contribution in each stage of the process is crucial, for, as Jean-Paul Sartre put it, the music on the page does not really exist until it is played and heard.

This view compliments Heschel's argument that one must *be* the music. Through the performance and reception of a piece of music, we make it our own. What we bring to the musical experience, our imaginations and perceptions, substantially comprises what the music ultimately is. As a living art, music takes on different meanings and associations depending on when and where, as well as for and by whom, it is performed. In much the same way, a *mitzvah* is given new life each time it is carried out. Most of these obligations were decreed long ago and in far away places. They are little more than "dead letter" unless and until they are enacted. And, as Heschel insisted, these sacred acts are only worthy of the name if they are done with complete attention and devotion.

1. Abraham Joshua Heschel, *God in Search of Man: A Philosophy of Judaism* (New York: Farrar, Straus & Giroux, 1955), 315.
2. Heschel, *God in Search of Man*, 315.
3. Aaron Copland, *Music and Imagination* (Cambridge: Harvard University Press, 1953), 2.

Absolute Music, Absolute Worship

There is a church in Albuquerque, New Mexico, that boasts of offering Sunday services "minus religion." It is called the Church of Beethoven, a congregation dedicated to presenting "professional live music performances of the highest quality, together with other artistic expressions from fields including poetry ... in a manner that transcends the commonplace." The church gathers each week for a one-hour program, typically comprised of a short musical selection, a poetry reading, a two-minute "celebration of silence," and a substantial work of chamber music. According to its founder, Felix Wurman (1958–2009), this service places music "as the principal element, rather than as an afterthought."

In some form or another, music has always played a part in the rituals of the world's religions. Melodic expression, it is widely maintained, helps prepare us for a spiritual experience. Yet music designed for sacred purposes is generally used in support of words. The term "worship music" primarily refers to song-settings of devotional poetry or prayer. This music is programmatic, guided by textual narratives and meant to convey specific extra-musical ideas and images. In contrast, most of the music performed at the Church of Beethoven is absolute, or music for its own sake. For example, a recent Sunday service consisted of Bach's Sonata in E-minor, Höller's SCAN for Solo Flute, and Mozart's Quartet for Flute, Violin, Viola and Cello. The intent behind such music is not necessarily religious. However, as the church insists, these performances can foster the uplift and communal bonding one would expect from a religious service — just without the dogma.

But, can this ostensibly secular music be considered sacred? More specifically, can our experience of this music inspire a divine encounter similar to that sought in more traditional worship settings? To address these questions, it is helpful to turn to the words of Zionist poet Naftali Herz Imber (1856–1909).

Imber noted in his 1894 essay, "Music of the Psalms," that music has a direct impact upon the life of the soul, and the power to impart a sense of the holy. According to Imber, "Music was the divine revealer long ere God chose to reveal Himself otherwise."[1] This suggests that there is something "wholly other" in music itself, independent of texts or rituals. There is scriptural support for this claim, most notably the prophet Elisha's call for music to be played so that he could channel the divine (2 Kings 3:15). And, as Imber wrote, music's sacred qualities have been known throughout history: "Music runs like a thread through all the ages and the dispensations, as a connecting link between God and man."[2]

Music has the potential to bring us into an awareness of a force greater than ourselves. This process can occur within or outside expressly religious contexts, and may be achieved with music made for many purposes, sacred and secular. The Church of Beethoven embraces this realization. It offers an alternative to conventional worship services, which are often cluttered with rules of theology and practice. Its service is, in a way, a "pure" experience, unhindered by agenda or ideology. It invites congregants to enter a state of absolute worship through the medium of absolute music.

1. Naftali Herz Imber, "The Music of the Psalms," in Jonathan L. Friedmann, comp., *Music in Jewish Thought: Selected Writings, 1890–1920* (Jefferson, NC: McFarland, 2009), 84.
2. Imber, "The Music of the Psalms," 82.

Fight Songs and Fighting Words

Synagogue composer Max Helfman (1901–1963) once said, "You may argue with a sermon, but you can never fight a melody."[1] At first glance, these words appear glaringly untrue. People "fight" melodies all time. As judgmental and selective creatures, we are quick to draw battle lines upon hearing music that falls outside our parameters of taste, or that we perceive as dull, outmoded, or poorly executed. Blanket statements like "I don't like country music" are usually precursors to the visceral repulsion felt when songs of the despised genre are played. And because musical taste is so much a part of how we define ourselves, we often get sucked into debates over bands, composers, performers, and styles—rhetorical exchanges that amount to a kind of self-defense. Still, with all this being said, there is a sense in which Helfman was right— namely, that sermons can be much worse.

Helfman's belief that melodies are not a source of conflict should be read in its proper context. He did not mean it as a generalization to be applied to all music, but as a specific reference to worship songs. In that setting, where music is an aid to a larger activity, there is considerably less resistance to sounds that might, when judged on their own, clash with one's musical standards. Cantors and congregants alike tend to hold their criticism in abeyance during services, as the goal is to engage in prayer and not to experience music for its own sake. Under such conditions, an entirely different rule of aesthetics is applied: a melody is considered "good" if it helps facilitate the prayer process. On purely musical grounds, this functionalist approach raises important questions of quality, musical literacy, respect for text, and so forth; but in the moment of prayer, even the most mundane or passé tune can be inspiring.

A sermon, however, is not afforded the same leniency. Unlike liturgical music, a thoroughly collective activity, sermons are highly personal. Though they generally seek to address issues that resonate with congregants and offer insights that apply to daily life, their content and the manner of delivery can arouse a range of reactions, positive and negative. One "may argue with a sermon," as Helfman put it, because of its abstractness, self-indulgence, political leaning, disjointedness, soft or harsh tone, simplicity or complexity, moralizing or relativizing, traditionalism or modernism — the list goes on. Sermons are, by definition, one person's opinion delivered to a captive audience. And while music can effortlessly transcend the divisiveness of language and unite people with differing interests and opposing points of view, sermons speak to the intellect, and are thus apt to cause disagreement, confusion, disappointment, or even downright hostility. Plus, no sermon is going to please everyone, and those that are designed to appease all factions generally come off as too passionless to be of any real value.

The contrasting responses to sermons and worship music shed light on crucial differences between these modes of communication. Notwithstanding the vehemence with which most of us cling to our musical preferences and reject the music we do not like, religious ritual creates an essentially neutral musical experience, in which the sacredness of the moment quenches the flames of musical taste. But the words of sermons, which fall outside the liturgical structure and expose the speaker's biases and outlook on life, are subject to immediate critique. It is in this vein that Helfman's words should be read: "You may argue with a sermon, but you can never fight a melody."

1. Philip Moddel, *Max Helfman: A Biographical Sketch* (Berkeley, CA: Judah L. Magnes, 1974), 62.

Musical Taste, Musical Fact

There is some truth to Henry Wadsworth Longfellow's familiar phrase, "Music is the universal language of mankind."[1] Despite the great assortment of sounds and styles produced by the world's music cultures, essentially all music can — at least to a degree — express feelings that reach across peoples, times, and generations. Even when the specific meaning and nuance of a piece escapes the notice of someone outside that tradition, it can nonetheless have a significant impact on the listener, intended or otherwise. Music is also universal in that there is no society without it. Musical tones are everywhere used to communicate, teach, enhance ceremonies, promote bonding, and perform other functions crucial to human life. Moreover, it is universally the case that each culture or subculture can — and often makes a point to — distinguish its own music from other kinds.

This latter phenomenon has led many to view their specific music with a sense of pride, possessiveness, and superiority. Not only do they recognize their sound as their own, they also pit their music against the music of other, perhaps competing, groups. So, for instance, one region of a country may insist that its folk music is better than that of neighboring regions, or may claim it as the country's "true" and "authentic" musical form. Similar sentiments arise when fans of one genre, such as Dixieland, see their favored tunes as more genuine and aesthetically perfect than the tunes of another genre, such as ragtime. Importantly, too, devotees of a musical style or group tend to experience bonding akin to the fellowship that occurs within ethnic and religious groups, and demonstrate their unity by attending concerts, joining fan clubs, participating in chat rooms, and the like.

These examples show that music, while sometimes lumped with life's auxiliary accompaniments, is actually a defining part of both individual and group identity. The passion with which most people cling to and espouse their musical preferences is evidenced in the way that musical taste is often hoisted to the level of musical fact. It is not enough for one to simply like a song or genre; such music is believed the most beautiful, interesting, moving, valid, and so on.

Perhaps not surprisingly, this elevating of partiality to verity is a major force in synagogue song. The ritualized, statutory nature of Jewish worship necessitates the establishment and use of equally recurrent prayer melodies. Over time, this musical corpus is viewed as "correct," even as its character depends on external factors like local norms, denominational standards, and congregational practice. In North America, for instance, Reform synagogues favor folk-rock, Renewal groups have New Age predilections, and Orthodox *shuls* utilize age-old European chant.

Set repertoires do, of course, serve practical aims in liturgical services of all types — Jewish, Christian, or otherwise — but Jews bestow upon their music an added layer of ethnicity. Their musical choices are not considered proper merely because they are familiar and linked to specific texts, but because they come to symbolize heritage, authenticity, and the Jewish soul itself. However, while this perception may reflect sincerely felt personal experiences, the astounding diversity of synagogue music makes any claim of an authoritative melody difficult to support. It is, then, safe to conclude that ideas about correct tunes stem from a confusion of subjective qualities, like familiarity, comfort, and taste, with more concrete notions of truth, legitimacy, and tradition.

1. Henry Wadsworth Longfellow, *The Prose Works of Henry Wadsworth Longfellow* (London: David Bogue, 1851), 305.

Ethnicity in Jewish Music

The fifth-century Greek historian Herodotus is credited with introducing the concept of ethnicity. Expanding on the term ethnos, meaning "nation," Herodotus defined Greek identity as kinship (*homaimon:* "of the same blood"), language (*homoglosson:* "speaking the same language"), and customs (*homotropon:* "of the same habits"). In modern usage, the terms ethnicity and ethnic group refer broadly to people who share a common ancestry and distinctive culture. A hallmark of these groups is the desire to preserve — with varying levels of modification — the stories, worldview, and behaviors of the ancestors. In the Jewish context, this aspiration underlies the sentiments of "continuity" and "from generation to generation." As a people historically scattered throughout the world and subject to the rule and influence of host cultures, Jews have always and everywhere sought to maintain distinguishing traits and practices, even as they adapt to their environments. It is through such concerted efforts that a sense of Jewish ethnic identity is both protected and asserted.

One of the many cultural features shared by the world's diverse Jewish communities is a high regard for music. This is especially important as music helps define individual and collective identity, expressing emotions, values, and concerns in a language more powerful than spoken words. Throughout the world, culturally specific music works to preserve and revitalize a people's heritage, celebrating those things that mark ethnicity: customs, language, history, lineage, and beliefs. This crucial function of music is amplified within historically marginalized groups — like the Jews — where music can reinforce internal cohesion and create a sonic defense against the onslaught of the majority culture.

But ethnic music, like most everything else, is rarely an insolated or stagnant enterprise; it interacts with and absorbs foreign characteristics while at the same time preserving a certain — if sometimes subtle — uniqueness. Musical acclimation is but one manifestation of a broader tension that shapes Jewish life: a longing for stability against a practical need to relate to the present. Without doubt, isolated Jewish groups, like the secluded enclaves of Yemen and Iraq, tend to be slower to change and more resistant to outside forces. In contrast, Jewish populations in modernized, accommodating societies, like post-emancipation Germany and the United States, are more likely to be exposed to and embrace the pervasive sounds of the region. Additional factors, such as attitude toward modernity and appeasement of the youth, also contribute to the degree and character of assimilation. But whether a community's stance is supportive or resistant to change, total avoidance of outside pressures is near impossible. It is true as well that even communities thoroughly influenced by music of non–Jewish origin retain a strong sense of cultural distinctiveness. This is partly because their songs incorporate Jewish aspects not necessarily found in the music itself: sacred history, calendar, holy tongue, fellowship, etc.

For this reason, musical adaptation should not be viewed as a hindrance but as a helpmate to Jewish self-preservation. The Jews' ability to select from regional sources for their own use is a clear indication of the durability and portability of Judaism. This active process is, in fact, the foundation from which all of Judaism's folk traditions developed, and is central to the construction and vitality of Jewish peoplehood. It can thus be concluded that, somewhat ironically, by modifying the past to meet the present and by using the environment to meet their own needs, Jewish groups fortify a link to ancestors and lay claim to being a people apart.

Historicism and Futurism

In his little book entitled *Art and the Question of Meaning,* Catholic theologian Hans Küng draws interesting parallels between espousing a limited view of God and elevating one style or school of art above all others. According to Küng, this exclusivism typically takes two forms: ideological historicism and ideological futurism. The first, historicism, refers to an aesthetic or religiosity centered on a specific past, as if art or theology had found its one and only true form in some long ago time. This position holds up the old as "a model, something to be imitated, not merely evoked."[1] The second approach, futurism, sees the latest artistic and theological expressions as the very best, as if every new technique or insight is, by virtue of its newness, a positive advancement. Proponents of this view believe "a new beginning [has] to be made again and again at zero" and see "every revolt [as a] great renewal."[2]

Though Küng's subject is visual art, his observations apply equally to music, where identical debates are waged between preservationists and innovationists. And the flaws he sees in these polarized stances on painting and God are also found in the musical realm. Ideological historicism, he argues, betrays not only "creative weakness," "intellectual impotence," and "anemic scholasticism," but a paralyzing belief in humanity's decline.[3] Ideological futurism, on the other hand, takes up the false notion that a radical break with tradition always results in something better, no matter how ephemeral the novel forms may be.

We can locate these two streams in synagogue song. Historicism is found among those who reject new settings of the liturgy, and judge familiar sounds—whether modal chants, folk tunes, or something else— as qualitatively superior. This group is correct in celebrating the beauty and religious efficacy of much of the older material; but stubborn adherence to one style at the exclusion of others is, as Nietzsche observed, a sort of "historical sickness."

The other tendency, futurism, is present with those who dismiss timeworn songs as outmoded or stale. This "musical ageism" is played out in virtually every generation, as youths predictably disavow the music of their parents and force their own preferences through the synagogue walls. Other futurists blanketly apply the "newer is better" outlook of the technological age to liturgical song, forgetting that heritage, tradition, and authenticity—concepts central to the Jewish religion—demand a considerable helping of long-established tunes.

These positions would be of little consequence if Jewish worship were a private matter. Like the collector who touts the supremacy of ragtime records or the indie rock connoisseur constantly seeking out undiscovered bands, historicism and futurism in Jewish sacred music would just be harmless personal tastes. But Jewish prayer is a collective activity, and the music it employs needs to resonate with people of varied backgrounds, interests, and ideological bents. And so, as Küng advises, the best remedy for dwelling too much in the past or looking too enthusiastically at the future is finding comfort in a present that thoughtfully balances a sense of heritage with an openness to new possibilities, and an awareness of the rich musical library available to aid the worship experience.

1. Hans Kung, *Art and the Question of Meaning* (New York: Crossroad, 1981), 40.
2. Kung, *Art and the Question of Meaning*, 42.
3. Kung, *Art and the Question of Meaning*, 41.

Music and the *Mitzvah* of Nostalgia

The modernization of Judaism, which took hold in the nineteenth century and has continued on a steady course to this day, has brought with it a slew of attitudes and behaviors hitherto antithetical to Jewish life. Commitment has given way to selectivity, insular communities have been replaced with personal autonomy, and unquestioned observance has been countered with unfettered rejection. This does not mean that the abandoned system is necessarily invalid or impossible to maintain—there are still thriving Orthodox communities throughout the world—nor does it imply that the old folkways are inherently superior to the possibilities afforded within the modern worldview—a charge often made in traditionalist circles. Rather, these remarks point to the reality that Judaism, once characterized by close-knit, tradition-oriented, and essentially stable groups, now finds expression in a variety of forms. Yet, regardless of whether the individual Jew is *shomer shabbas* or completely secular, there is a powerful sentiment shared by Jews of all stripes: nostalgia.

Nostalgia can be defined as the wistful affection or sentimental longing for a past seemingly better and more pure than the present. In some Orthodox communities, this is manifested in a romantic re-imagining of pre-modern Europe, where all Jewish men were learned and pious and all women were modest and happy in their supporting roles. For modern, secular Jews, nostalgia likewise involves romanticizing the ancestors' merits. However, while traditionalists might use old-world grandparents or more distant forebears as inspiration to become even more traditional, non-observant Jews tend to appreciate them from a distance: their virtues are espoused, their stories are mythologized, and the symbols of their devotion, like *tefillin* and *tzitzit*, are cherished as heirlooms and museum pieces, not as objects to be used. As Arnold Eisen has written, for Jews who are not bound to the *mitzvot*, nostalgia itself becomes a sort of commandment.[1]

The *mitzvah* of nostalgia can be fulfilled in a variety of ways, such as taking a tour of Israel's holy sites, collecting *mezuzot*, or contributing to the Chabad Telethon. Each of these examples not only involves a limited, non-binding experience of something specifically Jewish, but also financial support of interests representing a Jewish lifestyle beyond the patron's own level of commitment. Through such support, nostalgic Jews give a nod to their ancestors—real or imagined—and do their own part to ensure Jewish religious and cultural continuity, if by externalized means.

In addition to these individual avenues, the *mitzvah* of nostalgia is also performed in liberal synagogues, where Hassidic and Hassidic-inspired *niggunim* are sung with great regularity. Without doubt, this musical style has a degree of universal charm and spiritual efficacy that exists independent of its original setting, especially when presented as user-friendly sing-alongs. But by using these tunes in a context far removed from their sub-culture of origin—and all of the insulation, ritualistic rigor, and ethnic trappings it entails—liberal congregants tap into an idealized and non-intimidating version of an obligation-heavy

Jewish sect. In other words, a *niggun* is a safe entry-point for less-observant Jews to feel (loosely) connected to what is perceived as an "authentic" Jewish lifestyle — one which may or may not have been practiced by their forebears.

The popularity of *niggunim* is illustrative of the important place nostalgia holds in modern Judaism. Like other sentimental sources, *niggunim* afford Jews the opportunity to experience — however superficially — a way of life thought to be more virtuous than their own, without requiring any additional knowledge, piety, or change in routine. In this sense, the *niggun* is an ideal way of fulfilling the *mitzvah* of nostalgia: it is the music of commitment without the commitment.

1. Arnold M. Eisen, *Rethinking Modern Judaism: Ritual, Commandment, Community* (Chicago: University of Chicago Press, 1998), 156–187.

Musical *Minhag*

Rabbi Louis Jacobs defined Judaism as "the religion, philosophy, and way of life of the Jews."[1] Viewing the term through a religious lens, Jacobs located the essence of Judaism in a concrete system of beliefs and practices. Others, like scholars Jacob Neusner and William Scott Green, have found such definitions to be erroneous, as Judaism, the religion, is not always an accurate representation of the Jews, the ethnic group. There are a plethora of ways Jews can define themselves, ranging from the communitarian-religious-isolationist to the independent-secular-cosmopolitan. Grouping Jews into a strictly religious category entails a blurring of theology and sociology, and does not fully account for the fact that Jewish life has developed and continues to develop within specific and ever-changing circumstances. Despite traditionalist notions of Jewish constancy and uniformity, Judaism is, in the end, a fluid term encompassing an array of sometimes starkly contrasting notions and behaviors.

The problem of defining Judaism is not limited to discrepancies between religious and ethnic understandings; it is also seen in the diversity of Jewish religious expression. There are differences between and within the various Jewish branches and denominations that extend into virtually every area of thought and action. One way of describing these different approaches is by gauging the degree to which each group adheres to *halakha:* regulations or statements of law derived from the Bible and later rabbinic sources, which address religious and ostensibly non-religious matters. At the risk of overgeneralization, it can be said that groups who make claims to "authenticity" or "true Judaism" tout a fervent adherence to *halakhic* demands. This includes all forms of orthodoxy, though shades of austerity exist in the legal opinions of each branch. In contrast, liberal denominations give significantly more weight to personal autonomy and freedom of choice, and may even reject *halakhic* arguments altogether.

But espousal, qualified acceptance, or dismissal of Jewish legalism is not really an effective way to characterize a particular group. This is mainly because, regardless of their attitudes toward *halakha,* all manifestations of the Jewish religion take a protective stance when it comes to *minhagim:* non-legislated habitual practices that are highly revered and accepted as "tradition." Historically, many of these customs, usually developed among the lay people, have gained rabbinic approval. This seems a practical maneuver, as it would be foolish to rule against cherished customs that would likely persist with or without official sanction. Over time, these norms tend to assume the force of *halakha,* meaning that they are, in essence, codified for perpetuation. This is a phenomenon equally prevalent in traditionalist and liberal communities.

It is, then, possible to define the various types of Judaism through their unique customs, as well as their spins on widely practiced customs. A case in point is the *kippah,* an outward symbol of Jewish identity that resides in the realm of *minhag,* not *halakha.* Since the skullcap is all but absent from the biblical text and holds an ambiguous place in Talmudic and later literature — especially when it comes to the requirements, nature, and design of *kippot* — local customs have been freely developed, reinterpreted, and abrogated over the centuries. In Hassidic communities, for instance, men often wear fedoras with large black *kippot* underneath, while religious Zionists in Israel are sometimes called *kippot serugat* for the knitted head coverings they wear. In recent years crocheted "Kabbalist" *kippot* have gained popularity among Jews with a mystical bent, while many women in liberal synagogues wear *kippot* to demonstrate, among other things, their equality with men. With its almost universal acceptance, at least during worship, the wearing of *kippot* is no longer viewed as a mere custom, but as a guarded pseudo-law.

The elevated position of *minhagim* is also evident in synagogue song. Though there are a handful of *halakhic* rulings that touch on musical subjects, mostly concerning the use of instruments and the integrity of the cantor, music generally falls outside the reach of law. This is certainly true of melody choice, which has always been susceptible to changing trends and the influence of surrounding, non–Jewish cultures. In fact, in all of the *halakhic* writings stressing the need for cantors to be pious, sincere, and learned in Scripture, there is no requirement that they be knowledgeable about particular melodies or musical inflections.

Perhaps the best example of a musical custom-turned-quasi-law is the Ashkenazi *Mi-Sinai* tunes, a corpus of Festival and High Holy Day folk melodies that originated in Germany and France between the eleventh and fifteenth centuries. The Maharil (1358–1425), a renowned rabbinic authority of the time, decided that these beloved and entrenched tunes be given the same authority as if they were handed down to Moses on Sinai — that is, they should never be changed. This pronouncement stemmed in part from a desire to unify Ashkenazi practice; but it also shows that, inasmuch as these melodies were already ubiquitous, it was good policy to give them the seal of approval. These tunes continue to radiate legitimacy, so much so that a cantor who dares deviate from the *Mi-Sinai* setting of *Kol Nidrei*, for example, risks being booed from the *bimah*.

In a similar manner, the songs and/or chant patterns a congregation sings service after service take on a sense of being "genuine" and "correct." Most congregations cling to their favored liturgical settings and consider it an infraction to use the "wrong" setting. Though these prayer melodies are received by way of convention rather than official decree, they are looked upon as being a prescribed part of ceremonial ritual. Melodies of all types — old, new, art songs, camp songs, etc. — can become sanctioned sounds in a given community; their perceived properness is not rooted in their origin or style, but in their established usage. These musical conventions and other treasured *minhagim* are an organic outgrowth of a ritually oriented religion that necessitates a level of constancy, predictability, and standards of practice. And it is mainly through such customs that congregations define who they are, and who they are not, as Jews.

1. Louis Jacobs, "Judaism," in *Encyclopaedia Judaica*, vol. 11 (2007): 511.

Identity and Memory

Changing a melody for a prayer is one of the most contentious issues in synagogue ritual. Through continuous usage, certain melodies become inseparable from the prayers they accompany. Without doubt, some congregations are more open than others to musical changes, but as ethnomusicologist Mark Slobin explains, local custom is a powerful force. In his study of the American cantorate, Slobin found that even in Reform congregations, removed from the strictures of *nusach*, and *halakhic* concerns in general, there is widespread objection to deviating from "decided tastes" or "certain favorites."[1]

It is tempting to dismiss adherence to specific melodies as mere stubbornness or clinging to the familiar. To a large extent, the old axiom holds true: "People like what they know and know what they like." But I wish to propose two deeper reasons for this phenomenon: one social and one cognitive.

Sociologist Émile Durkheim (1858–1917) observed that periodic gatherings help to revive a congregation's sense of identity.[2] Group members may live most of their lives pursuing individual concerns, but the social aspect of their identities—the feeling of belonging and of a force greater than themselves—requires occasional gatherings. As Durkheim would put it, a group can revive its sense of self only by assembling. Crucial for this revitalization is the repetition of ritual elements, including music. Through shared and familiar religious experiences, individuals unite into a collective whole.

A 1917 study published by esteemed American rabbi, David de Sola Pool (1885–1970), further illustrates the degree to which melodies can define congregational identity. He compared Sephardic melodies sung in London, Manchester, Amsterdam, New York, Montreal, and eight other locations, and found that even the most popular congregational tunes exhibit melodic variations from synagogue to synagogue.[3] These alterations developed organically as the tunes were sung over a period of time. And the way each congregation sang these otherwise standard melodies became an audible symbol of the group itself. A change in their musical practice—whether "correcting" a song's performance or using a different melody—would have caused the congregation to lose, at least temporarily, a sense of itself.

There is also a cognitive reason behind the difficulty of changing congregational tunes. Neuroscientific research confirms what we know from experience to be true: a familiar melody stirs memories and emotions. Concetta M. Tomaino, director for The Institute for Music and Neurologic Function, observes, "Music ... can provide access not only to specific moods and memories, but also to the entire thought-structure and personality of the past."[4] Familiar songs are direct conduits to the past, both personal and collective; they immediately bring us back to specific times, places, feelings, relationships, and so on. Thus, in a profound way, time-honored synagogue songs connect congregants to their Jewish heritage.

The bond between melody and memory is also demonstrated in several recent studies on dementia. Dementia patients retain musical memories much longer than other memories. Even when the disease advances to the point where one cannot recognize family members, songs from a long-ago childhood are rarely forgotten. Patients frequently respond to familiar melodies by singing along, usually with the words, and often continue singing after the stimulus has stopped. In a similar (though less dramatic) way, familiar synagogue songs aid congregants in remembering prayer-texts—an important function, since most Jews are not fluent in the Hebrew language.

Synagogues typically utilize one or two melodies for any given prayer. Some might consider this an unfortunate reality, which deprives congregants of the rich and varied corpus of Jewish music. But establishing a set musical repertoire is both natural and valuable. While not necessarily musically fulfilling, repeated melodies do serve impor-tant social and cognitive functions. They are symbols of group identity, conveyers of memories and emotions, and tools for remembering sacred texts. They are, in short, an essential part of worship.

---

1. Mark Slobin, *Chosen Voices: The Story of the American Cantorate* (Urbana and Chicago: University of Illinois Press, 1989).

2. Émile Durkheim, *The Elementary Forms of Religious Life*, trans. Carol Cossman (New York: Oxford University Press, 2001).

3. David de Sola Pool, "The Music of the Synagogue," in Jonathan L. Friedmann, ed., *20th Century Synagogue Music: Essential Readings* (Woodland Hills, CA: Isaac Nathan, 2010), 18.

4. Deborah Mitchell, *How to Live Well with Early Alzheimer's: A Complete Program for Enhancing Your Quality of Life* (New York: Macmillan, 2010), 131.

Performing Identity

Performance approaches to the study of religion contend that the essence of a faith is not found in its fixed texts or rigid doctrines, but in the dynamic enactment of ritual. Viewing religious groups through an anthropological lens, scholars of this school seek to uncover how ceremonial activities, both scripted and non-scripted, generate ideas of culture, heritage, hierarchy, and transcendence. While it is true that the bases of belief and institutional structure are typically located in the sacred writings and oral traditions of a given group, it is not until these concepts are translated into practice that they actually become religious. This understanding recalls the original essence of the term religion, which derives from the Latin *religi*, meaning obligation. Regardless of how text-oriented or intellectually rich a faith is, mere convictions are not a way of life. It is only by performing specified duties—that is, by fulfilling ritual obligations—that religions truly come into being. And it is in the unique manner a group performs these tasks that its identity is formed.

One of the most basic and pervasive modes of Jewish ritual is singing. In both formal settings, like synagogue worship and lifecycle events, and casual gatherings, like Shabbat and holiday meals, song is a ubiquitous signifier of the occasion and, equally, a powerful marker of identity. From the perspective of performance scholars, the exact language of the songs, while crucial for stating the group's worldview, is secondary to the singing itself. This is because ritual song, in a literal sense, turns text into a living experience. As influential ritual studies professor Catherine Bell would have said, singing is a way of *doing* religion.

To better understand this phenomenon, it is worthwhile to explore musical choices of select Jewish groups. Though this exercise will be brief and generalized, it should nevertheless help identify, in a cursory way, why music plays such an important role in forming communal identity. The unaccompanied male singing of modal formulas (*nusach*) favored in Orthodox circles asserts a link to old ways and a rejection of contemporary, "foreign" styles. The guitar-driven folk-rock melodies found in many Reform synagogues proclaim that denomination's mission of social justice. The Renewal movement's incorporation of spiritual song forms from Middle Eastern, Indian, and other sources announces their multicultural and mystical tendencies. And the blend of *nusach* and contemporary songs heard in most Conservative services declares the movement's desired blending of past and present.

These broad observations are even more significant when we consider that the words these groups sing are, by and large, derived from the same Hebrew sources. The language and thematic content they sing mark the activity, occasion, and setting as Jewish, but it is the music and the way it is performed that signals what kind of Jews the worshipers are. To reiterate, these sonic choices are not merely an outgrowth of the group's affinities or ideology, but a primary way its self-understanding is shaped and defined. It can thus be said that a Jewish group is what it sings.

Diversity and Balance

Judaism is not monolithic. Dramatic differences exist between and among the Jews of North America, Israel, Europe, Latin America, Asia, North Africa, and elsewhere. In contemporary America, Jews divide themselves into a number of groups, including Orthodox, Conservative, Reform, Reconstructionist, Renewal, and Secular Humanist, not to mention the significant percentage of Jews who are unaffiliated. And many define their Jewish identities in distinctly non-religious terms, such as secular Zionism, Yiddishism, and other "cultural" forms.

Divergent practices, contrasting beliefs, and regional variants are defining features of Jewish Diaspora life. Seemingly endless variations make up what history professor Steven M. Lowenstein calls the "Jewish cultural tapestry."[1] Yet, even though Judaism is heterogeneous, most Jews feel deep ties to one another. This is expressed in *Klal Yisrael:* the shared sense of community and destiny among all Jews, regardless of background or ideology.

Throughout history and across the globe, Jewish groups have exhibited unique traits and distinctive customs. Though generally rooted in the same sacred stories, calendar, and historical consciousness, each Jewish community has its own ritual behaviors and preferences, styles of dress and decorum, holiday foods and decorations, and so on.

This variety owes mainly to the fact that Jews have always been influenced by their surroundings. Jewish communities have adapted to far-flung geographic and social settings, borrowing and "Judaizing" elements from the dominant culture. To be sure, the degree of outside influence has depended on the amount of direct contact between the Jews and their neighbors. As a general rule, groups in major population centers, like cities in Poland and Spain, were more strongly influenced than communities on the periphery, like those in Yemen and Iraq. But no group was completely free of foreign elements.

Judaism's multifarious nature is evidenced in the wide-ranging genres and traditions of Jewish music. In fact, scholars have long recognized that no single melody is common to all Jewish groups. Like the Jewish people, Jewish music does not exist in a vacuum. Whatever musical unity may have existed in the Temple ritual prior to the Diaspora has long since been erased by generation after generation of Jews living throughout the world, and adopting local sounds as their own. In the words of Slobin, "Basic to all Jewish musics is their close ties to the musical traditions of their non–Jewish neighbors."[2]

We are the inheritors of this fertile musical heritage. American Judaism is an amalgam of people and practices from around the world. German-Jewish immigrants brought a tradition of choral hymns to American soil. Eastern European Jews introduced *hazzanut*. Twentieth-century composers like Ernest Bloch and Leonard Bernstein expanded the limits of synagogue song. The 1970s brought guitars into the synagogue walls. Songwriters dabbling in an array of styles, from Sufi chant to Brazilian pop, have contributed to Jewish worship.

American synagogue music is characterized by a diversity of sound, both in terms of the music itself and its modes of presentation—cantorial, choral, sing-along, accompanied, unaccompanied, etc. The best services highlight this wonderful assortment, utilizing melodies of sundry origins, past and present. Not confined to a singular rite, most liberal congregations are free to construct a balanced service that draws from many styles. Such a service can be inspiring and entertaining, as well as a vibrant reminder of Judaism's manifold streams and sources.

1. Steven M. Lowenstein, *The Jewish Cultural Tapestry: International Jewish Folk Traditions* (New York: Oxford University Press, 2000).
2. Mark Slobin, "Learning the Lessons of Studying Jewish Music," *Judaism* 44:2 (1995): 222.

III

Holidays and Liturgy

Shabbat Singing

The most basic definition of the word "sacred" is that which is set apart from the ordinary. Religious communities throughout the world demarcate sacred space in otherwise unremarkable landscapes, revere sacred scriptures over worldly texts, and engage in sacred rituals removed from the activities of everyday life. And in almost every tradition, music helps draw attention to these holy things: houses of worship are filled with song, texts are chanted with melody, and ritual is accompanied by singing.

This close association of music and the sacred is not accidental. Singing marks a break from the normal mode of communication. Words set to music rise above the drone of everyday speech. Songs separate words of prayer from ordinary language. In short, music can inspire a sense of sacred time and place.

It is thus fitting that Shabbat is a day brimming with song. Shabbat is, after all, set apart by God from the rest of the week. As it is written: "On the seventh day God completed His work which He had done, and He abstained on the seventh day from all the work which he had done. God blessed the seventh day and sanctified it, because on it He had abstained from all His work which God created to make" (Gen. 2:2–3).

Many prominent figures in Jewish history have noted the suitability of singing on Shabbat. The great Spanish poet Judah Halevi (c. 1080–1141) wrote, "I will sing, O Sabbath, songs of love unto thee. For it is Fitting, O day that art precious to me."[1] Rabbi Isaiah Horowitz (1565–1630) suggested that the welcoming and departing of Shabbat be escorted by song.[2] And Hassidic master Rabbi Nachman of Breslov (1772–1810) taught that singing on Shabbat "will give you a new life and send joy into your soul. Then you will be able to bind yourself to God."[3]

Over the centuries, a vast library of Shabbat music has been amassed, from folk tunes and table songs (*zemirot*), to choral works and cantorial gems. Cantors and rabbis regularly introduce fresh musical settings into Shabbat services, and there is a seemingly endless supply of new Shabbat recordings and sheet music. As such, Shabbat should not only be understood as a day of rest, peace, and joy, but also a day of song.

1. Judah Halevi, "Sabbath Poem," quoted in Jonathan L. Friedmann, ed., *Quotations on Jewish Sacred Music* (Lanham, MD: Hamilton, 2011), 36.
2. Isaiah Horowitz, *Shnei Luhot ha–Brit* (1698).
3. Mordechai Staiman, *Niggun: Stories Behind the Chasidic Songs that Inspire Jews* (Lanham, MD: Jason Aronson, 1994), 34.

Music and the Moods of Shabbat

Certain types of music can effect positive changes on moods and behaviors. According to the American Music Therapy Association, music is especially helpful for treating people with anxiety, depression, learning impairments, developmental disorders, addictions, and chronic pain. An array of evidence-based studies confirms the health benefits of music, and music therapists work in places ranging from hospitals and rehabilitation centers to correctional facilities and halfway houses.

While the field of music therapy is relatively new, its roots extend back to ancient times. One of the earliest depictions of music's therapeutic function is found in the Hebrew Bible. Suffering from deep mental anguish, the aging King Saul directs his courtiers to locate "someone who is skilled in playing the lyre" (1 Sam. 16:14–16). They find David, whose soothing music alleviates Saul's troubled mind. The narrative relates: "Whenever the [evil] spirit of God came upon Saul, David would take the lyre and play it; Saul would find relief and feel better, and the evil spirit would leave him" (1 Sam. 16:23).

This account suggests an established connection between music and healing in ancient Israel. Without hesitation or mention of another curative method, Saul turns to music as a remedy for his psychological ills.

But, beyond describing music's efficacy in therapeutic settings, this passage sheds significant light on the role of music in religious services. In particular, it illustrates how musical sounds can inspire two moods closely associated with Shabbat worship: rest and peace.

The calming effect of synagogue music has long been noted. For Jews throughout the ages, prayer-songs have often provided relief from the stress and struggles of everyday life. A letter published in *The Jewish Daily Forward* in 1909 describes this purpose of synagogue song: "Sitting in the synagogue among people from back home and listening to the good cantor, I forgot my unhappy weekday life, the dirty shop, my boss the bloodsucker, and my pale, sick wife and my children. All of my America with its hurry-up life was forgotten."[1]

Release from worldly concerns is central to the notion of Shabbat rest. Rest in this context does not only mean the absence of work, but also an opportunity for renewal, reflection, refocusing, and remembering the truly important things in life. Just as David's music helped temporarily relieve Saul of his psychical chaos, much of Shabbat music is designed to stimulate clarity of mind.

Musical tones also led Saul to inner-peace, a primary aim of Shabbat observance. Shabbat peace is not conceived of on a grand scale, as in the absence of war. Rather, it refers to the tranquility that comes when individuals refrain from negative thoughts and emotions. The experiences of Saul and Jewish worshipers affirm music's ability to foster this peaceful mood.

The Talmud lists music among the human indulgences capable of restoring serenity of mind (BT *Berakhot* 57b). This quality of music appears in the biblical account of Saul and David, and lies at the root of the modern field of music therapy. In Jewish practice, the soothing effect of music is especially important on Shabbat, a day set aside for rest and peace.

1. Jonathan L. Friedmann, ed., *Quotations on Jewish Sacred Music* (Lanham, MD: Hamilton, 2011), 59.

Opening Songs on Shabbat

British conductor Sir Thomas Beecham wrote, "The function of music is to release us from the tyranny of conscious thought."[1] Music's impact is immediate and all consuming. Whatever thoughts may be swirling in one's mind can be swept away in a moment by musical sounds. This function of music has special importance on Shabbat, when Jews are instructed to remove themselves from the demands of the secular week. Just as the Torah states that God rested after six days of creation, Jews are to make Shabbat a day of rest for the mind, body, and spirit. But this sense of tranquility is not always easily achieved. All who enter the synagogue carry with them an array of worries and concerns. It is thus a primary purpose of Shabbat music, and the opening songs in particular, to help create a time and space in which the tyranny of thought can be overthrown.

Friday evening services often begin with introductory songs, emphasizing major themes of Shabbat. They can be grouped into three categories: songs of separation, songs of peace, and songs of goodness.

Among the most effective songs of separation are *niggunim:* wordless tunes with origins in Hassidic practice that are designed to rid the mind of extraneous thoughts. In this way, *niggunim* help forge a separation from the tensions of ordinary time and bring worshipers into a heightened awareness of the sacred moment.

Shabbat is also a day of peace. Peace (*shalom*) is more than the mere absence of war; it encompasses the harmony and wholeness sought on Shabbat. So, the phrase "*Shabbat Shalom*" is not just a greeting of peace to one another, but also, as musicologist Macy Nulman explains, an address to the day itself: "Sabbath, you are good, you are peaceful and blessed and are being accepted graciously and with great joy."[2] Many opening songs proclaim this message of peace, including *Ma Yafeh HaYom* (How Beautiful is this Day), *Shalom Aleichem* (Peace Be Unto You), and *Bim Bam Shabbat Shalom.*

Other introductory songs illuminate the goodness of Shabbat. Shabbat goodness means many things: warmth, kindness, tenderness, calmness, community, joy. Songs that celebrate this unique quality bring to mind all of these feelings and more. They include *Hinei Ma Tov*, which states how good and pleasant it is when people gather together, and *Ma Tovu*, which exclaims, "How good are your tents, O Jacob. Your dwelling places, O Israel."

In its most basic meaning, Shabbat is the cessation from work and all of the hassles and anxieties that come with it. Judaism recognizes the power of music in aiding this transition from six days of labor to a day of separation, peace, and goodness—a power best described by Rabbi Nachman of Breslov: "Through song, calamities can be removed."[3]

1. Harold Atkins and Archie Newman, eds., *Beecham Stories: Anecdotes, Sayings and Impressions of Sir Thomas Beecham* (London: Robson, 1978), 80.
2. Macy Nulman, *The Encyclopedia of the Sayings of the Jewish People* (Northvale, NJ: Jason Aronson, 1997), 222.
3. Nachman of Breslav, *Likkute Moharan*, quoted in Jonathan L. Friedmann, ed., *Quotations on Jewish Sacred Music* (Lanham, MD: Hamilton, 2011), 38.

Vayekhulu and the Renewal of Time

With the seventh-day Sabbath, Jews commemorate the completion of God's creation of the world. It is, in essence, a weekly reenactment of the biblical account, in which God, on the seventh day, "ceased from all the work of creation that He had done" (Gen. 2:2). In abstaining from the labors of ordinary life, Sabbath-observant Jews construct a worldly repetition of this divine act, and, in turn, afford themselves a weekly opportunity to renew their own lives. Much more than a symbolic event, the Sabbath constitutes what historian of religion Mircea Eliade called the "myth of the eternal return."[1] Through ritual recitation of the liturgy, rest from labor, and other ceremonial acts, the Jew returns weekly to the dawn of time. Such commemoration repeats the pre-eminent cosmogonic act: the creation of the world.

The foundation for the Sabbath is summarized liturgically in the Friday evening prayer *Vayekhulu*, which is taken from Genesis 2:1-3: "Thus the heaven and earth were finished, and all their legion. On the seventh day God completed His work which He had done, and He abstained on the seventh day from all the work which he had done. God blessed the seventh day and sanctified it, because on it He had abstained from all His work which God created to make."

The architects of the prayer book included *Vayekhulu* three times in the Friday night service: in the silent *Amidah*, directly after the *Amidah*, and before the *Kiddush*. This betrays an effort to ensure that the repetition of cosmology would not escape the worshipers' consciousness. Importantly, too, with the obvious exception of its appearance in the silent *Amidah, Vayekhulu* is usually chanted rather than spoken. This musical rendering helps further engender a sense of eternal time, as music linked to a particular text or event and repeated on a regular basis imparts the existence of a continuous stream.

Melodies attached to ceremonial rituals have the unique ability to connect one to the cycle of history, in which similar ceremonies have occurred and will occur again. But, not only does this music instantly recall memories and sentiments connected to the day, it also evokes the original event. As Eliade explained, rituals unfold in "sacred time," or "once upon a time"—that is, "when the ritual was performed for the first time by a god, an ancestor, or a hero."[2] For instance, prayer-songs of Hanukkah, like *Al Hanisim* and *Maoz Tzur*, transport the worshiper to the rededication of the Temple, while the chanting of the Song of the Sea reproduces the moment when the Israelites escaped Pharaoh's army.

In like manner, *Vayekhulu,* when sung to a familiar tune, can bring one into the distant, mythic moment when "heaven and earth were finished." Text and tones merge to make immediate the original act of creation, and the worshiper experiences—at least figuratively—what Eliade termed "the primordial gesture of the Lord."

1. Mircea Eliade, *The Myth of the Eternal Return* (New York: Pantheon, 1954).
2. Eliade, *The Myth of the Eternal Return,* 21.

Reinterpretation Through Song

Quotations from the Bible are found throughout the Jewish prayer book. Notable examples include the *Shema* (Deut. 6:4–9, 11:13–21; Num. 15:37–41) of morning and evening services, the introductory prayer *Ma Tovu* (Num. 24:5; Pss. 5:8, 26:8, 95:6, and 69:14), and the ancient Priestly Blessing (Num. 6:24–26). According to the index of the *Authorized Daily Prayer Book* (London, 1890), 74 of the 150 biblical psalms appear in the liturgy, either in whole or in part.[1] The transference of these and other passages from the Bible to the prayer book shows the extent to which Jewish religious expression depends on biblical themes and ideas. And, even though the setting changes, biblical quotes generally carry their original spirit into the liturgy. For instance, the praises that conclude the Psalter (145–150) retain their joyous intent when adapted to the daily *Pesukai Dezimra*, while the opening words of *Mi Chamocha* (Exod. 15:11) bring the elation of the Red Sea crossing into the worship service. But, there are times when the shift from biblical to liturgical settings necessitates the reinterpretation of a text's mood or meaning, a process usually helped along by music.

A case in point is the Shabbat prayer *Veshamru*, which comes from Exodus 31:16–17: "The people of Israel shall keep the Sabbath, observing it throughout the ages as a covenant for all time: it shall be a sign for all time between Me and the people of Israel. For in six days the Lord made the heaven and earth, and on the seventh day He rested from his labors." In two short verses, this proclamation relates the basic purpose of Shabbat: as God rested after six days of Creation, so we are to abstain from work on the seventh day.

Surprisingly, however, *Veshamru* was originally given as a stern command, not a blissful message. It came directly after the harsh decree: "You shall keep the Sabbath, for it is holy for you. He who profanes it shall be put to death: whoever does work on it, that person shall be cut off from among his kin" (Ex. 31:14). Read in this context, there appears little connection between Shabbat and its familiar themes of joy, peace, and tranquility.

Bringing the text's original flavor to the synagogue service would require first and foremost the abandonment of its musical settings, which range from meditative to exuberant. In their place, composer A. W. Binder suggested that music be used "of a martial character ... music through which we hear trumpet sounds bearing a command, expressing the significance of a holy pact, and of a covenant never to be broken."[2] Still, Binder conceded that such aggressive melodies would disturb "sweet peace and rest"—feelings that have become inextricably linked to Shabbat—and would thus fall quickly into disuse.

The attainment of relaxation is not aided by stiff or commanding tones. This is why most settings of *Veshamru*, from simple chant and folk melodies to choral works and contemporary prayer-songs, use musical conventions that elicit positive states, like happiness or contemplation. In keeping with the moods of Shabbat observance, these melodies are guided by the text's mention of rest, rather than the forceful tenor of the biblical passage.

1. Joseph H. Hertz, *The Authorized Daily Prayer Book* (New York: Bloch, 1987).
2. Abraham W. Binder, *"V'shomru:* A Century of Musical Interpretations," in Irene Heskes, ed., *Studies in Jewish Music: Collected Writings of A. W. Binder* (New York: Bloch, 1971), 52.

Thanksgiving Every Week

One hundred seventeen of the Bible's 150 psalms begin with superscriptions. These brief statements provide clues as to the psalms' origins and performance in the Jerusalem Temple. To take just two examples, the superscription for Psalm 3 indicates the author and historical context, "A psalm of David when he fled from his son Absalom," while Psalm 76 denotes musical instructions and authorship, "For the leader; with musical instruments. A Psalm of Asaph, a song." Unusual among these headings is that of Psalm 92. It does not identify an author, nor does it describe how or for whom the psalm was sung. All that is established is its apparent use on Shabbat: "A psalm. A song; for the Sabbath day."

Because Psalm 92 mentions no author, rabbinic commentators were free to imagine who composed it. They attributed the text to Adam, whom they pictured singing on the first Shabbat in the Garden of Eden. While it is unclear when Psalm 92 became connected with Shabbat or when it was sung in the Temple ritual, the rabbis asserted that the Levites sang a special psalm each day during the morning sacrifice, and that this was the one designated for the seventh day.

Outside of its superscription, Psalm 92 does not appear to have explicit ties to Shabbat. Some have noted that it contains seven instances of the Tetragrammaton (YHWH), which may refer to the seven days of Creation; but there is little in the psalm's subject matter to conjure images of Shabbat. It relates neither to the formation of the world nor to the day of rest. Instead, like many other biblical psalms, its main concern is the struggle against evil and the destruction of the wicked: "Though the wicked will sprout like grass, though all evildoers blossom, they will be destroyed forever" (v. 7).

As such, the rabbis sought a link between the eradication of evil and Shabbat. Viewing Shabbat as a symbol of ultimate perfection, peace, and tranquility, they understood the psalm to be a vision of an Edenic age when all evil will cease and every day will be Shabbat. For them,

Psalm 92 was "a song for the future, for the day that is entirely Shabbat and rest for all eternity" (*Tamid* 7:4).

The psalm does, however, offer a more obvious Shabbat theme. In the second verse, we read: "It is good to give thanks to God, to sing hymns to Your name, O Most High." On Shabbat, we express gratitude to God for the many blessings in our lives, for sustaining us through the workweek, and for releasing us from the stresses of ordinary time. According to Israel Abrahams (1858–1925), a leading Jewish scholar of his generation, the text's suitability for Shabbat "is found in its character as a thanksgiving psalm, eulogizing God's faithful providence and love in caring for our world, the marvelous works of His hands."[1] Psalm 92 reminds us that Shabbat is not only a day of rest, peace, and joy, but also a holiday of thanksgiving.

1. Israel Abrahams, *A Companion to the Authorized Prayer Book* (New York: Sepher-Hermon, 1966), 127.

The Modern Origins of an "Ancient" Tune

A familiar song often achieves a sense of timelessness. It transcends the confines of time and place, and the melody becomes inseparable from the text for which it was written. Through continued and repeated performance — both live and recorded — it tends to be stripped of its status as a human creation. The composer's identity is almost invariably forgotten, and the music becomes the "property" of the masses. A prime example of this is the popular *Shalom Aleichem* melody.

While presumed by many to be an old folk tune, the setting of *Shalom Aleichem* sung in most Ashkenazi synagogues was published in 1918 by Israel Goldfarb (1879–1967), a Polish-born American rabbi, cantor, and composer. Goldfarb served as rabbi and cantor of the Kane Street Synagogue in Brooklyn for more than a half century, and was professor at the Cantors Institute of the Jewish Theological Seminary, which he helped establish. During his lifetime, Goldfarb earned the title of "father of [Jewish] congregational singing," introducing compositions to his synagogue and around the Shabbat table that would eventually spread to Jewish communities far and wide.

Goldfarb published over a dozen songbooks containing original material and older melodies adapted for single voice or choir and keyboard accompaniment. He collaborated on several of these books with his brother Samuel, who was a choral director and Jewish music educator. A number of Goldfarb's compositions have become synagogue standards, including his *Magein Avot* (The Shield of Our Fathers) for Shabbat evening, and *Zochreinu* (Remember Us) for the High Holy Days. These pieces and others frequently appear in music collections under the heading of "traditional," "folksong," or other generic terms indicating that, not only are the editors or compilers unfamiliar with the songs' origins, but also that the tunes are so generally known as to be thought of as ancient.

With regards to *Shalom Aleichem*, Goldfarb noted that it had "traveled not only throughout [the United States] but throughout the world, so that many people came to believe that the song was handed down from Mt. Sinai by Moses."[1] Rabbi Morris Kertzer gave a similar report about his visit to India, where he heard an Indian Jew singing the melody. When he asked the man how he knew it, he replied "it came down by tradition from the ancestors."[2]

As far as Goldfarb was aware, no other melodies for *Shalom Aleichem* existed before he composed the tune. Instead, the prayer was "half-chanted" or "only recited" by men returning home from synagogue on Friday nights. And even this practice was limited to certain Orthodox communities, primarily in the Old World. It can therefore be argued that the introduction of Goldfarb's setting into the synagogue — either at the opening or closing of the Friday evening service — essentially saved the prayer from obscurity.

The melody's assumed antiquity stems largely from its successful use of the *Ahavah Rabbah* synagogue mode. *Ahavah Rabbah* is common to many Eastern European melodies, both Jewish and non–Jewish. It is characterized by the interval of an augmented second between its second and third scale degrees, as heard in the popular song *Hava Nagila*, and is widely considered the most "Jewish sounding" of the prayer modes. By setting *Shalom Aleichem* in these cherished tones, Goldfarb gave it a sense of reaching back to distant times.

---

1. Henry D. Michelman, "The Journey of a Hebrew Melody: Israel Goldfarb's *Shalom Aleichem*," *The Synagogue Journal* (Dec. 2006): 17.
2. Michelman, "The Journey of a Hebrew Melody," 17.

Springtime and the Song of Songs

"Oh, give me the kisses of your mouth, for your love is more delightful than wine." Thus begins the Song of Songs, the Bible's exquisite collection of love poetry. In eight short chapters, the Song explores the delicate relationship between two young lovers, each delighting in the physical charms of the other. No morals are drawn and there is no mention of God.

The Song's sensual and earthly character made its inclusion in the biblical canon controversial. To justify its sacred status, rabbis of the first century interpreted the Song as a description of the love between God and His chosen people. So important was this allegorical reading to the rabbis that Akiva wrote, "He who trills his voice in the chanting of the Song of Songs in the banquet-halls and makes it a secular song has no share in the world to come" (*Tosefta Sanhedrin* 12:10).

Still, it is likely that the Song was included in the Bible because, as an anthology of secular love poems, it played an important role in the culture of ancient Israel and the Second Temple period. Physical love was a popular subject in poetic traditions throughout the ancient world, and images similar to those conjured in the Song appear in Egyptian, Mesopotamian, and other literatures. As such, biblical scholars argue that portions of the Song were cherished expressions of Jewish sentiments long before the book was canonized.

To this day, the Song figures prominently in two characteristically springtime celebrations: Passover and weddings. Along with its commemoration of the Exodus, ritual meal, religious services, and numerous customs, Passover marks the beginning of spring; and the regeneration of nature, pleasant weather, and proverbial "love in the air" has forever linked springtime and weddings. The Song's themes of hopefulness, renewal, and deep affection capture the seasonal character of these occasions, as we read in the familiar passage: "For now the winter is past, the rains are over and gone. The blossoms have appeared in the land, the time for pruning has come; the song of the turtledove is heard in our land. The green figs form on the fig tree, the vines in blossom give off fragrance" (2:11–13).

In Sephardic custom, the Song is chanted at the *seder* table, following the reading of the *Haggadah*. Ashkenazi Jews traditionally chant the book in the synagogue during the intermediate Shabbat of Passover, prior to the Torah reading. Its simple, elegant, and emotive cantillation — specific to the three festivals (Sukkot, Passover, and Shavuot) — transports the community to a collective ancestral past.

Portions of the Song are also sung at Jewish wedding ceremonies. In that context, both the Song's literal and spiritual meanings have obvious relevance. As a metaphor for divine-human love, the Song brings sanctity to the wedding ceremony. The deepest meaning of matrimony is reflected in its portrayal of human intimacy and praise of the goodness of love. Wedding songs taken from the book include *Dodi Li*—"My beloved is mine and I am his" (2:16)—*El Ginat Egoz*—"I went down to the nut grove" (6:11)—*Hinach Yafeh*—"Ah, you are fair" (4:1)—and *Zeh Dodi*—"This is my beloved" (5:16).

With poetic imagery featuring birds, trees, fruit, and other symbols of fertility and renewal, the Song of Songs has long been associated with springtime. And, whether it is read literally or as a supernatural allegory, its message rings eternal: "Many waters cannot quench love, neither can floods drown it" (8:7).

Song of Redemption

Passover is a holiday of redemption. With the annual retelling of the Exodus drama, Jews are reminded of their ancestors' escape from the physical and spiritual shackles of Egyptian slavery. This theme is captured in the phrase *z'man cheiruteinu* (season of our freedom), which inspires the Jewish people to reflect on their past struggles, and give thanks for the blessings of the present.

Passover's redemptive message also led to the association of the holiday with ultimate redemption: the coming of the Messiah and rebuilding of the Jerusalem Temple. There is, in fact, a belief that the Jerusalem Temple will be rebuilt on the first night of Passover. And while building during a festival is *halakhically* forbidden, the Talmud states that the Temple will descend from heaven, and so does not require the strenuous labor of human hands (BT *Shebu.* 15b).

Out of this tradition emerged *Addir Hu* (Mighty is He), a hymn sung by Ashkenazi Jews at the conclusion of the *seder* meal. *Addir Hu* is one of several songs that were added to the *Haggadah* in the Middle Ages. It consists of two thematic elements: a list of God's attributes (greatness, majesty, dependability, grace, etc.), and a plea that He build the Temple "speedily in our days."

Leopold Zunz, the German-Jewish scholar who pioneered the critical investigation of Jewish literature, hymnody, and ritual, dated the text to the sixth or seventh century. However, it did not appear in printed form until the latter part of the fifteenth century, and was originally included in all festivals, not just Passover.

Addir Hu is sung to essentially the same tune throughout the world's Ashkenazi communities. The tune's popularity is evidenced by the fact that, in addition to being sung for the text of *Addir Hu*, it is commonly used for singing other prayers during the festival, like *Mi Chamocha* and parts of *Hallel*. For this reason, musicologist Eric Werner called it "the seasonal leitmotif of the entire Passover-tide."[1]

The melody took different forms before arriving at its present shape. The first known musical transcription was printed in a 1644 German *Haggadah*, but this primitive version, according to Rabbi Francis L. Cohen, was of "a droning intonation rather than a set melody."[2] By the eighteenth century, the tune as we know it today had spread throughout Germany and other parts of Europe, and found its way into several cantorial compositions. The melody has a distinctly Germanic character, and while not identical to any single folksong, contains motifs ubiquitous in *Gassenhauer* (street songs) from the sixteenth and seventeenth centuries.

The continued popularity of the *Addir Hu* melody can be explained, at least in part, by its simplicity and pleasantness. Like many folk tunes, it relies on primary harmonies (tonic, dominant, and subdominant), and stays within an octave range. Its decidedly major, easy-flowing, and singable melodic line captures perfectly the text's unequivocal praise of God and hopeful message of redemption. These elements combine to accomplish three central functions of Jewish sacred music: uniting individuals in a shared experience, uplifting the spirit, and elevating the prayer toward heaven.

---

1. Eric Werner, "The Tunes of the Haggadah," *Studies in Bibliography and Booklore* 7 (1965).

2. Francis L. Cohen, "Addir Hu," *The Jewish Encyclopedia* (New York: Funk and Wagnalls, 1901–1906), 187.

Sound of the Sea

The Red Sea crossing is the climax of the liberation narrative in the Book of Exodus. In response to their deliverance, Moses and the Israelites burst forth in exalted song, praising God for enabling their miraculous escape from the pursuing Egyptian army (15:1–18). Known as the Song of the Sea, this lyric poem is among the oldest texts in the Bible. It recounts in enthusiastic terms the drowning of Pharaoh's forces (vv. 4–12), God's guidance of Israel to the Promised Land (vv. 13–17), and His eternal rule (v. 18). Not mentioned, however, are key elements of the escape account, such as the splitting of the sea, the walls of water, and the crossing to dry land (14:26–29). But the Song was not a ballad; it was a triumphant hymn offered at freedom's shore. Rather than a recapitulation of a historical event, it was a musical celebration of God's redemptive power.

The Exodus from Egypt has been described as the creation story of the Israelites, with the emergence from the sea signifying a national rebirth. Viewed in this way, the Song of the Sea was not only a fitting response to a miraculous episode, but also the declaration of a newly freed nation. Additionally, the singing of the Song was the first corporate worship experience in the Bible, as well as its first instance of devotional music.

It is, of course, impossible to know for sure the exact manner in which the Song was intoned; while the text has been canonized and transmitted through the millennia, its original tune is irretrievably lost to history. Still, the Song's literary structure and the notion that it was at the same time spontaneous and collective indicate that it was originally sung as a call-and-response.

The significance of this passage is emphasized in the Torah scroll, where its verses are arranged in overlapping segments rather than the standard parallel columns. This unique layout may be meant to recall Israel's experience as brick-laying slaves, or represent the waves of the Red Sea. In synagogue practice, the text is not bound to the usual system of biblical chant, which follows prescribed musical patterns determined by a system of textual accents called *te'amim*. It exists instead as an independent tune that in sound and structure establishes a perceptible departure from the cantillation, and resembles a trumpet-call signaling a moment of victory.

It is fitting that this melody, known as the *Shirah* (Song), is one of the oldest in the Ashkenazi synagogue. The *Shirah*'s antiquity is evidenced in part by its strong pentatonic character, which is among the earliest established scales. There is also a close similarity between the Ashkenazi and Sephardic versions, suggesting that the tune might predate the development of these rites, or at least stems from an ancient cultural exchange. In fact, the features unique to either tune can be attributed to rhythmic rather than tonal differences. While in Ashkenazi synagogues the *Shirah* is chanted annually by a single reader, it is customary among Sephardim for the congregation to sing it together as part of the Shabbat liturgy — a practice that necessitated its conversion from free chant to a metrical tune.

In the past, these old features led scholars to the romantic notion that the melody goes back to Red Sea crossing itself. As David Aaron de Sola (1796–1860) put it, "Some have affirmed that what we now sing to the Song of Moses is the same [melody] Miriam and her companions sang."[1] While such a claim cannot be substantiated (and is highly unlikely), it does speak to the indelible link between the melody and this paramount event in Jewish sacred history. The tune works to consolidate the thoughts and sentiments of worshipers, transporting them to the moment when the Israelites escaped Pharaoh's army. Thus, for those familiar with its triumphant strains, the *Shirah* is more than an ancient folk melody; it is an audible symbol of Jewish deliverance and freedom.

1. David de Sola Pool, *The Ancient Melodies of the Liturgy of the Spanish and Portuguese Jews* (London: Wertheimer and Co., 1857), 15.

Akdamut and the Power of Song

Shavuot commemorates the revelation of Torah on Mount Sinai. Unlike most other Jewish holidays, it has no prescribed observances, aside from the prayer services and abstention from work that come with all festivals. It does, however, boast several customs, including the consumption of dairy products, the public reading of Ruth, and the decoration of homes and synagogues with greenery. There is also the longstanding practice of chanting *Akdamut Millin*—"Introduction to the Words [of the Ten Commandments]"—in the morning service prior to the Torah reading.

Akdamut is attributed to the eleventh-century rabbi Meir ben Isaac of Worms. It consists of a ninety-verse double alphabetical acrostic followed by an acrostic giving the author's name and the wish, "May he grow in Torah and in good deeds, Amen; Be strong and of good courage!" The poem was originally used as a prefatory hymn to the Aramaic translation of the Ten Commandments, which was read throughout Germany during the Middle Ages. While the poem celebrates the Jewish people, their love of Torah, and their longing for redemption, its language is esoteric, difficult to pronounce, and notoriously hard to translate. Nevertheless, it has remained a standard part of the Shavuot liturgy.

It seems an accident of history that a prayer of this length and abstruseness has persisted through the centuries. After all, its intended function—introducing the Aramaic version of the Ten Commandments—is no longer needed, and other liturgical poems of similar vintage fell into disuse long ago. *Akdamut* has, in fact, outlasted its relevance: it is used today without being understood and without serving a practical purpose. So why has it been retained?

Rabbi Jeffrey Hoffman gives one explanation for this curious survival in his article, "Akdamut: History, Folklore, and Meaning."[1] He writes that *Akdamut*'s initial popularity derived from its connection with the First Crusade, which devastated the Jewish communities of Worms, Mayence, and other Rhineland towns in the eleventh century. Amidst these dire circumstances, a Yiddish folk-tale was promulgated involving a monk-sorcerer who used black magic to murder over thirty thousand Jews. As the story goes, the Jewish community pleaded with the king for protection, and the monk conceded that he would end his murderous ways if the Jews produced a wonderworker with skills greater than his own. They searched tirelessly for such a person, but no one fit the bill. Just as all hope seemed lost, Rabbi Meir crossed the mystical river of Sambatyon, beyond which resided the ten lost tribes. There he found Dan, a hero-ancestor with magical powers rivaling those of the monk. Shavuot was nearing, and before Dan departed for battle, Rabbi Meir composed *Akdamut* and offered it to him as a blessing. Using incantations of mystical names of God, Dan defeated and killed the evil monk, and to mark the victory instituted the poem's annual recitation.

This popular tale brought a sense of uplift and self-assurance to a population ravaged by persecutions and plagues. As time passed, the myth became inseparably linked with *Akdamut*, and its chanting stirred feelings of justice and redemption — sentiments that strengthened the people's unity and resolve. As Hoffman argues, it was the emotions associated with the colorful origin story — not the obscure Aramaic — that made *Akdamut* a cherished piece of liturgy.

Hoffman's analysis does much to account for the text's appeal in the Middle Ages, but is less helpful for explaining why the prayer is still used when the Crusades reside in the distant, almost unfathomable past. A better reason may be the esteem given to its tune, sometimes referred to as the "*Akdamut* motif." This melody is sung throughout the Ashkenazi world, and claims great antiquity both because of its psalmodic style and because of its placement among the so-called *Mi-Sinai* tunes. It is likely that the melody predated the *Akdamut* text, and it long ago traveled to the evening *Kiddush* for the three festivals as well. As such, the tune serves as a seasonal signifier, and the emotions and memories it conjures exist apart from — and can exceed the importance of — the texts to which it is set. Certainly with *Akdamut*, the focus is less on the puzzling words than on the simple, pleasing tune, which enhances the festive atmosphere of the day.

Akdamut is not the only liturgical text that owes its preservation to melody. This is also true for *Kol Nidrei*, an archaic legal formula scribed in Aramaic and often cited as a "proof text" by anti–Semites, *El Maleh Rachamim*, a memorial prayer comprised of cryptic language and mystical imagery, and *Shalom Aleichem*, which, before Israel Goldfarb wrote his ubiquitous tune, was a little-known poem with no proper melody. These and other examples demonstrate the power of music to capture the mood and spirit of sacred time, and to aid the survival of even the most obscure and apparently irrelevant texts.

1. Jeffrey Hoffman, "Akdamut: History, Folklore, and Meaning," *Jewish Quarterly Review* 99:2 (2009): 161–183.

Songs of Renewal

Rosh Hashanah and Yom Kippur are days of renewal. They are sacred times when virtually all Jews feel obliged to attend synagogue services, and the Jewish world is infused with heightened feelings of conviction and solidarity. More so than any other occasion, the High Holy Days have the ability to "recharge" a sense of Jewishness and communal bonding. On a personal level, these holidays provide a focal point for thoughts and emotions, and an opportunity for soul searching and rejuvenation. On a collective level, they reinforce a sense of connection to ancestors, tradition, and one another.

Much of this revitalizing impact owes to the music of the High Holy Days. Time-honored music of the synagogue serves as a powerful reminder of our shared history and common heritage. In Ashkenazi tradition, this is perhaps best demonstrated by the widespread use of *Mi-Sinai* tunes: melody-types traditionally believed to have been transmitted to Moses on Sinai. These tunes, developed in southern Germany and eastern France between the eleventh and fifteenth centuries C.E., comprise the signature sounds of Rosh Hashanah and Yom Kippur. Throughout the world, Ashkenazi communities hear these melodies during High Holy Day services. They unite Jews who might otherwise be religiously or geographically dispersed, and instantly recall memories and sentiments tied to these sacred days.

Mi-Sinai tunes include the High Holy Day settings of *Bar'chu, Mi Chamocha, Chatzi Kaddish, Aleinu Gadol, Kol Nidrei,* and many others. These melodies are intimately linked to the prayers they accompany, and Jews have long insisted that no other melodies should be used in their place. It is therefore curious to note that these tunes did not originate as synagogue songs, but as creative responses to devastations brought on by the Crusades.

From 1096 well into the fourteenth century, the Jews of Western Europe were faced with an ongoing series of atrocities. In response, two kinds of songs arose: lamentations, voicing Jewish plight and memorializing martyrs, and hymns of praise, glorifying God and offering hope against hope. Though most of these texts are now forgotten, their melodies have remained a powerful and unifying force for Jews around the world. The migration of these tunes into the fixed liturgy of Rosh Hashanah and Yom Kippur is a testament to their ability to capture and convey petition and praise — the dual themes of the holidays. While we are far removed from the existential fears and dangers of crusader times, the effect of these melodies is largely the same: they bring worshipers into heightened feelings of community, reverence, and contrition.

Mi-Sinai tunes set the tone and atmosphere of the High Holy Days. When worshipers gather together and experience these melodies, they are transported from ordinary concerns to a revived sense of Jewish identity and community-mindedness. The music enables them to reach levels of devotion that would otherwise seem unattainable, and helps to renew their souls for the year to come.

Moses, Music and Eurocentrism

It is not known for sure when the term *Mi-Sinai* was first applied to fixed melodies sung on the High Holidays and portions of the Three Festivals. Some scholars suggest the designation was coined by Idelsohn (1882–1938), though hints of the term appear in earlier literature. Whatever the case, the *Mi-Sinai* label is based on the writings of Jacob Moelin (the Maharil, c. 1365–1427), a prominent Talmudist and legal authority who codified the customs of German Jews. Among other things, he ruled that longstanding melodies sung for key holy day texts be treated as if they were handed down to Moses on Sinai — that is, they should never be changed. With this decree and the perpetual usage it prescribed, these tunes, which originated in the medieval Rhineland and have roots in secular street songs of the region, became the most revered sounds of the Ashkenazi synagogue.

As is clear from Moelin's pronouncement, "songs from Sinai" was not meant as a literal concept. We have no record of what melodies (if any) Moses sang on that holy mountain, and even if they were transmitted orally through the generations, they would have retained none of their original character. Still, there are Jews, especially in observant circles, who maintain that Moses sang these tunes. This position is the product of an unquestioning piety, which accepts fantastic ideas as truth and, quite often, turns metaphors into statements of fact. Specific to *Mi-Sinai* tunes is a willful ignorance of both the term's symbolism and the music's indebtedness to Germanic conventions.

It is one thing to use the classification *Mi-Sinai* to raise the tunes' standing and ensure their preservation, and something else entirely to believe these melodies actually originated with Moses. Such a position goes beyond mere romanticism, as it posits that Israelite melodies were not only retained, but, remarkably, sounded Central European. Aside from a musical impossibility, this presumption is tainted with Ashkenazi bias. These tunes are wholly different from the High Holiday and Festival music of Sephardic and Mizrahi rites, and the rich memories and associations they carry are limited to the descendants of European Jews. Thus, while we can, perhaps, excuse the thought of these German melodies reaching back to Bible times as charmingly naïve, a more cynical analysis would place it within a larger narrative that sees the practices of European Jews as *the* genuine way.

This worldview can be traced to the eleventh century, when the hegemony of Jewish life shifted from the Middle East to the European continent. Gradually and inevitably, cultural elements were borrowed and Judaized from this host environment, and remnants of "orientalism" were replaced with European influences. Not insignificantly, *Mi-Sinai* tunes also began to develop during the eleventh century, and quickly became the defining sounds of Ashkenaz. On a deep level, these melodies, which were simultaneously Jewish and German, helped mark Europe as the new center of the Jewish world, and, whether their connection to Sinai was taken literally or figuratively, declared a powerful message: despite being far removed in time and place from their ancestral homeland, European Jewish practice was so authentic as to be worthy of Moses himself.

Modern-day Jews who assert the literalness of *Mi-Sinai* melodies are similarly motivated by a desire to legitimize their diasporic folkways. By upholding a connection to Moses through these tunes, they create a sense of uninterrupted Jewishness. But, however gratifying this belief may be, it is hard to escape its Eurocentric overtones. Tracing German music to the Sinai revelation is only possible if one views Western musical norms as both universal and timeless.

In the end, though, it probably matters little whether *Mi-Sinai* melodies are backdated to antiquity or appreciated for the medieval creations they really are. For Ashkenazi Jews everywhere and of all levels of observance, the music brings on a flood of personal and collective sentiments. So, in this emotional sense at least, the tunes are almost as powerful as they would be coming from Moses himself.

The Curious Case of *Kol Nidrei*

It is impossible to locate within a group as ancient and diverse as the Jews a single melody or motif that can be deemed "exclusively Jewish." Jews have lived in and adapted to widely varied places throughout the millennia, borrowing elements from their host environments and Judaizing them to serve their cultural needs. As a result, what is called Jewish music is in fact a heterogeneous amalgam of sounds culled from and inspired by virtually all conceivable genres, old and new. Even folksongs and the modes of cantillation and prayer-chant owe their Jewish identity to usage rather than some innate musical quality.

With similar observations in mind, musicologist Curt Sachs devised his well-known definition: "Jewish music is that music which is made by Jews, for Jews, as Jews."[1] This description is appropriately functional: it identifies Jewish music by its purpose rather than its sonic features. As long as a piece is composed by a Jew, written with a Jewish audience in mind, and has expressly Jewish content, lyrical or thematic, it is, according to Sachs, Jewish. These parameters would exclude pieces like *White Christmas* and *Rhapsody in Blue*, both of which were written by Jews (Berlin and Gershwin respectively) but have no discernable Judaic themes. Likewise, songs such as "Celebration" and "YMCA" are not made Jewish by virtue of being fixtures of *b'nai mitzvah* parties.

When we move beyond these obvious examples, however, Sachs's definition becomes more problematic. This is especially so when we consider music that is undeniably Jewish in terms of content and performance setting, but was composed by a non–Jew. And lest we assume that such pieces can be easily stripped of their Jewish label, we need only consider a work riddled with Jewish sentiment and associations: Max Bruch's *Kol Nidrei* for solo cello and orchestra.

Bruch (1838–1920) was a German Protestant with no Jewish ancestry, and his arrangement of *Kol Nidrei* was part of a wider exploration of folksongs of the world. Based on a version of the Yom Kippur melody sung by his friend, Berlin's chief cantor Abraham J. Lichtenstein, Bruch's setting takes many creative liberties, including a middle section that adapts Isaac Nathan's melody for a Lord Byron poem, "O Weep for Those that Wept on Babel's Stream." Bruch made clear that his aim was not to write something of religious value, but to use Jewish sources for his own artistic expression: "Even though I am a Protestant, as an artist I deeply felt the outstanding beauty of these melodies and therefore I gladly spread them through my arrangement."[2] Still, Bruch's *Kol Nidrei* is regularly placed among the most majestic pieces in the Jewish music library, and few would question its Hebraic aesthetic. Yet, no matter how often it is played on Yom Kippur or how strongly it resonates in the Jewish imagination, the piece is not, in Sachs's view, Jewish.

Other works face a similar judgment on account of their composer's non–Jewish status, including Shostakovich's *From Jewish Folk Poetry* and the klezmer projects of jazz clarinetist Don Byron. In cases like these, listeners are required to disregard their intuitive presumptions of Jewishness, however intense they may be. It is, then, perhaps wise to expand Sachs's definition to include all music that utilizes Jewish sources and is heard in Jewish contexts, whether or not it came from a Jewish pen. After all, it is the music that touches the listener, not the religious or ethnic affiliation of the composer.

1. Curt Sachs, First International Congress of Jewish Music (1957).
2. Max Bruch, Letter to Eduard Birnbaum, Breslau, 4 December 1889.

The Sound of Sincerity

There is a well-known Hassidic story of a shepherd boy who came to a synagogue to pray. As he entered the sanctuary, he was immediately struck by the words and melodies swirling about. Imitating the bearded men who filled the room, he opened a prayer book and began swaying back and forth, hoping that this gesture would somehow tap him into the worship experience. But he was illiterate, and the Hebrew letters that skipped across the page appeared to him an incoherent jumble. And so he sat down in quiet frustration. After some time had passed, the boy felt his hand reaching into his pocket, as if moved by the spirit of God. He drew out a small wooden flute with which he led his flock, and began playing a simple, spontaneous melody. As his flute became louder and louder, the men's prayers turned to complaints, and commotion filled the synagogue. The rabbi demanded that the boy be brought before him;

but instead of denouncing his apparent desecration, he scolded the congregation: "Until this very moment, all your prayers and supplications had been rejected by the Lord, but these simple and humble notes, sprouted from deep down this child's clean and tender heart, were what broke the barriers that separate the people of Israel from God, and moved with their fervor the great God of compassion."

Some versions of this tale have the Ba'al Shem Tov or Levi Yitzchok of Berditchev playing the part of the rabbi, and several take place during Rosh Hashanah or Yom Kippur. These details are significant. First, attributing the remarks to a revered rabbi adds legitimacy to the approval of the boy's melodic prayer. Second, though Orthodox custom strongly prohibits the playing of instruments on holy days, the rabbi makes an exception on account of the boy's pure and pious motives. Third, High Holiday services are the most ritually intricate and liturgically complex of the Jewish year, and thus an impromptu, non-verbal prayer seems especially out of place. All of this drives home the point that sincere devotion, no matter when, where, or how it is offered, is always preferable to merely "going through the motions" of statutory prayer.

This message has relevance for today. Most American Jews are not fluent readers of the prayer book, and have only cursory knowledge of its history, theology, and internal structure. And, when presented with English translations of the texts, it is not uncommon for congregants to become confused or offended by certain concepts, which were developed in places and periods seemingly at variance with our own. Such discomfort can, like the shepherd boy's illiteracy, create a barrier to wholehearted worship; but, like the boy's flute playing, the singing of prayers can help us connect to God, even if we do not completely understand or agree with every word we sing.

It should be noted as well that the role of Jewish sacred music is, as implied in the story of the shepherd boy, amplified during the High Holidays. As mentioned, these exalted services are filled with especially dense and difficult language, covering topics as supernatural as the Book of Life and as dire as modes of death. But, at the same time, High Holiday tunes are among the most immediate, stirring, and aesthetically satisfying of all Jewish music. For example, while *Kol Nidrei*, an outmoded Aramaic legal formula, is by itself a dry and uninspiring text, its plaintive melody instantly brings worshipers into the spirit of Yom Kippur; and though some might object to the gendered language of *Avinu Malkeinu*— "Our Father, Our King"—it is hard to resist the emotional pull of its folk tune. Thus, like the shepherd's flute, synagogue melodies can arouse genuine devotion in a way more powerful than words.

Rejoicing in Torah

Anthropologists have long noted the relationship of religion and dance. From the earliest human societies to the present, dance has been a part of religious stories, rites, ceremonies, and celebrations. Prehistoric cave paintings include images of ritual dance, and dancing figures appear on the walls of Egyptian tombs. Philosopher of religion Gerardus van der Leeuw (1890–1950) summed up dance's role in religion this way: "the man who invented the dance did not only discover himself, he discovered God. For he stepped into a new dimension of his existence.... The man who dances discovers that there is a power which enables him to give a new character to his own movement: by dancing to a fixed beat [he develops] a new essence."[1]

The Hebrew Bible recognizes the spiritual nature of dance. Miriam and the Israelite women danced ecstatically after crossing the Red Sea (Exod. 15:20). King David danced in front of the Holy Ark (2 Sam 6:14). The Psalms depict dancing as a form of divine praise (e.g., Pss. 149:3; 150:4). In present-day Jewish practice, the religious function of dance is most clearly displayed in the celebration of *Simchat Torah* (Rejoicing in Torah), which commemorates the completion of the annual reading of the Torah scroll.

The custom of celebrating the end of a Torah reading cycle began in the Talmudic period. The Talmud places this celebration on "the second day of *Shemini Atzeret*" (BT *Megilla* 31a), which over time became known as *Simchat Torah*. The occasion is marked by the chanting of the final words of Deuteronomy, followed by the opening passage of Genesis—a practice symbolizing that the Torah is, like life itself, a never-ending circle. As many congregants as possible are given the honor of reciting a blessing over the Torah, and the scroll is danced around the synagogue seven times.

Dancing on *Simchat Torah* represents several things. First, it illustrates that the Torah is a living document: it is a constant source of inspiration, enrichment, and joy. Rather than a museum piece confined to a dusty case, the Torah is a document that demands our physical embrace. Second, dancing marks a release from the solemnity of the High Holy Day season. While the Days of Awe are characterized by pensiveness and introspection, *Simchat Torah* is a distinctly non-intellectual holiday, calling for outward expressions of exuberance rather than inward reflections on complex liturgy. As Samuel Beckett wrote, "Dance first. Think later. It's the natural order." Third, dancing with the scroll communicates our gratitude for having completed another year of life, and our thankfulness for being the recipients of the rich heritage of Torah.

It goes without saying that *Simchat Torah* dancing is accompanied by music. Popular songs for the holiday include *Ivdu et Hashem* ("Serve God with gladness; come before Him with joyous song"), *Mitzvah Gedolah* ("It is a great mitzvah to always be happy"), and *V'samachta B'chagecha* ("You shall rejoice on your festival, and you shall be completely joyous"). Through these songs and the dances they accompany, worshipers experience the purpose of the day: rejoicing in Torah.

1. Gerardus van der Leeuw, *Sacred and Profane Beauty: The Holy in Art* (New York: Oxford University Press: 2006), 73.

Songs of Victory and Light

Each Jewish holiday has its own essence. Yom Kippur, for instance, is a day of contrition and repentance, while Purim is a time of jollity and frivolity. The Torah identifies Sukkot as "The Season of Our Joy," Passover as "The Season of Our Freedom," and Shavuot as "The Season of the Giving of Our Torah." These themes, elucidated in Scripture and liturgy, are made palpable through song. Upon hearing or singing a favorite holiday melody, one's mood turns instantly to the spirit of the moment. This effect is achieved equally with the solemn strains of *Avinu Malkeinu* and the bright sounds of *Ani Purim*. Quite literally, the music sets the tone of the day.

It is therefore appropriate that most of the music specific to Hanukkah is in an uplifting vein. Hanukkah commemorates the Maccabean victory over the Syrian-Greeks, and the rededication of the

Temple that followed. The Talmud (BT *Shabbat* 21b) adds that there was only enough oil at the ceremony to fuel the ritual flame for one day. But, miraculously, the oil burned for eight days. These two aspects of the story — one historical and one mythic — give the holiday its festive atmosphere, and spurred the creation of a number of cheerful melodies. These range from silly tunes, like "I Have a Little Dreydl," to more substantive songs, like *Mi Yimalel*.

The custom of singing joyful songs on Hanukkah is rooted in the original ceremony. The events surrounding Hanukkah are recorded in First and Second Maccabees. These books were left out of the Hebrew Bible, but did make the canon of some churches, including Catholic and Eastern Orthodox. They relate that the rededication began on the twenty-fifth day of Kislev — which became the start of Hanukkah — and lasted eight days. The books also hint that festive music was used to mark the occasion.

There are two main reasons why the celebration probably included music. First, it was a convention in biblical times to announce victories with song and dance. This was, for example, the manner in which the Israelites proclaimed their escape from Egypt (Exod. 15:1–21). Second, the Maccabee narratives describe rejoicing, which in biblical terms is almost a synonym for singing. The link between song and joy is made explicit in several psalms (Pss. 9, 16, 32, and 68), and over forty others allude to this connection.

In First Maccabees, we read that the Jews "joyfully offered burnt offerings" (4:56) and "celebrated for eight days with rejoicing" (10:6) — language that implies musical accompaniment.

It is difficult to imagine a Hanukkah gathering bereft of joyful tunes. They capture the ethos of the holiday, and provide the emotional underpinning for stories of victory and miraculous light. These songs of glee — silly and exalted alike — hearken back to the original event, when the Jews rejoiced in the Holy Temple.

The *Maoz Tzur* Melody: Sacred or Sinful?

"O mighty stronghold of my salvation, to praise You is a delight." These words begin the popular Hanukkah hymn *Maoz Tzur*. Written by an unknown thirteenth-century poet, *Maoz Tzur* expresses hope for the reestablishment of the Jerusalem Temple, recounts the Jews' deliverance from Egyptian bondage, the Babylonian exile, Haman's plot, and tells of the miracle of Hanukkah.

Like many Jewish prayers, *Maoz Tzur* is cherished more for its traditional melody than its poetry or theology. As early as the fifteenth century, the tune was in wide use among Ashkenazi Jews, and has since become a theme song of Hanukkah. The melody is often used for the singing of *Mi Chamocha* during the eight-day holiday, and instrumental renditions have been known to conjure the same emotions as when the text is sung. It is therefore interesting to note that the tune has distinctly non–Jewish origins.

Scholars have identified several German gentile sources of the *Maoz Tzur*. Among them is the folk-song "*So weiss ich eins,*" which Martin Luther also adapted to a church chorale. The melody's origins troubled Leib Glantz (1898–1964), one of the twentieth century's most gifted cantors. In a 1956 article, Glantz questioned if *Maoz Tzur* can "really be our 'national' Hanukkah song."[1] He was concerned that the "borrowed" melody was so strongly linked to a holiday celebrating the Maccabees' struggle against assimilation. "The Hanukkah holiday," Glantz wrote, "annually reminds us that for centuries the Jewish people lived as minorities among other nations, and had to struggle constantly in order to avoid integrating the customs and culture of those among whom they lived." On this ground, he labeled *Maoz Tzur* a "sin."

In an effort to rectify the seeming absurdity of the tune, Glantz offered a new setting of *Maoz Tzur* based on the chant for the blessing of the *Hanukkiah* candles. "Hopefully," he wrote, "this *Maoz Tzur* will capture the hearts of those who yearn for true and authentic culture."[2] Glantz's attempt to replace the old tune failed; but this has little to do with the merits of his own composition. The traditional *Maoz Tzur* is a folksong — a song that belongs to and resonates with the Jewish people. Like other folksongs, it has no known composers and developed through the process of oral transmission. Passed on from generation to generation, it is a vessel containing collective memories and emotions of the Hanukkah festival.

Maoz Tzur should not be judged on the basis of its sources. It has come to be, in both usage and sentiment, a thoroughly Jewish song. As Eric Werner reminded us, "It matters little that many folksongs are of non–Jewish origin.... The decisive fact is that the songs which are generally classified as typically Jewish are being sung at present by Jews exclusively."[3]

1. Leib Glantz, "The Sin of *Maoz Tzur*,'" in Jerry Glantz, ed., *Leib Glantz: The Man Who Spoke to God* (Tel Aviv: Tel Aviv Institute of Jewish Liturgical Music, 2008), 449–451
2. Glantz, "The Sin of *Maoz Tzur*,'" 450.
3. Irene Heskes, *Passport to Jewish Music: Its History, Traditions, and Culture* (New York: Tara, 1994), 26.

Making Noise

Judaism is in many ways a religion of adaptation. In ancient times, the Israelites constantly struggled to define themselves against surrounding and conquering cultures, taking in and Judaizing certain elements, like ceremonial garb, while rejecting others, like idol worship. In the Diaspora, the tension between integration and resistance has had a constant and powerful impact on Jewish practice and identity. As a minority people living in diverse regions of the globe, Jews have historically engaged in careful cultural borrowing, absorbing and reinterpreting aspects of the dominant society while at the same time retaining a sense of Jewishness. This process has resulted in the great assortment of rituals, clothing, music, cuisine, literature, and other cultural features that make up the complex fabric of world Jewry. Just as Heschel observed that "no religion is an island,"[1] no manifestation of Judaism has ever been completely isolated from outside contacts or influences.

Numerous Jewish customs developed by way of adaptation, though their foreign origins are usually forgotten. A case in point is the *grogger*, a Purim noisemaker comprised of two early percussion instruments: a bull-roller and a scraper. While this rattle is integral to the public reading of the Esther Scroll, and thus has a distinctly Jewish character, it is probably a carry over from a widespread ancient practice of scaring away evil spirits at the outgoing and incoming of seasons.

Purim comes at the beginning of spring, and therefore lends itself to this noisemaking custom. The architects of the ritual replaced the pagan notion of evil spirits with Haman, the evil man of the Purim saga; and the shaking of *groggers* at the mention of his name is a way of symbolically scaring him off. But, there is also a deeper meaning to this raucous activity. The rabbis saw in the Book of Esther a battle between God's forces, Esther and Mordecai, and Israel's eternal enemy, Amalek. Esther 3:1 ties Haman to the Amalekites through his father, Hammedatha the Agagite (Agag was an Amalekite). This places him in the bloodline of those who, following an attack on the Israelites during their exodus from Egypt (Deut. 25:18), became known as the epitome of evil and as the Jews' main existential rivals. The Torah even decrees that any memory of the Amalek nation is to be erased (Deut 25:19). As such, sounding the *grogger* with the chanting of Haman's name is a way of (figuratively) wiping him and his lineage from our memories.

Confronting Haman with cacophonous sounds is common to most Jewish groups, though the method of producing such noise takes several forms. The *grogger* as we know it first appeared in France and Germany during the thirteenth century, and is a staple of the Ashkenazi celebration. An earlier practice involved writing Haman's name on two smooth stones and clanging them together until the name was blotted out. Italian Jews instituted the blowing of trumpets, while Persian Jews have the custom of beating drums.

Though these noisemaking methods are, on their surface, symbolic ways of eradicating Haman and his evil plot, underlying them is a profound message of Jewish survival. As modifications of the ancient superstitious act of chasing away the lingering spirits of winter, these practices exemplify the adaptability and ingenuity that have ensured Judaism's persistence through the ages.

1. Abraham Joshua Heschel, "No Religion Is an Island," *Union Seminary Quarterly Review* 21:2 (1966): 117–134.

Music, Midrash and *Megillah*

Music is often used to paint tone pictures illustrating overt or implicit messages of a text. Ascending scales, for example, may accompany lyrics about going up, while slow, dark tones may be employed for lyrics expressing despair. The dramatizing function of music in Jewish worship is sometimes referred to as "musical *midrash*." This term is typically applied in a generic sense, indicating that music has the capacity to clarify a theme or give a specific meaning to a sacred text. For this reason, all synagogue music can be viewed as *midrashic:* it gives an added layer of interpretation to the fixed word. On Purim, however, this concept takes on a very literal meaning.

The Scroll of Esther is the most "secular" of the biblical books. It makes no mention of God, the Temple, piety, prayer, or Jewish practice. Added to this, it treats a rather serious subject, the threat of the Jews' annihilation, in a comic style. The story's depiction of the rowdy Persian court and drunken king, along with its hyperbolic, mocking tone, are well suited for the carnivalesque holiday of Purim, but less appropriate for a holy narrative. As Bible scholar Adele Berlin writes, "The plot glories in revelry and bawdiness, and this may be the primary reason for the absence of God's name."[1]

Because of all this, the book's inclusion in the biblical canon did not come easy. And once it was received, great efforts were made to resolve the omission of divinity. Rabbinic responses ranged from the notion that God's presence was concealed because of Israel's neglect of Torah, to the discovery of God's name hidden acrostically in the verse, "*Yavo Hamelekh V'Haman Hayom*" ("The King and Haman will come today") — the first letters of which spell out the tetragrammaton YHVH.

Some *midrashic* responses to God's absence are expressed musically during the chanting of the Scroll. Midrash Esther 2:11, for example, states that the vessels used at Ahasuerus' feast were taken from the Jerusalem Temple by Nebuchadnezzer in 586 BCE. To draw attention to this commentary, the verse mentioning the vessels is not chanted in the joyous Esther trope, but takes the mournful mode of Lamentations, invoking the Ninth of Av — the day commemorating the Temple's destruction. Another melodic departure occurs at Esther 6:1, when we are told of King Ahasuerus' night of sleeplessness. According to Midrash Esther 10:1, God, the King of kings, also lost sleep that night on account of His people's terrible plight. This verse is therefore sung with the elevated melody of *Ha-Melekh* (The King), a prayer of God's supremacy and exaltedness found in the morning services of Rosh Hashanah and Yom Kippur.

These are but a sampling of *Megillah* chant excursions based directly on *midrash*. Using carefully inserted musical clues — obvious to those familiar with melodies sung throughout the year — *midrashic* insights come to life, and the sacred nature of the text is revealed. This musical symbolism brings a divine awareness to the Esther scroll and recalls the Temple's destruction and subsequent exile — elements central to the rabbis' "deep reading" of the text. The chanting of the scroll thus shows the integration possible between *midrashic* and musical commentaries.

1. Adele Berlin, *Esther: JPS Bible Commentary* (Philadelphia: Jewish Publication Society, 2001), xvi.

Tension and Release

Music theorists since Aristotle have recognized tension as one of music's most fundamental properties. Like a coiled spring that is pushed and pulled, musical passages portray a cyclic dance, traveling through increases and decreases in intensity on their way to a resting position. Human beings seem hardwired to perceive this musical interplay. We feel musical tension on a primal level, as if it were a visceral or kinesthetic response. When musical suspense reaches its height, our muscles tighten, and with musical resolution, our muscles relax. Of course, no tone, interval, or harmony is intrinsically tense. Rather, the impression of tension stems from culturally derived expectations, which may differ from place to place. But, regardless of how it is generated, our intuitive perception of this musical property is the source of much of music's emotional impact.

Tension and release is especially integral to sacred music. The prayers of most liturgical traditions are arranged to convey dramatic movement. Calculated transitions occur both within and between prayers, moving from introduction to introspection, petition to praise, contrition to elation, and so on. These thematic developments — sometimes stark and other times subtle — take worshipers on a journey through the gamut of religious concepts and sentiments. But, like any lyrical text, prayers often depend on musical assistance to reach their desired effect. This is because music, much more than spoken words, can help clarify and magnify moods and feelings implicit in the text. And, again, these emotions are evoked in large part through musical tension and release.

To give just one example from Jewish liturgy, a drastic change occurs in the evening service when *Mi Chamocha* moves into *Hashkiveinu*. *Mi Chamocha* commemorates the moment when Moses, Miriam, and the Israelites crossed the Red Sea and burst out in exuberant song and dance. This highpoint in Jewish history is captured in the prayer's opening and closing lines, which are taken directly from the Exodus account: "Who is like you among the gods that are worshiped" (Exod. 15:1), and "The Lord will reign forever" (Exod. 15:18). Musical settings that are faithful to the spirit of this text incorporate dynamic swells, joyful tones, strong rhythmic pulse, and other devises that help bring out its energy and ecstasy.

In contrast, the *Hashkiveinu* prayer, which comes directly after *Mi Chamocha*, is a gentle petition asking God to grant peaceful rest and rejuvenation. Whereas *Mi Chamocha* is an enthusiastic call to celebration, *Hashkiveinu* has a relaxed and meditative quality suited for soft and easy-flowing music. The prayer is, in essence, a liturgical lullaby, and its musical setting should fit accordingly.

Tension and resolution can be used to aid the dramatic movement found not only within these prayers, but also between them. While *Mi Chamocha* recalls the anxiety and exhilaration experienced as the Israelites fled Pharaoh's army and reached the shore of freedom's sea, the dominant theme of *Hashkiveinu* is release from the stresses of waking life. When sung side-by-side, these prayers illustrate both the theatrical aspect of Jewish liturgy, and the emotionalizing force of musical tension and release.

Aleinu: Its Storied Past and Sacred Melodies

Jewish liturgy is a portal to the past. Beyond its immediate function in worship, a prayer can tell us much about the history of Jewish thought and culture. The liturgical texts that comprise our services are not only spiritually efficacious, but also historically valuable. This is certainly true of the *Aleinu* (It is our duty), which extols God's unity and sovereignty.

Aleinu was first introduced into the *Malkhuyyot* (Kingships) section of the Rosh Hashanah additional service (*musaf*) liturgy. This original placement is fitting, as *Aleinu* calls for a time when all people will accept God as their King. By the twelfth century, the text found its way into the daily morning service as a concluding prayer, and was later added to the end of the afternoon and evening services. In this concluding role, *Aleinu* reaffirms that God is the sole and supreme ruler of the universe — a crucial declaration according to Rabbi Yisrael Meir Kagen (1838–1933): "Lest people should think that we worship the moon when we joyously go out to great it, we recite this prayer, which closes with *ayn od*, saying that the Lord alone is God and none beside Him."[1]

Aleinu has been ascribed to several authors. There is a popular myth that Joshua wrote the prayer when he conquered Jericho. Others attribute the prayer to the Rav (Abba Arika), a third-century leader of the Jewish academy in Babylonia. Yet another tradition places *Aleinu* in the Second Temple Period (516 B.C.E.—70 C.E.), with the Men of the Great Assembly. This early date is supported by the prayer's reference to the Temple practice of prostration: ".... we bend our knees, bow, and acknowledge our thanks before the King of kings."

The prayer became the subject of controversy during the Middle Ages. In 1400 a baptized Jew spread a rumor that the passage "for they bow down to vanity and emptiness and pray to a god who does not save" was an attack on Christianity.[2] In support of this claim, he noted that the numerical equivalent of the word "emptiness" (*varik*) is the same as "Yeshua," the Hebrew name for Jesus. And because *varik* is also related to the word *rok*, meaning "spittle," it was customary for Jews to spit during this phrase — a practice anti-Jewish author Johann Andreas Eisenmenger (1655–1704) interpreted as a further insult to Christianity.

In France and Germany, censors insisted that this passage be deleted. In 1703 the Prussian government in Berlin even appointed special commissioners to make sure that the cantor did not sing these words. Many rabbis tried to prove these accusations wrong, arguing that the passage is based on a pre–Christian text, Isaiah 45:20, and that if Rav was the author, it was scribed in a non–Christian land. But the censors renewed their attacks in 1716 and 1750, and the passage was eventually expunged from most Ashkenazi prayer books.

Because of its theme of God's eternal kingship, *Aleinu* also came to be associated with Jewish martyrdom. Most notably, the prayer was chanted during the 1171 massacre in Blois, France. Jews of the town were accused of murdering a Christian child during Passover. This was the first time that the accusation of ritual murder, known as the "blood libel," was made in continental Europe, and as a result some thirty Jews were burned at the stake. There are three reports extant that describe the victims singing *Aleinu* as they died amid the flames. One is an eyewitness account sent to Rabbi Jacob of Orleans, which reads in part: "When the flames blazed and licked the bodies of the victims, they raised their voices in a unison melody; at first it was a low chant and afterwards a high-sounding melody. The people [gentiles] came and said: 'Which of your songs is this? For we have never heard such a melody from you before.' Yet we knew it very well, for it was the chant of the *Aleinu*."[3] Another report adds that the gentiles "henceforth used the chant in their church"; and Eric Werner did in fact locate the melody in the *Sanctus* of the Ninth Mass of the Virgin.[4]

The melody these martyrs sang was the *Mi-Sinai* tune from the *Malkhuyyot* portion of the High Holy Day liturgy. A similarly honored melody for *Aleinu* permeates all other services. It is a creation of Salomon Sulzer (1804–1890), the Austrian cantor-composer known as the "father of the modern cantorate." Like the High Holy Day tune, this melody has become "traditional" in the truest sense of the term: it is long established, regularly chanted, and universally known. Many of Sulzer's pieces remain synagogue standards, including the familiar tunes for *Shema*, *Hodo Eretz*, and *Ki Mitziyon*. And it is interesting to note that virtually all of Sulzer's music in popular use is in three-quarter time, reflecting his affinity for the waltzes of his native Vienna.

Aleinu is a prayer rich in both religious and historical significance. It captures succinctly the theological assertions of God's kingship and the chosen status of His people. Its origins, controversial language, use as a martyr's prayer, and musical settings tell of a storied and sometimes tragic past. But the fact that *Aleinu* is still sung thrice daily is evidence of its lasting relevance and spiritual value. Like the Jews themselves, it refuses to perish.

1. Macy Nulman, *The Encyclopedia of Jewish Music* (Northvale, NJ: Jason Aronson, 1996), 24.
2. Alan Unterman, *The Jews: Their Religious Beliefs and Practices* (Sussex: Sussex Academic Press, 1996), 30.
3. R. Barukh ben David, quoted in Werner, *A Voice Still Heard: The Sacred Songs of the Ashkenazic Jews* (University Park: Pennsylvania University Press, 1976), 43.
4. Werner, *A Voice Still Heard*, 43, 44.

Adon Olam: Master of the World

Adon Olam is one of the few strictly metrical hymns in the Jewish liturgy. Each line contains two rhythmically balanced phrases and ends with the syllable "*ra*" (e.g., *Adon olam asher malach, b'terem kol y'tzir nivra*). Its subject is God's eternality, uniqueness, omnipotence, and providence. In the words of liturgist Ismar Elbogen, it is "a prayer of purest poetry and universal religious content."[1] Because of its smoothness of language and purity of sentiments, *Adon Olam* holds a place of unusual significance in Jewish worship. It figures prominently in all rites, and has been set to innumerable melodies.

Adon Olam is most commonly ascribed to Solomon ibn Gabirol, the famous eleventh-century Spanish philosopher and liturgical poet. In Ashkenazi liturgy, it is comprised of ten lines, while in the Sephardic world it appears with twelve, fifteen, or sixteen lines. The original place of the prayer was at the beginning of the weekday morning service, where it was sung to inspire reverence and devotion among those preparing for worship. This was especially appropriate, according to the Gaon of Vilna, as the morning service is attributed to Abraham, who was the first to call God *Adon* (Gen. 15:2).

The prayer later found its way into other rituals. Its reference to sleep—"Into his hand I shall entrust my spirit, when I go to sleep and I shall awaken"—earned it a place in the bedtime prayers. Its closing words—"God is with me, I shall not fear"—made it suitable for the deathbed. In Morocco, *Adon Olam* is chanted before the bride is led to the *chupah;* and congregations everywhere sing it at the conclusion of both morning and evening services, using it as a climactic statement of exuberant praise.

Adon Olam boasts perhaps the most melodies of any Jewish prayer, rivaling only *Lecha Dodi* in the sheer volume of its musical settings. According to Rabbi Francis L. Cohen, "This song is sung to many different tunes, and can be sung to virtually any."[2] Most synagogue composers have written at least one setting of the prayer, ranging from congregational to sophisticated choral pieces. In Ashkenazi practice one setting is more widely known than any other: the melody by Russian born cantor-composer Eliezer Gerovitsch (1844–1924). Gerovitsch was both a Talmudic scholar and a thoroughly trained musician. Possessed with a keen understanding of the Hebrew language, Jewish theology, and music, Gerovitsch took a pre-existing folk melody and adapted it to the text of *Adon Olam*, the result being his world-famous tune.

This process of constructing a new musical composition on an already existing one, known as contrafact, is a common feature of Jewish music. Many cherished melodies are built upon or bear a resemblance to earlier songs. In the case of *Adon Olam*, not only was Gerovitsch's version created in this manner, but there are contemporary examples of congregations singing the prayer to the Beatles' "Yellow Submarine," the Hawaiian classic "Aloha 'Oe," and a host of other popular tunes. Notwithstanding the blurring of secular and sacred such adaptations entail, the very existence of this practice testifies to the role of the Hebrew language in making a song sound "Jewish." As Cantor William Sharlin wrote, "Language has the enormous power to transform the music which accompanies it. It is the very taste, the feel, the association, the context of the language. It's so powerful that you can put almost anything against that language and you are going to experience it as a Jewish experience."[3]

1. Ismar Elbogen, *Jewish Liturgy: A Comprehensive History*, trans. Raymond P. Scheindlin (Philadelphia: Jewish Publication Society, 1993), 77.
2. Francis L. Cohen, "Adon Olam," *Jewish Encyclopedia* (New York: Funk and Wagnalls, 1901–1906), 205.
3. William Sharlin, "Trust the Process: My Life in Sacred Song," in Jonathan L. Friedmann, ed., *Perspectives on Jewish Music: Secular and Sacred* (Lanham, MD: Lexington, 2009), 122.

The Myth of *Ein Keloheinu*

Synagogue songs are often given invented origins. There are at least four reasons that account for this phenomenon. First, it may reflect a desire to elevate the status or authority of a tune. This is achieved, for instance, with the title *Mi-Sinai*, which sends a number of medieval High Holy Day and Festival melodies back to Moses on Sinai. Second, false origins can make a piece seem more authentic or universal. This is a motive for calling a song "traditional" or "folk tune," even if it was written recently and/or by a known composer. Third, imagined beginnings may be linked to theological concepts, such as the Hassidic understanding of God as author of all music. In this view, any melody can be returned to its divine source if sung with devotional lyrics or as a wordless *niggun*. Fourth, a song's mythic roots may be the product of sensationalism. Perhaps the best illustration of this is the widespread rumor that the familiar setting of *Ein Keloheinu* is actually a German drinking song.

The hymn *Ein Keloheinu* (There Is None Like Our God) has several musical settings, but none is more popular than the tune by German composer Julius Freudenthal (1805–1874). Written in 1841, it is among the best-known and frequently sung melodies of the Ashkenazi synagogue. Like other songs of the nineteenth-century Reform, *Ein Keloheinu* exhibits characteristics of a Lutheran hymn, and is thoroughly German in flavor. However, the notion that it is an adaptation of an existing German tune, sacred or secular, is not based in history, but in the misreading of musicological data and a desire to give a titillating back-story to an otherwise innocent composition.

Cantor Sam Weiss has traced the confusion surrounding *Ein Keloheinu* to Idelsohn's classic text, *Jewish Music in Its Historical Development* (1929). Idelsohn wrote, "This tune has the typical German melodic line, and in its first part resembles a German melody [*Grosser Gott wir loben Dich*]."[1] It is important to note that Idelsohn did not assert that *Ein Keloheinu* was taken from the German song, but merely that there is a similarity between their first four measures. And, though it had been in use for some time, *Grosser Gott wir loben Dich* was first published one year after Freudenthal's *Ein Keloheinu*. Moreover, the German tune is a church hymn, not a drinking song. Nevertheless, this slight (and probably coincidental) resemblance was picked up and exaggerated by later scholars, who claimed that *Ein Keloheinu* derived from the hymn, and the connection eventually morphed into the story of the Jewish tune coming from a German tavern.

This origin seemed reasonable enough, given the stereotypical image of German drinkers. And those critical of the use of Germanic music in the synagogue seized upon the story as a way to belittle the entire nineteenth-century genre. Weiss explains: "It is very tempting to grasp at whatever German sounding synagogue music that has endured and stereotype it as an illustration of that sordid activity, regardless of its actual history."[2]

But not all who perpetuate the drinking song story do so in order to demean the melody. It is human nature to be attracted to juicy details and hidden truths, real or imagined. "*Ein Keloheinu*—Freudenthal melody" is hardly compelling. "*Ein Keloheinu*—German hymn" lacks pizzazz. But "*Ein Keloheinu*—German drinking song" is rife with intrigue. There is something irresistible about the notion of a sacred melody emerging from the dark and dingy halls of a German watering hole. For this reason, the myth of *Ein Keloheinu* is not likely to go away.

1. Abraham Z. Idelsohn, *Jewish Music in Its Historical Development* (New York: Henry Holt and Co., 1929), 238.
2. Sam Weiss, "Ein Keloheinu," *Chazzanut Online* (2002). <http://www.chazzanut.com/articles/on-ein-keloheinu.html>

The Religious Roots of *Hava Nagila*

Of the vast library of Jewish songs, *Hava Nagila* is certainly one of the most well known. Since emerging in early twentieth-century Palestine, *Hava Nagila* has become a perennial favorite at gatherings of all sorts, Jewish and non–Jewish alike. It has been recorded by an array of performers, ranging from Harry Belafonte to Bob Dylan, and can even be heard over the loudspeakers at major sporting events. But, despite its secular uses and universal appeal, the song's history discloses its sacred origins.

In the early 1900s, musicologist Idelsohn was busy collecting folk melodies from Jewish groups that had settled in Jerusalem from places like Russia, Germany, Yemen, and Morocco. He transcribed and published these songs in his monumental ten-volume anthology, *Thesaurus of Hebrew Oriental Melodies* (1914–32).[1] Part of Idelsohn's aim in assembling this work was the creation of a national music in Palestine that would help unify its diverse Jewish population. To this end, he attached Hebrew lyrics to a number of the folk melodies he collected, including one that would become *Hava Nagila.*

During the course of his research, Idelsohn encountered the Sadigorer Hassidim from Bukovina, and recorded several of their wordless *niggunim*. He was especially taken by one of these tunes, which he felt resonated with the message of Psalm 118: "This is the day the Lord has made, let us rejoice and be glad" (v. 24). He modified these simple words to form the lyrics of *Hava Nagila*, removing reference to God and adding a theme of solidarity: "Let us rejoice and be glad. Let us sing and be glad. Awake brothers with a joyful heart."

Idelsohn explained the genesis of this musical concoction: "The tune originated at the court in Sadigora (Bukovina) and was brought to Jerusalem. In 1915 I wrote it down. In 1918 I needed a popular tune for a performance of my mixed choir in Jerusalem. My choice fell upon this tune which I arranged in four parts and for which I wrote a Hebrew text. The choir sang it and it apparently caught the imagination of the people, for the next day men and women were singing the song throughout Jerusalem. In no time it spread throughout the country, and thence throughout the world."[2]

It is clear that Idelsohn wished *Hava Nagila* to be a popular — that is, secular — song. He purposely obscured the melody's original spiritual purpose, and eliminated the theological content of the text. Even so, the song retains the fervor of the Hassidic *niggun*, and exudes the joy of the Psalm. Though adaptation and usage have masked its religious character, *Hava Nagila* remains connected to the sacred realm.

1. Abraham Z. Idelsohn, *Thesaurus of Hebrew Oriental Melodies* (Leipzig: Friedrich Hofmeister, 1914–1933).
2. Abraham Z. Idelsohn, *Jewish Music in Its Historical Development* (New York: Henry Holt and Co., 1929), xiv.

IV

Cantors, Choirs and Congregations

The Cantor at the Center of the World

Most world religions have a concept of the *axis mundi,* an object or location marking the center of the world where Heaven connects with the Earth below. This sacred symbol can be a natural object, like a boulder or tree, or something made by human hands, like a pagoda or totem pole. In many cases, these divine-earthly intersections are situated in high places, where material existence seems in closest proximity to the world beyond. According to historian of religion Mircea Eliade, who popularized the term *axis mundi,* these holy centers are "replicas of the cosmic mountain,"[1] where divine contact first occurred and is perpetually maintained. In the Jewish vision of the universe, the Jerusalem Temple once stood as this sacred locale. However, since its destruction in 70 C.E., and despite the reverence given to its remaining wall, no specially appointed space is any longer necessary for Jewish worship. Rather, the *axis mundi* has, in a sense, shifted to the people themselves.

Judaism asserts that a link between Heaven and Earth is established through a *minyan:* a gathering of ten Jews anywhere that, by virtue of praying together, invites the presence of God. And though synagogues are convenient places for achieving this end, it is not the architecture but the worshipers assembled within that possess a degree of sanctity.

Yet, even as the group merges as a religious unit, an individual has long been singled out to pray on its behalf. This person is the cantor, or *sheliach tzibbur*, whose role is to ensure that God hears the congregation's collective petition and praise. On a deeper level, then, while the assembly comprises the holy ground, it is the cantor's voice that creates a direct channel connecting the congregation to God. In this symbolic way, the cantor is positioned at the center of the world.

Throughout Jewish legal and theological writings, it is stressed that the cantor is not a performer but a spokesperson. He or she is charged with converting, through song, an assemblage of individuals into a liturgical body, and transmitting its prayers to the divine. In the words of renowned cantor Benzion Miller, the cantor is "an intermediary ... a lawyer, pleading a case for [a] client."[2] And though vocal flourishes are highly valued within the cantorial craft, these outpourings are not aimed to impress or entertain, but to elucidate the grandeur of the liturgy, enhance the devotional atmosphere, and, most importantly, serve as a launching pad by which prayers are sent heavenward.

Like a church steeple reaching into the sky, the cantor's song rises above the physical plane, carrying with it the collective hopes and fears, joys and sorrows, praise and gratitude of the congregation. And, like a lightning rod affixed atop a skyscraper, the cantor attracts and harnesses heavenly energy, enabling it to permeate the worshiping community. Whenever and wherever the cantor offers communal prayers, he or she is transformed into an *axis mundi*, where humanity and divinity intersect.

1. Mircea Eliade, *The Sacred and the Profane: The Nature of Religion* (New York: Harcourt, 1959), 39.
2. Gigi Yellen, "Scales out of Shul," *Hadassah Magazine* 88:9 (2007): 50.

Singing and Prophecy

The biblical prophets were particularly passionate people. As mouthpieces of God, they advocated for the downtrodden, denounced hypocrisy, and condemned immoral behavior. Their emotions ran high, spilling into their divine communications. Whether consumed with rage or jubilation, they made their feelings clear. The words they proclaimed frequently took the form of psalms, a poetic genre that covers the gamut of human emotions. And, just as the psalms were sung by priestly choirs, there is evidence that the prophets turned to singing when delivering their messages. The urgency and intensity they felt could not be contained in speech alone; only the heightened language of music could adequately transmit their holy declarations.

These observations point to a phenomenon known to faith traditions throughout the world: singing can stimulate encounters with the divine. Of course, the prophets were believed to be specially commissioned by God, and so had a direct connection to the heavenly realm. But in many instances, they still required the aid of singing to amplify this channel of communication. A similar function of song is prevalent in modern times, as worshipers regularly sing prayers to God. It is widely held that singing can generate a palpable sense of the divine presence. Like the prophets of the Bible, worshipers have the opportunity to interact with God through musical utterances. This is what Yiddish novelist Joseph Opatoshu had in mind when he wrote, "Through true song one may rise to the power of prophecy."[1]

The link between singing and prophesying is further demonstrated by the word *chozeh*, a biblical term for prophet meaning "seer." In Rabbinic Hebrew, this term became *chazzan* (cantor), referring to the individual who sings the liturgy in Jewish services. That this word means both prophet and cantor indicates a visionary dimension of the cantor's vocation. The cantor serves as a *sheliach tzibbur*—"messenger of the congregation"—sending the community's prayers heavenward on the wings of song. Thus, cantors—and all others who sing prayers—have a modicum of prophetic ability in that they communicate directly with God through song.

1. Joseph Opatoshu, *In Polish Woods* (Philadelphia: Jewish Publication Society, 1921), 162.

Cantors and Levites

Cantorial students are often met with surprise when they mention that their schooling takes five years. "That seems like a long time," is a typical response, "don't you already know how to sing?" And when a young cantor takes his or her first pulpit, it is not uncommon for congregants to naïvely ask, "Are you planning to become a rabbi, or are you just going to be a cantor?" Questions like these are illustrative of the ignorance surrounding the cantorial craft. Most people assume that the cantor's job begins and ends on the *bimah,* and so the years of courses on chaplaincy, philosophy, Jewish history, biblical criticism, *halakhah,* and so forth seem at best tangential and at worst a waste of time and money. And since the rabbi is the public face of Judaism and plays the grandiose part of a congregation's "spiritual leader," there is a general lack of awareness among non–Jews of what a cantor is, and a widespread perception in Jewish circles that the cantor holds a secondary position to that of the rabbi. Moreover, since the West tends to view music (and vocal music in particular) as a form of entertainment, cantors are not usually hired or fired based on their depth of knowledge or insight, but on how well they "perform."

Despite all of this, the five-year program of cantorial studies is appropriate. Not only does the profession demand extensive musical training, liturgical competence, and mastery of a range of non-musical subjects, but Levitical singers, the biblical forerunners of the cantor's vocation, also underwent five years of intensive study. According to Numbers 8:24, a five-year training period was required for all Levitical work beginning at twenty-five. Some of the Levites were schooled as Temple architects, masons, gardeners, accountants, scribes, educators, and street sweepers, while a select group was given the exalted task of performing and supervising the music of divine worship.

Given that music in those days was passed on orally, and so large quantities of liturgical songs had to be memorized, the actual training (informal though it may have been) most likely began much earlier than the prescribed age of twenty-five. This is confirmed in a rabbinic account (BT *Arakhin* 13b), which states that junior choristers of Levite stock regularly added their voices to Temple song. This practice of apprenticeship is reminiscent of the mentor-pupil relationship that characterized cantorial instruction prior to the establishment of professional schools, and persists to this day, either as a primary or supplementary path to the cantorate. Like the child singers of the Temple service, musical development in modern times usually begins at a very young age, and many cantors-to-be first learn to lead services through participation in synagogue choirs.

Much of the puzzlement over why cantorial school takes five years can be chalked up to differences between outsiders and insiders. For outsiders unappreciative of the intricacies of liturgical music or unacquainted with the numerous duties in the cantor's job description — ranging from spiritual counseling to fundraising — five years might appear an excessive amount of time. But for insiders, whose musical and Judaic training begins long before and extends well beyond graduation, five years of formal schooling can seem too short a duration. As with the Levitical singers of the Jerusalem Temple, the cantor's holy work requires great devotion, refined skills, and a lifetime of dedicated study.

More Than a Voice

The office of the *hazzan* (cantor) as we know it today has its roots in the geonic period (589–1038). It was during that time that the *hazzan*, who had primarily functioned as synagogue caretaker, became a permanent service leader. The role and prestige of *hazzanim* continued to grow through the Middle Ages, when many were afforded long tenures, healthy salaries, and communal tax exemptions. In those days as well it became commonplace for congregations to seek out *hazzanim* more for their vocal skills than their piety or Torah learning. In response to this clamoring to hear the best voices — a phenomenon akin to "sacred entertainment" — fixed qualifications for the *hazzan* were gradually established. In addition to possessing a pleasant voice, it was ruled that he should be married, have a beard, have deep knowledge of the liturgy, be of blameless character, and have a good reputation in the community. In other words, the true sacred singer was not just an impressive performer, but also a man of devotion and integrity.

This combination of virtue and vocal skill remains the cantorial ideal in all denominations, from the most Orthodox, whose conception of the cantorate is shaped by these legal requirements, to the most liberal, who, while not guided by rabbinic rulings, give similar emphasis to character. Nevertheless, history contains numerous examples of cantors who captivated worshipers with acrobatic voices, but were, in their everyday dealings, far from exemplary. Several singers of this sort are well known; some are even legends of the art form. However, it is not my purpose to single out names, regardless of the severity of their off-*bimah* shenanigans. Rather, I wish to examine the opposite end of the cantorial spectrum — namely, those who had plain voices yet, due to their sincerity of expression, were considered masters of the craft.

Unable to reach the vocal heights of their virtuosic colleagues, these cantors turned inward, delivering the liturgy in tones saturated with the beauty of sincerity. Chief among such cantors was Nissi Belzer (1824–1906) of Berditchev, who traveled with his choir from village to village, drawing in audiences with his uniquely engrossing approach. The impact of his singing is captured in a story told by Pinchos Jassinowsky (1886–1954), himself a famed cantor of the golden age: "Once Nissi Belzer and his choir conducted a Sabbath service in a small town. The company was scheduled to depart for another town, but the inhabitants pleaded that they remain with them for another Sabbath service. This was obviously impossible. The people, seeing that neither pleas nor offers of more money were of any avail, stationed themselves on the outskirts of the city, and when the coaches bearing the singers approached they demolished the wheels and compelled them to stay over."[1] Though Belzer's voice was not particularly musical, his impassioned singing and skillful choral direction were so exhilarating that worshipers resorted to aggressive tactics in order to keep him around.

There are many other examples of cantors who are admired for their character rather than their vocal displays. This does not, though, mean that the idyllic merging of virtue and virtuosity is impossible to achieve. For instance, Yossele Rosenblatt, widely considered the greatest cantor of all time, and Yitzchak Meir Helfgot, among the most acclaimed cantors of today, are both placed at the top of their profession largely because their vocal feats coincide with religious devotion. And whether the person is Belzer, Rosenblatt, or a cantor at the local *shul*, the same principle applies: singing to God requires much more than a beautiful voice.

1. Pinchos Jassinowski, "Hazzanim and Hazzanut," in Jonathan L. Friedmann, ed., *20th Century Synagogue Music: Essential Readings* (Woodland Hills, CA: Isaac Nathan, 2010), 84.

The Cantorial Ideal

The popular image of the cantor is of a virtuosic singer adept at interpreting prayers through flexible vocalisms and melodic embellishments. This was the style characteristic of the "Golden Age" of cantorial music in America, a period between the World Wars that witnessed the rise of European-born cantors to the status of star performers and recording artists. These cantors represented a powerful link to the Old World, utilizing familiar folksong elements and improvising within the hallowed prayer modes. Traveling from synagogue to synagogue, they brought hope and inspiration to a mostly immigrant population laboring to adapt to an American way of life. As musicologist Irene Heskes put it, "[the cantors] entertained, comforted, and inspired struggling immigrant factory workers, tradesmen and storekeepers; and their liturgical artistry truly bridged the old *shtetl* with the modern city tenement."[1]

Beloved cantors of this period included Yossele Rosenblatt (1882–1933), Mordecai Hershman (1888–1940), Gershon Sirota (1874–1943), and other remarkable musicians who thrilled audiences with concerts, prayer services, radio appearances, and phonograph recordings. Even though their style of singing is no longer the norm in synagogue ritual, they remain for many a symbol of what a cantor is or should be. A magnificent voice, it is commonly thought, is what defines a magnificent cantor.

Surprisingly, however, being an outstanding singer is low on the list of legal requirements for the cantorate. In the *halakhic* literature, a cantor's humility, piety, affability, Jewish knowledge, dedication to family, and reputation in the community are all valued above vocal skills. The cantor is to be a *sheliach tzibbur*— messenger of the congregation — concerned with transmitting the prayers of the congregation to God rather than drawing attention to him or herself. The opposite of this ideal is a cantor whose vocal artistry is the central focus. Unfortunately, many of the star cantors of the "Golden Age" fell into this latter category, as Rabbi Sam L. Jacobson explained: "Some cantors possessing superior vocal powers were not above prostituting their sacred offices to a means of self-aggrandizement, and personal jealousies on this account were not unknown. The result is readily imaginable."[2]

Of course, a cantor who is a skilled and knowledgeable vocalist and musician can elevate the worship experience to greater emotional and spiritual heights. And the Talmud remarks, "Who is considered conversant with prayers...? He who is skilled in chanting, who has a pleasant voice" (BT *Ta'anit* 16a). But, the best cantors are not "just" singers, in the sense of performers. They understand their role as intermediaries, singing prayers on behalf of the congregation and directed toward the heavenly realm. According to Cantor William Sharlin, the cantor should aim to move, not to impress. "If a *chazzan,* or cantor, is driven to be moved, as well as to move," Sharlin writes, "he or she will be able to give up being impressive. Ultimately, it is the person who touches the congregant, not the baritone, contralto, tenor, or soprano."[3] A congregation may be entertained by a great voice, but it is impacted more deeply by a cantor's sincerity of motive and expression.

1. Irene Heskes, "The Golden Age of Cantorial Artistry," in Velvel Pasternak and Noah Schall, ed., The *Golden Age of Cantors: Musical Masterpieces of the Synagogue* (New York: Tara, 1991), 7.
2. Sam L. Jacobson, "The Music of the Jews," in Jonathan L. Friedmann, ed., *Music in Jewish Thought: Selected Writings, 1890–1920* (Jefferson, NC: McFarland, 2009), 33.
3. William Sharlin, "Why Can't a Woman Chant like a Man?," in Jonathan L. Friedmann and Brad Stetson, eds., *Jewish Sacred Music and Jewish Identity: Continuity and Fragmentation* (St. Paul, MN: Paragon House, 2008), 97.

The Cantor's Prayer

Today, most cantors come to the profession with extensive performance backgrounds, and though they are aware of the differences between *bimah* and concert stage, cannot help but bring an element of entertainment to the service. This is not necessarily a bad thing, as the prayer book has dramatic overtones begging for musical treatment, and synagogue-goers, like all human beings, are attracted to and inspired by artistic expression. Even so, the cantor must remember that he or she is not a singer in the show business sense, but an intermediary whose role is to transmit the people's prayers to God. As such, while beautiful voices are certainly welcome in the service, the synagogue is no place for ego-driven performance.

Jewish authorities have long cautioned against self-absorbed synagogue song. For example, Nathan Hannover's seventeenth-century prayer book *Sha-arei Tziyon* asserts that God only answers the prayers of a cantor who is completely attentive to the needs of the community, and recommends that cantors reflect on the verse "Love your neighbor as yourself" (Lev. 19:18) prior to leading a service.[1] The Rebbe of Kossov (1795–1854) wrote similarly that the cantor is the "vessel through which flow the prayers and yearnings of his people. He therefore has to associate himself with the activity of his people. Then he can fully represent them."[2]

This theme is also found in *Hineni*, a plaintive meditation from the High Holiday liturgy, generally referred to as "the cantor's prayer." Admittedly, the customary way of delivering this text might appear egocentric. It is usually chanted as the cantor walks slowly down the center aisle toward the pulpit — placing him or her in a figurative spotlight — and most settings include "show-off" elements like ornamented runs, stylized turns, and expansive tonal and dynamic range. But *Hineni* is a prayer of self-effacing supplication, and its choreography and expressive melodies are meant to represent the cantor's trepidation as he or she approaches God to plea on behalf of the congregation.

Hineni begins with an admission of humanity's insignificance before God: "Behold me of little merit, trembling and afraid, as I stand before You to plead for Your people. O gracious God, the One enthroned by Israel's praises, God of compassion and love, accept my petition and that of my people. Let them not be put to shame because of me, nor I because of them." The lengthy text continues in this vein, asking that prayers be accepted on high in spite of the shortcomings of those who offer them.

Humility is a vital attribute for all Jews, not just the cantor. It is the foundation of other key virtues, like compassion, charity, and cooperation; and Judaism stresses that, no matter how grand one's station in life, everyone is an imperfect and fragile creature dependent on God's grace and compassion. So, while *Hineni* specifically addresses the activity of prayer, it can be taken as a reminder to be humble in all endeavors.

1. Nathan Hannover, quoted in Max Wohlberg, "The Hazzan as Spokesman of the Congregation," *Journal of Synagogue Music* 20, no. 2 (1990): 31.
2. Rebbe of Kossov, quoted in Wohlberg, "The Hazzan as Spokesman," 31.

Cantors, Rabbis, Hitters and Pitchers

In his memoir, *Thirty-Four Years on the Bimah*, Cantor Harry Newman recounts several confrontations he had with clergy partners during his career. On one occasion, a rabbi requested a list of the music in the synagogue's repertoire, intending to dictate which settings to use in the service. Newman answered with sharp words that most cantors would think, but few would dare to say: "My ... response was that he could give me a list of subjects that he wanted to speak about, and I would let him know what his sermon would be about."[1] However humorous this exchange may appear, it touches upon on a crucial, though hardly discussed, aspect of the rabbi-cantor relationship: respect for one another's expertise.

Musical selection and sermon topics are domains understandably guarded by these specially trained professionals, and just as it is not the cantor's place to determine the rabbi's sermon, it is presumptuous for a rabbi to tell a cantor what to sing. To be sure, as with any working partnership, friendly recommendations can be instructive; but suggestions are not the same as declarations. And though a cantor is not likely to interfere in the rabbi's sermon-writing process, rabbis tend to be less reserved in asserting their melodic preferences. This is due mainly to the fact that, unlike the highly personal sermon, worship music is in essence the people's property, especially in synagogues saturated with congregational tunes. As a result, complaints of disrespect are usually heard from the cantor's side of the pulpit.

To better understand this dynamic, it is helpful to use a baseball analogy. Pitchers specialize in throwing the ball. In the American League, they are substituted in the batting order by designated hitters, and in the National League are by and large regarded as easy outs. The amount of time, energy, and focus required for developing pitches, refining mechanics, improving location, and so on places severe limits on a pitcher's batting practice, and his vital role of delivering the baseball excuses his general lack of offensive prowess. In other words, pitchers are paid to throw, not to hit. Still, because pitchers are familiar with the basics of batting — both because they occasionally swing the bat and because they face batters for a living — they might fancy themselves qualified to give hitting advice to their teammates. But such tips can be taken as insults, since they involve an expert in one area of the game telling a player with a different skill set what to do. Likewise, most pitchers would be offended if batters— who square off against pitchers and may have some pitching experience — were to critique the fine points of their technique.

This baseball illustration is somewhat hypothetical, as professionalism, respect, and a desire to maintain a happy dugout prevent most players from offering unwanted guidance. A similar level of respect should be the foundation of clergy relations. Even as rabbis—who add their voices to synagogue song and may have musical backgrounds—and cantors—who listen to sermons and may themselves be skilled orators—might feel justified intruding upon each other's craft, they should be careful not to overstep their roles. And when input is offered regarding melodies or sermons, it should be done so in humble dialogue rather than forceful decrees.

1. Harry Newman, *Thirty-Four Years on the Bimah: Vignettes of a "Professional" Jew* (Bloomington, IN: AuthorHouse, 2007), 22.

The Choir in Jewish History

King David is credited with establishing the first Israelite orchestra and choir, with the purpose of enhancing the spiritual mood of sacred services. Most of the musicians and singers David employed came from the tribe of Levi. As we read in I Chronicles 15: "David told the leaders of the Levites to appoint their brothers, the singers, with musical instruments, harps, lyres, and cymbals, joyfully making their voices heard."

The *Mishnah* (*Arakhin* 2:6) states that in Jerusalem's Second Temple, "There were never fewer than twelve Levites standing on the platform [as a choir] but there was no limit on the maximum number of singers." The singing of the Levitical choir was a constant accessory to the sacrificial ritual.

Following the destruction of the Second Temple in 70 C.E., the Rabbis abolished the sacrificial rite and its accompanying instrumental and vocal music. So, even as most other elements central to the Jewish tradition survived the destruction, the Levites refused to divulge their "trade secrets," and their musical culture was lost.

Still, the Jews longed for the elevating sounds of the choir. Even Maimonides, the twelfth-century Jewish philosopher, permitted choirs to sing God's praise in synagogue and at religious feasts. In the Middle Ages, some Ashkenazi services included two singers who stood with the cantor, providing musical support. For the most part, the singers would hum chords or pedal points, rhythmic accompaniments, and other harmony lines.

Professional synagogue choirs were established as early as the sixteenth century, following the artistic model of the European churches. Choirs of six to eight members would sing prayers like *Aleinu, Ein Keloheinu,* and *Adon Olam.* Not surprisingly, there were some who objected to this practice; but Solomon Hazzan of Metz, in his manual for cantors, argued that, "just as it is impossible for the earth to exist without wind," a cantor cannot exist without choristers.[1]

Among the few synagogue choral composers of this period, the most celebrated was Salamone Rossi (1570–1630), court composer to the dukes of Mantua. Rossi published a collection of thirty-three Jewish motets, displaying the beauty and elegance of the late Italian Renaissance. But, it was not until the nineteenth century, with the emancipation and enlightenment of European Jewry, that choral singing became a regular feature of the synagogue.

The early Reform movement abolished the office of the cantor, giving musical responsibilities to choirs of men and women, who sang with an organ in the manner of a Lutheran service. Before long, a more moderate reform took hold, and synagogue musicians such as Salomon Sulzer (1804–1890) and Louis Lewandowski (1823–1894) composed music and conducted four-part choirs that complemented the cantors' solos. The nineteenth century also witnessed the creation of male *a cappella* choirs in Orthodox synagogues, following the example of modern German Orthodox leader, Rabbi Samson Raphael Hirsch (1808–1888), who introduced a professional choir in Frankfurt.

The first synagogue choir in the United States was organized in 1818, at New York's Congregation Shearith Israel. In 1897, the Reform movement published its first *Union Hymnal,* comprising 129 hymns for four-part choir. Though its musical style was virtually indistinguishable from Protestant hymns, the *Union Hymnal* sparked the enthusiastic development of synagogue choral music in America, which reached its highpoint in the mid-twentieth century, with composers like Max Helfman, Max Janowski, Samuel Adler, A. W. Binder, Herbert Fromm, and William Sharlin.

---

1. Francis L. Cohen, "Choir," in *Jewish Encyclopedia,* vol. 4 (New York: Funk and Wagnalls, 1901–1906), 41.

The Music of Heaven on Earth

At the dedication of Solomon's Temple, the "trumpeters and the singers joined in unison to praise and extol the Lord" (2 Chr. 5:13). This liturgical function reached full force in the Second Temple. There is, however, a tradition that places choral music much earlier than the Jerusalem Temple. When the tragic character Job asks God why his life has been thrown into chaos, God reprimands him, saying that since he was not present at the creation of the world, he has no right to ask such questions: "Where were you when I laid the earth's foundations...? Who set its cornerstone, when the morning stars sang together and all the divine beings shouted for joy?" (Job 38:4–7). Aside from reminding us that life is a mystery known only to God, this passage introduces the music of the "Celestial Choir": a perfect symphony produced by the interaction of planets and stars. This choir is as old as creation itself, and the harmony it yields is a resounding testament to the order God gave to the universe.

Though this concept probably originated with the Greek philosopher Pythagoras (c. 570–c. 495 B.C.E.), it seeped into Jewish thought first with Job and later in the writings of Philo of Alexandria (20 B.C.E.–50 C.E.). Philo explained that when Moses ascended Mount Sinai to receive the words of Torah, strains of heavenly music filled his ears. Several medieval Jewish scholars picked up on the notion of cosmic music, including Maimonides (1135–1204), who wrote that the planets produce sounds in their daily movements across space.

Significantly, too, first-century rabbi Simeon bar Yochai posited that there are angelic choristers who sing according to the rules set forth by the celestial bodies. "Hearken well to the music of the spheres," bar Yochai told his students. "There are choirs of angels intoning the music and harmony of the spheres."[1] The image of angelic choirs singing in the heavenly realm is sometimes used as a model for choirs here on Earth. Just as these spiritual beings come together to sing ethereal songs, the Levites joined their voices in harmonious praise; and all subsequent Jewish choirs — whether professional or volunteer — work to create a unified sound suggestive of the music produced above.

But synagogue choirs do not only make harmony in the musical sense. A choir is a cohesive unit comprised of many constituent parts, and its proper functioning depends on each person's willingness to forgo ego, set aside differences, listen to one another, coordinate breathing, and follow the tones, rhythms, dynamics, and articulation of the music — all of which results in a temporary dissolving of self-awareness and, in its place, a profound sense of collective identity. When choir members gather to sing, they focus their efforts to achieve a common purpose. Like the planets in the solar system and the angels of God, each member comes with a distinct personality and a unique vocal instrument; and, like the music of the spheres, these individual features melt away into a larger sound. What is heard is not Mars, the angel Uriel, or a single baritone, but a harmonious blend of many voices. For this reason, choral singing can be called the music of heaven on earth.

1. Irene Heskes, *Passport to Jewish Music: Its History, Traditions, and Culture* (New York: Tara, 1994), 112.

Unity, Participation and the Choral Experience

Jewish affiliation in America is voluntary. Not only is America a pluralistic nation, where citizens are free to explore different faiths or opt out of religion altogether, but American Judaism is characterized by denominationalism, "*shul* shopping," and the ability to define one's Jewish identity through organizations or activities found outside the synagogue walls. Self-identifying Jews may attend services regularly or be regulars at the local deli; they may be ritually observant, or observant fans of a Jewish celebrity. In this environment, characterized by fragmentation and diversity of expression, few things are more effective in bringing Jews together or encouraging involvement in Jewish life than synagogue choirs.

A recent survey conducted by the Zamir Choral Foundation shows the extent to which Jewish choral singing promotes feelings of solidarity and interest in broader areas of Judaism. Results from 2,000 respondents indicate that choir members are more likely to volunteer for other Jewish groups and give to Jewish charities than the general Jewish population. These findings add to the already substantial evidence that choral singing improves physical health, cognitive abilities, social skills, and overall mood. According to Diane Tickton Shuster, co-director of the study, "Sometimes, being involved in a Jewish choir is [a person's] entry point into Jewish life, and we didn't know that before."[1]

Seventy-three percent of survey respondents said that choral singing strengthens their bonds to fellow Jews. The Foundation's director, Matthew Lazar, notes that Jewish choirs are among the rare places where Jews of varying backgrounds, religious leanings, and political persuasions have an opportunity to do something Jewish together. These ordinarily divisive issues are put aside as members join one another in shared purpose and common song. "Choir is the embodiment of *klal Yisrael* [Jewish solidarity]," Lazar states. "It's transdenominational and, even more importantly, it's transpolitical...."[2]

The survey also indicates that seventy-three percent of choir members volunteer under other Jewish auspices, compared to only twenty-five percent of the general Jewish population. And seventy-three percent of choir members give to Jewish causes, versus forty-one percent of other Jews. Strikingly, these numbers suggest that many who do not otherwise participate in Jewish life become active through choral singing. The choral experience ignites a passion for things Jewish, and a deeper concern for and involvement in the Jewish world.

The primary role of the synagogue choir is to enhance the beauty and inspiration of religious services. But this is not the only benefit of Jewish choral singing. While there is much that separates American Jews, singing in a choir helps build a sense of cohesion, belonging, and dedication to the Jewish people. In a time and setting where Jewish affiliation and participation are increasingly optional, taking part in a synagogue choir can stimulate further engagement in Judaism. In short, Jewish singing leads to Jewish living.

1. Sue Fishkoff, "Survey Indicates Jewish Singing Spurs Jewish Engagement," *Jewish Journal of Greater Los Angeles* 25:28 (2010): 27.
2. Fishkoff, "Survey Indicates," 35.

From Choir to Congregation

One of the central aims of Jewish worship is to unite participants in thought, energy, and action. This goal is reflected in the prayer book, which is permeated with collective language, notions of peoplehood, and references to common mission and ancestry. These elements, combined with the shared experience of worship, have inspired group singing throughout the ages. Inevitably, too, this congregational urge has impacted other types of synagogue music, with cantors attaching "singsong" sections to their recitatives and choral pieces often dissolving into unison tunes.

The influence of congregational singing can be traced back to the Jerusalem Temple, when worshipers strove to add their voices to the music of Levitical choirs. Such participation was achieved through responsorial singing, in which the choir sang intricate passages and the laity responded with formulaic statements. Some of these responses are recorded in the Book of Psalms, such as "Blessed be the Lord," "Amen and Amen," and "His faithfulness is forever." These would have appeased the congregants' compulsion to "sing unto God," even as they were not wholly familiar with the psalm texts or the manner of their performance. Other psalms have superscriptions suggesting popular melodies to which the words could be sung — a method likely used to facilitate communal involvement. Examples include *Al Shoshanim*, "On the Lillies" (Pss. 45; 69; 80), *Al Tashchet*, "Do Not Destroy" (Pss. 57–59), and *Al Ayelet ha-Shachar*, "On the Hind of the Morning" (Ps. 22).

Tensions between choral and congregational song were especially pronounced during the nineteenth century. The reformation that spread across Western Europe brought with it a choral style rooted in the sonic vocabulary of Christian worship. Mixed choirs sang refined settings of the liturgy while congregants, who had been accustomed to chanting the liturgy themselves, listened from the pews. But the people would not be silenced, as German synagogue composer Louis Lewandowski (1821–1894) explained: "With the introduction of choral music, congregations were prevented *a priori* from direct participation in the services, because of the artistic nature of choral singing.... After a short while, out of a desire for equal participation, congregations adopted the melody, or soprano line, singing together with the choir in two, three and four octaves. The other voices [of the choir] were thus overwhelmed, and the artistic form was entirely destroyed."[1]

Many congregational tunes used today likewise originated as choral pieces. As choirs gradually faded from most American synagogues during the latter half of the twentieth century, select pieces were retained in simplified verse-refrain sing-along form. Familiar examples include

Lewandowski's *Lecha Dodi*, Sulzer's *Ki Mitziyon*, Gerovitsch's *Adon Olam*, Ephros's *Lecha Adonai*, Janowski's *Sim Shalom*, and Helfman's *Hashkiveinu*.

The transformation of choral compositions to congregational tunes places obvious restrictions on melodic range, harmonic complexity, emotive capacity, and other properties of the original settings. By definition, any tune suitable for group singing must be inviting to all in attendance, even the least musically proficient. Yet, while this is perhaps lamentable from an aesthetic standpoint, there is much to be said for the profound sense of fellowship and liturgical ownership that comes with participatory song. And in the current environment, where choirs are on the verge of extinction and group singing dominates, it should not be overlooked that, without their conversion into congregational melodies, these once-choral pieces would probably never be sung at all.

1. Louis Lewandowski, *Kol Rinnah U'T'fillah* (Berlin, 1871).

Why Congregations Sing

Most religious traditions endorse private, personal devotion, especially during significant junctures in one's life, good and bad. However, the social nature of religion necessitates the institution of corporate worship, which is ascribed equal, if not greater, importance than individual prayer. Religion always involves community: it is learned in social contexts and requires a system of social relations and functions. In both Judaism and Christianity, the congregation is the most significant and influential level of social organization. And in both faiths, communal singing is among the most ubiquitous, and arguably most powerful, forms of collective expression.

Though the specific uses, content, and stated rationale for group singing may differ from congregation to congregation, when examined broadly, the pervasive incorporation of participatory music in religious services can be attributed to the three fundamental relationships it promotes: between humanity and God, between the individual and his/her personal history, and between members of a community. A brief overview of these relationships will yield a useful foundation for appreciating the social and religious import of congregational song.

First, congregational music typically contains condensed theological statements, which serve to educate participants about the nature of God and strengthen their relationship to Him. In this category, we find hymns and other liturgical poetry that utilize linguistic devises to compress and contain their messages. Among other things, they employ familiar idioms, clichés, recurring words and phrases, repeated choruses, and metric devises like rhyme, assonance, and alliteration — all of which restrict the amount of syllables and types of words that can be squeezed into a given verse. It is also the case that texts set to relatively simple and/or familiar melodies are better remembered than those that are only read or spoken. Such melodies include sequential information and an order for encoding and recalling lyrics, which substantially mitigates the possibility of misplacing or skipping words.

Second, congregational music serves to connect individuals to a sense of personal history and heritage. Recent neuroscientific research confirms what has long been known from experience: a familiar melody stirs vivid memories and emotions. These songs are direct conduits to the past, both personal and collective; they immediately bring us back to particular times, places, people, and feelings. Evidence of this is found in a series of interviews church music scholar Don E. Saliers conducted with elderly women at Bethel United Methodist Church in Charleston, South Carolina. When he asked the women to identify their favorite church hymns, they gave conventional answers from late nineteenth and early twentieth-century gospel material. As the interviewees recalled these songs, they spoke of "hearing their grandmother's voice," "leaning against their mother's breast," hearing the "squeak of the parlor organ," and attending weddings, funerals, and Sunday evening gatherings. The texts and music were tied to the narrative quality of the women's religious identities, and, in Saliers's words, "evoked a marvelous range of life experiences and relationships."[1]

Third, congregational song helps stimulate and fortify bonds between congregants. The religious concepts and feelings housed in hymns and other prayer-songs, while certainly having personal significance, are intertwined with the context of their ritual presentation: the public worship service. Corporate songs help communities define and affirm who they are and what they stand for. Though in most cases they are the work of a single author with a single viewpoint, they are meant to be universal in appeal and usage, at least within a given group. A song's communal intention and performance assure that its social quality remains central even when an individual calls it to mind in a private moment. Worshipers remember not only the words and melodies of these sacred compositions, but also the group context in which they were sung and the shared sentiments they embody.

Because religion is at core a social enterprise, it is appropriate that singing–along with activities like text study and festive meals–takes place in group settings. And because community is in essence an integrated web of relationships, it is fitting that communal song is, as discussed above, so much about relationships: between the people and God, between individuals and their pasts, and between constituent members. Thus, while it is possible to identify other reasons congregants might sing together, these three functions are sufficient justification for the time-honored practice.

1. Don E. Saliers, *Music and Theology* (Nashville, TN: Abingdon, 2007), 6.

A Blended Sound

Commenting on the importance of singing in Jewish prayer, kabbalistic poet Menachem de Lonzano (1550–c.1624) wrote: "He whose voice is bad and unpleasant, and who cannot perform hymns and songs according to their tunes and who cannot remember melodies: even to a man like him it is allotted to raise his voice."[1] The principle that everyone, even the so-called "tone deaf," should sing out to God has roots in the Book of Psalms, and finds support in Jewish communities throughout the world, where melody is the preferred means of presenting the liturgy, Bible, and even Talmud. But for those who are self-conscious about singing, the prospect of raising the voice in prayer and praise can at times seem more terrifying than transcendent. This feeling is exacerbated in our technological age, when people are less likely to experience live music than to hear the professionally produced and polished sounds of the recording industry—the quality of which sets an unrealistic measure for judging our own music making. So, while insecure voices might occasionally sing forth in the safety of the car, shower, or living room, they are not typically inclined to do so in public. That is unless the setting happens to be a worship service.

Houses of prayer are among the few remaining environments in Western society where people are expected to sing. Despite the gradual transformation of the populace from creators to consumers of music, congregational song continues to hold a prominent place in religious life. The ease with which worshipers possessing a range of vocal confidence and skill join together in these songs can be attributed to several converging factors, including the simplicity of the music, the warmth of the community, and a sense of religious obligation. Perhaps the most compelling reason why strong and weak singers happily participate in collective prayer-songs is found in the writings of Congregational minister Reuben T. Robinson (1792–1868).

Robinson explained that "rude and uncultivated voices" contribute to congregational music in a way analogous to the "wolf stop" of a church organ: "a pipe which produces most inharmonious sounds, but which are overborne by the music of the other stops, and so made to swell the general harmony."[2] And while we would not want to hear the "wolf stop" alone, "with a sufficient volume of musical sound, we can understand how grand the effect may be."[3] In like manner, the "discordant sounds" produced by certain congregants might not be pleasing by themselves, but when blended with others, can support, encourage, and enhance the music's "swelling tide."

With this, Robinson went beyond merely stating that congregational song allows for insecure singers to hide within the larger sound, and gain the rewards of devotional singing — improved mood, liturgical participation, connection to God and community, etc.— without the fear of scrutiny or humiliation. Rather, he argued that the music itself benefits from all voices, whether course, refined, or somewhere in between. It is, after all, through their blending that the community asserts its true character and achieves its fullest sonic expression. No matter how ragged or imperfect the result, this vocal merging is a splendid fulfillment of the psalmist's decree that all the faithful come together to "Sing unto God."

1. Jonathan L. Friedmann, ed., *Quotations on Jewish Scared Music* (Lanham, MD: Hamilton, 2011), 37.
2. Reuben T. Robinson, "Congregational Singing," *The Congregational Review* (1868): 273.
3. Robinson, "Congregational Singing," 273.

The Limits of Congregational Singing

Many liberal American synagogues rely heavily on congregational singing. A typical Shabbat evening or morning service might consist of a melodic journey through the prayer book led by a cantor, rabbi, soloist, or song leader, and accompanied by guitar, piano, live band, or a combination of all three. This inclusive atmosphere encourages participation, stimulates group cohesion, and invites even the least musical congregants to lend their voices. In some ways, congregational song seems a fitting expression of Judaism's communal orientation. Such music resonates naturally with a faith that favors collectivity over individualism and solidarity over isolation. Yet, there is a danger in over-programming congregational music. Utilizing group song at the expense of other modalities places substantial limits not only on musical options, but also on the functions the music can potentially perform.

Congregational songs need to be basic enough to be sung by everyone in attendance. Songs of this type are normally in verse and refrain form, contrasting a melody that is repeated to different texts (the verse) with another that has the same text each time it occurs (the refrain, or chorus). The length of these sections is usually eight or sixteen measures, and the texts tend to be broken into short, digestible phrases containing repeated words or syllables. The melodies are almost always comprised of predictable rhythmic and melodic patterns, and their pitches rarely span more than an octave. These characteristics largely account for why these songs are both accessible and memorable.

Because participation is the main goal of this music, congregations most often adopt melodies that can be easily sung by old and young, expert and novice alike. This restricts not only which songs can be chosen (some are too complex for popular use), but also decreases the likelihood of other types of music finding a place in the service. Indeed, the preference for simple "sing-along" tunes has contributed to the demise of choral singing in most synagogues, as well as the diminishing role of the cantor as solo interpreter of the liturgy. In this environment, "just listening" is deemed stale, passive, and even antithetical to the religious experience. Dependency on congregational song also limits the range of feelings that can be facilitated through music. To be sure, all devotional music is functional: it is designed to accompany the activity of prayer, not to be enjoyed for its own sake. As such, the value of worship music is dependent more on what it does than what it sounds like. Group songs are certainly apt for serving a cohesive function; but they are far less capable of accomplishing other important aims, such as introspection, meditation, and inspiration. These fundamental components of worship are best achieved through listening to cantorial and choral music, which are open to a greater variety of harmonies and intervals, rhythms and dynamics, pitches and durations, and overall nuance of expression.

There is little doubt that congregational singing plays an important part in the worship service. It is, perhaps, the most direct way of fostering a palpable sense of unity among worshipers. However, over-emphasizing group song and excluding more complex material constrains music's ability to stimulate a variety of responses and serve an array of functions. Music's potential to enhance the worship service is minimized when too much focus is given to this or any other single type of song.

Good and Friendly Music

The positive effects of congregational song are well known. Along with promoting the usual health benefits associated with singing, congregational music encourages liturgical literacy, fortifies communal ties, strengthens religious identity, bolsters a sense of heritage, and so on. These good outcomes, whether intellectually grasped or simply felt, have contributed to the pervasiveness of group singing across denominations and creeds. However, even as these rewards are closely linked to communal song, it is important to remember that not all participatory tunes are equal. As with any medicine or educational method, some are more fruitful than others.

Group singing has dominated liberal Jewish services in America since the latter part of the twentieth century. With this has come a marked increase in liturgical fluency and strengthened community bonds, but also the less desirable consequences of restricted repertoires and over-simplified music. Limited repertoires are formed when congregations use the same settings week after week, grow comfortable in these repeated sounds, and adopt the melodies as their own. And on the rare occasions when a new melody is welcomed into the service, it tends to be highly simplistic and conventional — the sort of tune that is familiar before it is ever heard.

In both cases, there is a strong desire to sing what is already known, whether this familiarity comes from repetition or the ordinariness of the new tune, as well as a preference for accessible melodies, no matter how humdrum or watered-down they may be. And while these simple songs are useful for bringing congregants into the singing fold and may be pleasing to the ear, they are generally less apt to achieve the "higher" aims of spiritual contemplation and divine communion.

This begs the question: can a melody be simultaneously participatory and transcendent? The answer to this lies in a quotation from British minister, composer, and musicologist Erik Routley (1917–1982): "Give us the best music we can have, but make it friendly to the people."[1] This concise statement stresses the creation and selection of congregational tunes that are at the same time singable and sophisticated. Like many before and since his time, Routley recognized the crucial role hymns play in the formation and expression of Christian faith; yet he was dissatisfied with melodies of poor substance and form, which cater to the lowest common denominator. In their place, he desired songs that are complex enough to have a deep religious impact, but straightforward enough to invite participation.

In practice, this ideal is rarely met. Congregational music in churches and synagogues alike is usually chosen for its "catchiness" rather than its capacity to inspire worshipers or generate a sense of the divine presence. And though it is true that more sophisticated music can be more demanding and take more time to perfect, a steady diet of superficial tunes can lead to spiritual malnourishment and a false impression that faith and struggle are somehow antithetical. For these reasons and more, it is wise to embrace Routley's call for music that is of the highest quality, but still "friendly to the people."

---

1. Erik Routley, *The Church and Music: An Enquiry into the History, the Nature, and the Scope of Christian Judgment on Music* (London: Gerald Duckworth and Co., 1950), 161.

Appendix:
Jewish Music Research

This bibliography lists books and monographs valuable for the broader study of Jewish music. Included are works representing several decades of scholarship, and written from varied perspectives and disciplinary approaches. Those pursuing research in Jewish music should also be aware of the five journals dedicated to the subject, *Musica Judaica* (American Society for Jewish Music, New York), *Journal of Synagogue Music* (Cantors Assembly, New York), *Journal of Jewish Music and Liturgy* (Cantorial Council of America, New York), *Yuval* (Hebrew University of Jerusalem), and *Orbis Musicae* (Tel Aviv University), as well as the many articles on Jewish music published in other learned journals.

Adaqi, Yehiel, and Uri Sharvit. *A Treasury of Yemenite Jewish Chants.* Jerusalem: The Israeli Institute for Sacred Music, 1981.

Adler, Israel. *Hebrew Notated Manuscript Sources up to Circa 1840: A Descriptive Catalogue with a Checklist of Printed Sources.* Munich: G. Henle Verlag, 1989.

_____, ed. *Hebrew Writings Concerning Music in Manuscripts and Printed Books from Geonic Times up to 1800.* Munich: G. Henle, 1975.

_____. *Musical Life and Traditions of the Portuguese Jewish Community of Amsterdam in the 18th Century.* Jerusalem: Magnes, 1974.

_____. *The Study of Jewish Music: A Bibliographical Guide.* Jerusalem: Magnes, 1995.

Adler, Israel, Frank Alvarez-Pereyre, Edwin Seroussi, and Lea Shalem, eds. *Jewish Oral Traditions: An Interdisciplinary Approach.* Jerusalem: Magnes, 1994.

Adler, Israel, Bathja Bayer, and Eliyahu Schliefer, eds. *The Abraham Zvi Idelsohn Memorial Volume.* Jerusalem: Magnes, 1986.

Adler, Israel, and Judith Cohen. *A. Z. Idelsohn Archives in the Jewish National and University Library: Catalogue.* Jerusalem: Magnes, 1976.

Appleton, Lewis. *Bibliography of Jewish Vocal Music.* New York: National Jewish Book Council, 1968.
Armistead, Samuel G., and Joseph H. Silverman. *Folk Literature of the Sephardic Jews, Vol. 2: Judeo-Spanish Ballads from Oral Tradition.* Berkeley: University of California Press, 1986.
_____. *The Judeo-Spanish Ballad Chapbooks of Yacob Abraham Yona.* Berkeley: University of California Press, 1971.
Avenary, Hanoch. *The Ashkenazic Tradition of Biblical Chant Between 1500 and 1900: Documentation and Musical Analysis.* Tel Aviv: Tel Aviv University Press, 1978.
_____. *Encounters of East and West in Music: Selected Writings.* Tel Aviv: Tel Aviv University Press, 1979.
_____. *Spanish-Portuguese Synagogue Music in Nineteenth-Century Reform Sources from Hamburg: Ancient Tradition in the Dawn of Modernity.* Jerusalem: Magnes, 1996.
_____. *Studies in Hebrew, Syrian and Greek Liturgical Recitative.* Jerusalem: Israel Music Institute, 1963.
Bacht, Nikolaus. *Music, Theatre and Politics in Germany: 1848 to the Third Reich.* Brookfield, VT: Ashgate, 2006.
Bahat, Avner, ed. *Jewish Music Listening Center Catalogue.* Tel Aviv: Museum of the Jewish Diaspora, 1984.
Bahat, Avner, and Naomi Bahat. *Saperi Tama: The Diwan Songs of the Jews of Central Yemen.* Tel Aviv: The Museum of the Jewish Diaspora, 1995.
Baker, Paula Eisenstein, and Robert S. Nelson, eds. *Leo Zeitlin: Chamber Music.* Middleton, WI: A–R Editions, 2009.
Barton, William Eleazer. *The Psalms and Their Story: A Study of the Psalms as Revealed to Old Testament History, with a Preliminary Study of Hebrew Poetry and Music.* Boston and Chicago: Pilgrim, 1898.
Bassan, Jacqueline. *From Shul to Cool: The Romantic Jewish Roots of American Popular Music.* New York: Jay Street, 2003.
Bauer, Susan. *From the Khupe to KlezKamp: The Process of Change and Forms of Reinterpretation of Klezmer Music in New York.* Berlin: Piranha, 1999.
Beeber, Steven Lee. *The Heebie-Jeebies at CBGB's: A Secret History of Jewish Punk.* Chicago: Chicago Review Press, 2006.
Benarde, Scott. *Stars of David: Rock 'n' Roll's Jewish Stories.* Lebanon, NH: Brandeis University Press, 2003.
Bennett, Roger, and Josh Kun. *And You Shall Know Us by the Trail of Our Vinyl: The Jewish Past as Told by the Records We Have Loved and Lost.* New York: Crown, 2008.
Bergovski, Moshe. *Old Jewish Folk Music.* Trans. Mark Slobin. Philadelphia: University of Pennsylvania Press, 1982.
Bernard, Andrew. *The Sound of Sacred Time: A Basic Music Theory Textbook to Teach the Jewish Prayer Modes.* Charlotte, NC: Temple Beth El, 2005.
Bernstein, Leonard. *Findings.* New York: Simon and Schuster, 1972.
Billig, Michael. *Rock 'n' Roll Jews.* Syracuse, NY: Syracuse University Press, 2001.
Binder, Abraham W. *Biblical Chant.* New York: Philosophical Library, 1959.
_____. *The Jewish Music Movement in America: An Informal Lecture.* New York: National Jewish Music Council, 1975.
Birnbaum, Edouard. *Jewish Musicians at the Court of the Mantuan Dukes.* Trans. and ed. Judith Cohen. Tel Aviv: Tel Aviv University Press, 1978.
Bohlman, Philip V. *Jewish Music and Modernity.* New York: Oxford University Press, 2008.

_____, ed. *Jewish Musical Modernism, Old and New*. Chicago: University of Chicago Press, 2008.

_____. *"The Land Where Two Streams Flow": Music in the German-Jewish Community of Israel*. Urbana and Chicago: University of Illinois Press, 1989.

_____. *The World Centre for Jewish Music in Palestine, 1936–1940: Jewish Musical Life on the Eve of World War II*. New York: Oxford University Press, 1992.

Bohlman, Philip V., and Otto Holzapfel, eds. *The Folk Music of Ashkenaz*. Middleton, WI: A–R Editions, 2001.

Bor, Josef. *The Terezin Requiem*. Trans. Edith Pargeter. New York: Avon, 1977.

Botstein, Leon, and Werner Hanak, eds. *Vienna: Jews and the City of Music*. Princeton: Princeton University Press, 2004.

Braun, Joachim. *Jews and Jewish Elements in Soviet Music: A Study of a Socio-national Problem in Music*. Jerusalem: Israeli Music, 1978.

_____. *Music in Ancient Israel/Palestine: Archaeological, Written, and Comparative Sources*. Grand Rapids, MI: Wm. B. Eerdmans, 2002.

_____. *On Jewish Music: Past and Present*. New York: Peter Lang, 2006.

Brener, Milton E. *Richard Wagner and the Jews*. Jefferson, NC: McFarland & Company, 2006.

Brinkmann, Reinhold, and Christoph Wolff, eds. *Driven into Paradise: The Musical Migration from Nazi Germany to the United States*. Berkeley: University of California Press, 1999.

Brinner, Benjamin. *Playing Across a Divide: Israeli-Palestinian Musical Encounters*. New York: Oxford University Press, 2009.

Burgh, Theodore W. *Listening to the Artifacts: Music Culture in Ancient Palestine*. New York: Continuum, 2006.

Chicural, Steven R. *George Gershwin's Songbook: Influences of Jewish Music, Ragtime, and Jazz*. Lexington: University of Kentucky, 1989.

Clark, Caryl. *Haydn's Jews: Representation and Reception on the Operatic Stage*. Cambridge: Cambridge University Press, 2009.

Cohen, A. Irma. *An Introduction to Jewish Music in Eight Illustrated Lectures*. New York: Bloch, 1923.

Cohen, Judah M. *The Making of a Reform Jewish Cantor: Musical Authority, Cultural Investment*. Bloomington: Indiana University Press, 2009.

Cohen, Judith, ed. *Proceedings of the World Congress of Jewish Music*. Tel Aviv: Institute for the Translation of Hebrew Literature, 1982.

Cohen, Mark R. *The Autobiography of a Seventeenth-Century Venetian Rabbi: Leon Modena's Life of Judah*. Princeton: Princeton University Press, 1988.

Cohen, Rich. *Machers and Rockers: Chess Records and the Business of Rock and Roll*. New York: W. W. Norton, 2004.

Cohen, Yehudah. *Ne'im Zemirot Yisrael: Musika U-Musika'im BeYisrael*. Tel Aviv: Am Oved Productions, 1990.

Cohn, Hans. *Risen from the Ashes: Tales of a Musical Messenger*. Lanham, MD: Hamilton, 2005.

Cook, Nicolas. *The Schenker Project: Culture, Race and Music Theory in Fin-de-Siècle Vienna*. New York: Oxford University Press, 2007.

Corenthal, Michael. *Cohen on the Telephone: A History of Jewish Recorded Humor and Popular Music*. Milwaukee, WI: Yesterday's Memories, 1984.

Davidson, Charles. *From Szatmar to the New World: Max Wohlberg, American Cantor*. New York: Jewish Theological Seminary, 2001.

_____. *Immunim Be-Nusach Ha-Tefillah: A Study Text and Workbook for the Jewish Prayer Modes*. Elkins Park, PA: Ashbourne Music, 1996.

_____. *Immunim Be-Nusach Ha-Tefillah II: Hallel* (A Study Text and Workbook). Elkins Park, PA: Ashbourne Music, 2004.

De Vries, Willem. *Sonderstab Musik: Music Confiscations by the Eisatzstab Reichsleiter Rosenberg under the Nazi Occupation of Western Europe*. Amsterdam: Amsterdam University Press, 1996.

Edelman, Marsha Bryan. *A Bibliography of Jewish Music*. New York: The Hebrew Arts School, 1986.

_____. *Discovering Jewish Music*. Philadelphia: Jewish Publication Society, 2003.

Eisenstein, Judith K. *Heritage of Music: The Music of the Jewish People*. Wyncote, PA: Reconstructionist Press, 1981.

Engel, Carl. *The Music of the Most Ancient Nations: Particularly of the Assyrians, Egyptians and Hebrews, with Special References to Recent Discoveries in Western Asia and in Egypt*. London: J. Murray, 1864.

Epstein, Lawrence. *The Haunted Smile: The Story of Jewish Comedians in America*. New York: Perseus/Public Affairs, 2001.

Erdman, Harley. *Staging the Jew: The Performance of an American Ethnicity, 1860–1920*. New Brunswick, NJ: Rutgers University Press, 1997.

Evans, Allan. *Ignaz Friedman: Romantic Master Pianist*. Bloomington: Indiana University Press, 2009.

Ewen, David. *Hebrew Music: A Study and an Interpretation*. New York: Bloch, 1931.

Feinberg, Sheldon. *Hava Nagila: The Story Behind the Song and Its Composer*. New York: Shapolsky, 1988.

Fénelon, Fania. *The Musicians of Auschwitz*. Trans. Judith Landry. London: Michael Joseph, 1977.

Fields, Armond. *Sophie Tucker: First Lady of Show Business*. Jefferson, NC: McFarland & Company, 2003.

Filar, Marian, and Charles Patterson. *From Buchenwald to Carnegie Hall*. Jackson: University Press of Mississippi, 2002.

Flam, Gila. *Singing for Survival: Songs of the Lodz Ghetto, 1940–1945*. Urbana and Chicago: University of Illinois Press, 1992.

Fleisher, Robert. *Twenty Israeli Composers: Voices of a Culture*. Detroit: Wayne State University Press, 1997.

Flender, Reinhard. *Hebrew Psalmody: A Structural Investigation*. Jerusalem: Magnes, 1992.

Fligel, Hyman. *Zavel Zilberts: His Life and Works*. New York: Shlusinger Brothers, 1971.

Freed, Isadore. *Harmonizing the Jewish Modes*. New York: Sacred Music Press, 1958.

Freedman, Jonathan. *Klezmer America: Jewishness, Ethnicity, Modernity*. New York: Columbia University Press, 2007.

Freeland, Michael. *Music Man: The Story of Frank Simon*. London: Vallentine-Mitchell, 1994.

Friedmann, Jonathan L. *Music and Jewish Religious Experience: Social and Theological Essays*. Saarbrücken: VDM Verlag, 2010.

_____, comp. *Music in Jewish Thought: Selected Writings, 1890–1920*. Jefferson, NC: McFarland & Company, 2009.

_____, ed. *Perspectives on Jewish Music: Secular and Sacred*. Lanham, MD: Lexington, 2009.

_____, ed. *Quotations on Jewish Sacred Music*. Lanham, MD: Hamilton, 2011.

Friedmann, Jonathan L., and Brad Stetson, eds. *Jewish Sacred Music and Jewish Identity: Continuity and Fragmentation.* St. Paul, MN: Paragon House, 2008.
Fromm, Herbert. *On Jewish Music: A Composer's View.* New York: Bloch, 1978.
Fruhauf, Tina. *The Organ and Its Music in German-Jewish Culture.* New York: Oxford University Press, 2009.
Gerson-Kiwi, Edith. *The Legacy of Jewish Music Through the Ages.* Jerusalem: World Zionist Organization, 1963.
_____. *Migrations and Mutations of the Music in East and West: Selected Writings.* Tel Aviv: Tel Aviv University Press, 1980.
Gilbert, Shirli. *Music in the Holocaust: Confronting Life in the Nazi Ghettos and Camps.* New York: Oxford University Press, 2007.
Gilbert, Sylvia. *Jewish Music from Bible to Broadway: A Short History of Jewish Music.* Nashville, TN: Winston-Derek Publishers, 1995.
Glantz, Jerry, ed. *Leib Glantz: The Man Who Spoke to God.* Tel Aviv: The Tel Aviv Institute for Jewish Liturgical Music, 2008.
Glazerson, Matisyahu. *Music and Kabbala.* Jerusalem: Raz-Ot Institute, 1988.
Goldin, Max. *On Musical Connections Between Jews and the Neighboring Peoples of Eastern and Western Europe.* Amherst: University of Massachusetts Press, 1989.
Goldsmith, Martin. *The Inextinguishable Symphony: A True Story of Music and Love in Nazi Germany.* New York: John Wiley and Sons, 2000.
Golomov, Daliah, and Ben-Zion Orgad, eds. *Madrich leHa'azanah liYetsirot Yisra'eliyot.* Tel Aviv: HaMercaz HaMatodi LeMuzikah, 1984.
Gorali, Moshe. *AMLI Studies in Music Bibliography.* Haifa: The Haifa Music Museum and AMLI Library, 1974.
_____. *The Old Testament in Music.* Jerusalem: Maron, 1993.
Gottlieb, Jack. *Funny, It Doesn't Sound Jewish: How Yiddish Songs and Synagogue Melodies Influenced Tin Pan Alley.* New York: State University Press of New York, 2004.
_____. *Working with Bernstein: A Memoir.* New York: Amadeus, 2010.
Gradenwitz, Peter. *Music and Musicians in Israel,* 3rd ed. Tel Aviv: Israeli Music, 1978.
_____. *The Music of Israel: From the Biblical Era to Modern Times.* Portland, OR: Amadeus, 1996.
Grossman, Elayne Robinson, and Ben Steinberg. *One People, One Voice: How to Organize a Jewish Community Chorus and Choral Festival.* New York: Jewish Music Council of the Jewish Welfare Board, 1989.
Guttman, Hadassah. *The Music of Paul Ben-Haim: A Performance Guide.* Metuchen, NJ: Scarecrow, 1992.
Harrán, Don. *In Search of Harmony: Hebrew and Humanist Elements in Sixteenth-Century Musical Thought.* Neuhausen-Stuttgart: Haensler-Verlag, 1988.
_____. *Salamone Rossi: Jewish Musician in Late Renaissance Mantua.* Oxford: Oxford University Press, 1999.
Heller, Charles. *What to Listen for in Jewish Music.* Toronto: Ecanthus Press, 2006.
Herzog, Avigdor. *The Psalm Singing of the Jews of San'a.* Tel Aviv: Israel Music Institute, 1968.
Heskes, Irene. *Passport to Jewish Music: Its History, Traditions, and Culture.* New York: Tara, 1994.
_____. *The Resource Book of Jewish Music.* Westport, CT: Greenwood, 1985.
_____, ed. *Studies in Jewish Music: Collected Writings of A.W. Binder.* New York: Bloch, 1971.

Heskes, Irene, and Suzanne Bloch. *Ernest Bloch, Creative Spirit: A Source Book.* New York: Jewish Music Council of the Jewish Welfare Board, 1976.

Heskes, Irene, and Arthur Wolfson, eds. *The Historic Contribution of Russian Jews to Jewish Music.* New York: Jewish Music Council of the Jewish Welfare Board, 1967.

Hirsch, Lilly E. *A Jewish Orchestra in Nazi Germany: Musical Politics and the Berlin Jewish Culture League.* Ann Arbor: University of Michigan Press, 2010.

Hirschberg, Jehoash. *Music in the Jewish Community of Palestine 1880–1948: A Social History.* New York: Oxford University Press, 1996.

_____. *Paul Ben-Haim: His Life and Works.* Trans. Nathan Friedgut. Jerusalem: Israeli Music, 1990.

Hoffman, Lawrence A., and Janet R. Walton, eds. *Sacred Sound and Social Change: Liturgical Music in Jewish and Christian Experience.* Notre Dame: University of Notre Dame Press, 1992.

Hoffman, Shlomo. *Hamusikah Betalmud.* Tel Aviv: Israeli Music Institute, 1989.

Holde, Arthur. *Jews in Music: From the Age of Enlightenment to the Present.* New York: Philosophical Library, 1959.

Horowitz, Amy. *Mediterranean Israeli Music and the Politics of the Aesthetic.* Detroit: Wayne State University Press, 2010.

Idelsohn, Abraham Z. *Jewish Music: Its Historical Development.* New York: Holt, Rinehart, and Winston: 1929.

_____. *Manual of Musical Illustrations for Hebrew Union College Lectures of Abraham Z. Idelsohn on Jewish Music and Jewish Liturgy.* Cincinnati, OH: Hebrew Union College, 1926.

_____. *Thesaurus of Hebrew Oriental Melodies* (10 volumes). Leipzig: Friedrich Hofmeister, 1914–1933.

Irwin, Joyce, ed. *Sacred Sound: Music in Religious Thought and Practice.* Chico, CA: Scholars, 1983.

Isaacs, Ronald H. *Jewish Music: Its History, People, and Song.* Northvale, NJ: Jason Aronson, 1997.

Isaacson, Michael. *Jewish Music as Midrash: What Makes Music Jewish?* Los Angeles: Egg Cream Music, 2007.

Jacobson, Joshua R. *Chanting the Hebrew Bible: The Complete Guide to the Art of Cantillation.* Philadelphia: Jewish Publication Society, 2002.

_____. *A Selective Annotated Bibliography of Jewish and Israeli Choral Music.* Newton, MA: HaZamir Publications, 1990.

Jaffe, Kenneth. *Solo Vocal Works on Jewish Themes: A Bibliography of Jewish Composers.* Lanham, MD: Scarecrow, 2011.

Jani, Emilio. *My Voice Saved Me: Auschwitz 180046.* Milan: Centuaro Editrice, 1961.

Kaczerginsky, Shmuel. *Songs of the Ghettos and Concentration Camps.* New York: CYCO Bicher Farlag, 1948.

Kalib, Sholom. *The Musical Tradition of the Eastern European Synagogue.* Syracuse, New York: Syracuse University Press, 2002.

Kalisch, Shoshana. *Yes, We Sang.* New York: Harper and Row, 1985.

Kantor, Kenneth Aaron. *Jews on Tin Pan Alley: The Jewish Contribution to American Popular Music, 1830–1940.* Jersey City, NJ: Ktav Publishing, 1982.

Karas, Joza. *Music in Terezin: 1941–1945.* New York: Beaufort, 1985.

Kater, Michael H. *Composers of the Nazi Period: Eight Portraits.* New York: Oxford University Press, 2000.

_____. *The Twisted Muse: Musicians and Their Music in the Third Reich*. New York: Oxford University Press, 1997.
Kater, Michael H., and Riethmüller Albrecht, eds. *Music and Nazism: Art under Tyranny, 1933–1945*. Laaber: Laaber-Verlag, 2003.
Katz, Isreal J. *Judeo-Spanish Traditional Ballads from Jerusalem, Vol. 1*. New York: Institute of Medieval Music, 1972.
_____. *Judeo-Spanish Traditional Ballads from Jerusalem, Vol. 2*. New York: Institute of Medieval Music, 1975.
Katz, Jacob. *The Darker Side of Genius: Richard Wagner's Anti-Semitism*. Hanover, NH: University Press of New England, 1986.
Katz, Mickey. *Papa, Play for Me: The Autobiography of Mickey Katz*. Middletown, CT: Wesleyan University Press, 2002.
Katz, Ruth. *The Lachmann Problem: An Unsung Chapter in Comparative Musicology*. Jerusalem: Magnes, 2003.
Kelman, Ari Y. *Station Identification: The Culture of Yiddish Radio in New York*. New York: New York University Press, 2009.
Keren, Zvi. *Contemporary Israeli Music: Its Sources and Stylistic Development*. Ramat Gan: Bar Ilan University Press, 1980.
Kligman, Mark L. *Maqam and Liturgy: Ritual, Music, and Aesthetics of Syrian Jews in Brooklyn*. Detroit: Wayne State University Press, 2009.
Knittel, K. M. *Seeing Mahler: Music and the Language of Antisemitism in Fin-de-Siècle [ZH1]Vienna*. Surrey: Ashgate, 2010.
Koskoff, Ellen. *Music in Lubavitcher Life*. Urbana and Chicago: University of Illinois Press, 2000.
Krakower, Dora Brenner. *Trusting the Song that Sings Within: Pioneer Woman Cantor*. Ontario: Azure, 1997.
Kushner, David Z. *The Ernest Bloch Companion*. Westport, CT: Greenwood Press, 2001.
Lachmann, Robert. *Jewish Cantillation and Songs in the Island of Djerba*. Jerusalem: Azriel, 1940.
Laks, Szyman. *Music of Another World*. Trans. Chester Kisiel. Evanston, IL: Northwestern University Press, 1989.
Lambert, Philip. *To Broadway, To Life! The Musical Theater of Bock and Harnick*. New York: Oxford University Press, 2011.
Landman, Leo. *The Cantor: An Historical Perspective*. New York: Yeshiva University Press, 1972.
Lane, Stewart F. *Jews on Broadway: An Historical Survey of Performers, Playwrights, Composers, Lyricists and Producers*. Jefferson, NC: McFarland & Company, 2011.
Lehman, David. *A Fine Romance: Jewish Songwriters, American Songs*. New York: Schocken, 2009.
Levi, Erik. *Music in the Third Reich*. New York: St. Martin's, 1994.
Levin, Neil, ed. *Salomon Sulzer*. Bregenz: Land Voraruberg, 1991.
_____, ed. *Songs of the American Jewish Experience*. Chicago: Board of JewishEducation, 1976.
_____. *Z'mirot Anthology*. Cedarhurst, NY: Tara Publications, 1981.
Levin, Theodore. *The Hundred Thousand Fools of Gold: Musical Travels in Central Asia*. Bloomington: Indiana University Press, 1998.
Levine, Gilbert. *The Pope's Maestro*. San Francisco: Jossey-Bass, 2010.
Levine, Joseph A. *Rise and Be Seated: The Ups and Downs of Jewish Worship*.Northvale, NJ: Jason Aronson, 2000.

———. *Synagogue Music in America*. Crown Point, IN: White Cliffs Media, 1989.
Levine, Lee. *The Ancient Synagogue: The First Thousand Years*. New Haven, CT: Yale University Press, 2000.
Levy, Isaac. *Anthologia de Liturgia Judaeo-Espagnoles* (10 volumes). Jerusalem: Ministry of Education and Culture, 1974.
———. *Chants judéo-espagnoles*. London: World Sephardi Foundation, 1973.
Loeffler, James Benjamin. *The Most Musical Nation: Jews and Culture in the Late Russian Empire*. New Haven, CT: Yale University Press, 2010.
Lyman, Darryl. *Great Jews in Music*. Middle Village, NY: Jonathan David, 1986.
Manushkin, Fran. *Come, Let Us Be Joyful! The Story of Hava Nagila*. New York: Union of American Hebrew Congregations, 2000.
Mazor, Yaacov, and Andre Hajdu. *The Hasidic Dance-Nigun: A Study Collection and Its Classification Analysis*. Jerusalem: Magnes, 1974.
McKinnon, James. *The Temple, the Church, and Early Western Chant*. Brookfield, VT: Ashgate, 1998.
Melnick, Jeffrey. *A Right to Sing the Blues: African Americans, Jews, and American Popular Song*. Cambridge: Harvard University Press, 2001.
Mendelsohn, Ezra, ed. *Modern Jews and Their Musical Agendas*. New York: Oxford University Press, 1993.
Meyer, Michael. *The Politics of Music in the Third Reich*. New York: Peter Lang, 1991.
Moddel, Philip. *Joseph Achron*. Tel Aviv: Israeli Music Productions, 1966.
———. *Max Helfman: A Biographical Sketch*. Berkeley: Judah L. Magnes, 1974.
Monod, David. *Settling Scores: German Music, Denazification, and the Americans, 1945–1953*. Chapel Hill: University of North Carolina Press, 2005.
Montagu, Jeremy. *Musical Instruments of the Bible*. Lanham, MD: Scarecrow Press, 2002.
Mordecai, Yardeini. *Words and Music: A Selection from his Writings*. Ed. Max Rosenfeld. New York: Yiddisher Kultur Farband, 1986.
Moricz, Klara. *Jewish Identities: Nationalism, Racism, and Utopianism in Twentieth-Century Music*. Berkeley: University of California Press, 2008.
Most, Andrea. *Making Americans: Jews and the Broadway Musical*. Cambridge: Harvard University Press, 2004.
Musleah, Rachel. *Songs of the Jews of Calcutta*. Owing Mills, MD: Tara, 1991.
Nathan, Hans, ed. *Israeli Folk Music: Songs of the Early Pioneers*. Madison, WI: A-R Editions, 1994.
Newman, Harry. *Thirty-Four Years on the Bimah: Vignettes of my life as a "Professional" Jew*. Bloomington, IN: AuthorHouse, 2007.
Newman, Richard. *Alma Rosé: Vienna to Auschwitz*. Portland, OR: Amadeus Press, 2000.
Newman, Joel, and Fritz Rikko. *A Thematic Index to the Works of Salamon Rossi*. Hackensack, NJ: Boonin, 1972.
Niekerk, Carl. *Reading Mahler: German Culture and Jewish Identity in Fin-de-Siècle Vienna*. Rochester, NY: Camden House, 2010.
Nulman, Macy. *Concepts of Jewish Prayer and Music*. New York: Yeshiva University Press, 1985.
———. *Concise Encyclopedia of Jewish Music*. New York: McGraw-Hill, 1975.
———, ed. *Essays of Jewish Music and Prayer*. New York: Yeshiva University Press, 2005.
Orenstein, Walter. *The Cantor's Manual of Jewish Law*. Northvale, NJ: Jason Aronson, 1994.

Paloma, Vanessa. *Mystic Siren: Woman's Voice in the Balance of Creation*. Santa Fe, NM: Gaon, 2007.

Pasternak, Velvel. *Beyond Hava Nagila*. Owing Mills, MD: Tara, 1999.

———. *The Jewish Music Companion: Historical Overview, Personalities, Annotated Folksongs*. New York: Tara, 2003.

Pasternak, Velvel, and Noah Schall. *The Golden Age of Cantors: Musical Masterpieces of the Synagogue*. New York: Tara, 1991.

Peyser, Joan. *Bernstein: A Biography*. New York: William Morrow, 1987.

Pinson, DovBer. *Inner Rhythms: The Kabbalah of Music*. Northvale, NJ: Jason Aronson, 2000.

Piris, Eliyahu. *The Music of the Mountain Jews*. Jerusalem: Jewish Music Research Centre, 1999.

Portnoy, Marshall, and Josée Wolff. *The Art of Torah Cantillation*. New York: Union of American Hebrew Congregations, 2000.

———. *The Art of Cantillation, Vol. 2 (Haftarah and M'gillot)*. New York: Union of American Hebrew Congregations, 2001.

Rabinovitch, Israel. *Of Jewish Music: Ancient and Modern*. Translated by A. M. Klein. Montreal: The Book Center, 1952.

Ravina, Menasheh. *"Hatikvah": Mekoro Shel Ha-himmon, Toledotav Utkhunotav Behashva'ah Lehimnomim Shel Umot Aherot*. Tel Aviv: Arielei, 1968.

Regev, Motti, and Edwin Seroussi. *Popular Music and National Culture in Israel*. Berkeley: University of California Press, 2004.

Rikko, Fritz, ed. *Hashirim Asher Lish'lomo*. New York: Jewish Theological Seminary of America, 1973.

Ringer, Alexander L. *Arnold Schoenberg: The Composer as Jew*. New York: Clarendon, 1990.

Rogin, Michael. *Blackface, White Noise: Jewish Immigrants in the Hollywood Melting Pot*. Berkeley: University of California Press, 1992.

Rogovoy, Seth. *The Essential Klezmer: A Music Lover's Guide to Jewish Roots and Soul Music, from the Old World to the Jazz Age to the Downtown Avant-Garde*. Chapel Hill, NC: Alonquin Books of Chapel Hill, 2000.

Rose, Paul Lawrence. *Wagner: Race and Revolution*. New Haven, CT: Yale University Press, 1992.

Rosen, Jody. *White Christmas: The Story of an American Song*. New York: Scribner, 2002.

Rosen-Bayewitz, Passi. *Shiloah: Discovering Jewish Identity through Oral/Folk History: A Source Book*. New York: Institute for Jewish Life, 1976.

Rosenbaum, Samuel. *A Guide to Haftarah Chanting*. Hoboken, New York: Ktav, 1973.

———. *A Guide to Torah Chanting*. Hoboken, NY: Ktav, 1973.

Rosenblatt, Samuel. *Yossele Rosenblatt: The Story of His Life*. New York: Cantors Assembly, 2005.

Rosenfeld, Lulla. *Bright Star of Exile: Jacob Adler and the Yiddish Theater*. New York: Thomas Y. Crowell, 1977.

Rosowsky, Solomon. *The Cantillation of the Bible*. New York: The Reconstructionist Press, 1957.

Rossen, Jane Mink, and Uri Sharvit. *Fusion of Traditions: Liturgical Music in the Copenhagen Synagogue*. Odense: Syddansk Universitetsforlag, 2006.

Rothmüller, Aron Marko. *The Music of the Jews: An Historical Appreciation*. Cranbury, NJ: A. S. Barnes, 1967.

Rubin, Emanuel, and John H. Baron. *Music in Jewish History and Culture.* Sterling Heights, MI: Harmonie Park, 2006.
Rubin, Ruth. *Voices of a People: The Story of Yiddish Folksong.* New York: McGraw-Hill, 1963.
Saleski, Gdal. *Famous Musicians of Jewish Origin.* New York: Bloch, 1949
Saminsky, Lazare. *Music of the Ghetto and the Bible.* New York: Bloch, 1934.
Sandrew, Nahma. *Vagabond Stars: A World History of Yiddish Theater.* New York: Limelight Editions, 1986.
Sapoznik, Henry. *Klezmer: Jewish Music from Old World to Our World.* New York: Schirmer, 1999.
Schiller, David M. *Bloch, Schoenberg, and Bernstein: Assimilating Jewish Music.* New York: Oxford University Press, 2003.
Schneider, Gertrude, ed. *Mordechai Gebirtig: His Poetic and Musical Legacy.* Westport, CT: Praeger, 2000.
Sendrey, Alfred. *Bibliography of Jewish Music.* New York: Columbia University Press, 1951.
_____. *Music in Ancient Israel.* New York: Philosophical Library, 1969.
_____. *Music in the Social and Religious Life of Antiquity.* Rutherford, NJ: Fairleigh Dickinson University, 1974.
_____. *Music of the Jews in the Diaspora.* New York: Thomas Yoseloff, 1970.
Sendrey, Alfred, and Milton Norton. *David's Harp: The Story of Music in Biblical Times.* New York: New American Library, 1964.
Serge, Marcella. *Bibliography of Jewish Music Bibliographies.* Haifa: The Haifa Music Museum & AMLI Library, 1970.
Seroussi, Edwin. *Popular Music in Israel: The First Fifty Years.* Cambridge: Harvard College Library, 1996.
_____. *Spanish-Portuguese Synagogue Music in Nineteenth-Century Reform Sources from Hamburg: Ancient Tradition in the Dawn of Modernity.* Jerusalem: Magnes, 1996.
Shelemay, Kay Kaufman. *Let Jasmine Rain Down: Song and Remembrance among Syrian Jews.* Chicago: University of Chicago Press, 1998.
_____. *Music, Ritual and Falasha History.* East Lansing, MI: African Studies Center, Michigan State University, 1986.
_____. *A Song of Longing: An Ethiopian Journey.* Urbana and Chicago: University of Illinois Press, 1991.
Shiloah, Amnon. *The Dimension of Music in Islamic and Jewish Culture.* Brookfield, VT: Ashgate, 1993.
_____. *Jewish Musical Traditions.* Detroit, MI: Wayne State University Press, 1995.
_____. *Music and Its Virtues in Islamic and Jewish Writings.* Burlington, VT: Ashgate, 2007.
Shiloah, Amnon, and Ruth Tenne. *Music Subjects in the Zohar Texts and Indices.* Jerusalem: Magnes, 1977.
Silverman, Jerry. *The Undying Flame: Ballads and Songs of the Holocaust.* Syracuse, NY: Syracuse University Press, 2002.
Slavicky, Milan. *Gideon Klein: A Fragment of Life and Work.* Trans. Dagmar Steinova. Prague: Helvetica Tempora, 1995.
Slobin, Mark, ed. *American Klezmer: Its Roots and Offshoots.* Berkeley: University of California Press, 2002.
_____. *Chosen Voices: The Story of the American Cantorate.* Chicago: University of Illinois Press, 2002.

———. *Fiddler on the Move: Exploring the Klezmer World*. New York: Oxford University Press, 2003.
———, ed. *Jewish Instrumental Folk Music: The Collections and Writings of Moshe Beregovski*. Syracuse, NY: Syracuse University Press, 2001.
———. *Tenement Songs: The Popular Music of the Jewish Immigrants*. Urbana and Chicago: University of Illinois Press, 1996.
Smith, Chani Haran. *Tuning the Soul: Music as a Spiritual Process in the Teachings of Rabbi Nahman of Bratzlav*. Boston: Brill, 2010.
Smith, John Arthur. *Music in Ancient Judaism and Early Christianity*. Burlington, VT: Ashgate, 2011.
Smoira-Roll, Michal. *Folk Music in Israel: An Analysis Attempted*. Tel Aviv: Israeli Music Institute, 1963.
Soltes, Avraham. *Off the Willows: The Rebirth of Modern Jewish Music*. New York: Bloch, 1970.
Sposato, Jeffrey. *The Price of Assimilation: Felix Mendelssohn and the Nineteenth Century Anti-Semitic Tradition*. New York: Oxford University Press, 2008.
Staiman, Mordecai. *Niggun: Stories Behind the Chasidic Songs that Inspire Jews*. Northvale, NJ: Jason Aronson, 1994.
Stanton, Steve, and Alexander Knapp, eds. *Proceedings of the First International Conference on Jewish Music 1994*. London: City University, Jewish Music Heritage Trust, 1994.
Steinberg, Michael P. *Judaism Musical and Unmusical*. Chicago: University of Chicago Press, 2007.
Steinweis, Alan E. *Art, Ideology, and Economics in Nazi Germany: The Reich Chambers of Music, Theater, and the Visual Arts*. Chapel Hill: The University of North Carolina Press, 2006.
Stevens, Lewis. *Composers of Classical Music of Jewish Descent*. London: Vallentine-Mitchell, 2005.
Strassberg, Robert. *Ernest Bloch: Voice in the Wilderness*. Los Angeles: California State University Press, 1977.
Stratton, Jon. *Jews, Race and Popular Music*. Burlington, VT: Ashgate, 2009.
Strom, Yale. *The Book of Klezmer: The History, the Music, the Folklore*. Chicago: Chicago Review, 2002.
Summit, Jeffery A. *The Lord's Song in a Strange Land: Music and Identity in Contemporary Jewish Worship*. New York: Oxford University Press, 2000.
Sutton, Silvia Hamui. *Cantos Judeo-españoles: Simbología Poética y Visión Del Mundo*. Santa Fe, NM: Gaon, 2008.
Swerling, Norman P. *Music of the Sephardic Jews of Curacao: Romemu-Exale*. New York: Tara, 1998.
Tischler, Alice. *A Descriptive Bibliography of Art Music by Israeli Composers*. Warren, MI: Harmonie Park, 1988.
Vigoda, Samuel. *Legendary Voices*. New York: M. P., 1981.
Vinaver, Chemjo. *Anthology of Hassidic Music*. Jerusalem: Jewish Music Centre, 1985.
———. *Anthology of Jewish Music*. New York: E. B. Marks, 1955.
Weiner, Marc A. *Richard Wagner and the Anti-Semitic Imagination*. Lincoln: University of Nebraska Press, 1995.
Weisenberg, Joey. *Building Singing Communities: A Practical Guide to Unlocking the Power of Music in Jewish Prayer*. New York: Segula, 2011.
Weisgall, Deborah. *A Joyful Noise: Claiming the Songs of My Father*. New York: Grove Press, 2000.

Weisser, Albert. *The Modern Renaissance of Jewish Music: Events and Figures, Eastern Europe and America.* New York: Bloch, 1954.

Wellesz, Egon, ed. *Music in the Old Testament.* London: Oxford University Press, 1970.

Werner, Eric. ed. *Contributions to the Historical Study of Jewish Music.* New York: Ktav, 1972.

———. *A Voice Still Heard: The Sacred Songs of Ashkenazi Jews.* University Park: Pennsylvania State University Press, 1976.

———. *From Generation to Generation.* New York: American Conference of Cantors, 1967.

———. *Hebrew Music: Anthology of Music.* Edited by K. G. Fellerer. Cologne: Arno Folk Verlag, 1961.

———. *Mendelssohn: A New Image of the Composer and His Age.* Trans. Dika Newlin. New York: Free Press, 1963.

———. *The Sacred Bridge: The Interdependence of Liturgy and Music in Synagogue and Church During the First Millennium.* New York: Columbia University Press, 1959.

———. *The Sacred Bridge II: The Interdependence of Liturgy and Music in Synagogue and Church During the First Millennium.* New York: Ktav, 1984.

Werner, Eric, and Arthur Berger. *Reviews of Selected Recordings of Jewish Music.* New York: National Jewish Music Council, 1953.

Westheimer, Ruth Karola. *Musically Speaking: A Life Through Song.* Philadelphia:University of Pennsylvania Press, 2003.

Whitfield, Stephen J. *In Search of American Culture.* Hanover, MA: Brandeis University Press, 1999.

Wright, Jill Gold. *Creating America on Stage: How Jewish Composers and Lyricists Pioneered American Musical Theater.* Saarbrücken: VDM Verlag, 2009.

Yardeini, Mordecai. *Fifty Years of Yiddish Song in America.* New York: Jewish Music Alliance, 1964.

———. *Words and Music.* New York: Yiddish Kultur Farband, 1986.

Zimmerman, Akiva. *B'ron Yahad: Essays, Research and Notes on Hazzanut and Jewish Music.* Tel Aviv: Central Cantorial Archive, 1988.

———. *S'harei Ron: The Cantorate in Responsa.* Tel Aviv: Bron Yahad, 1992.

Zorn, John, ed. *Arcana I: Musicians on Music.* New York: Tzadik Books, 2001.

———. *Arcana II: Musicians on Music.* New York: Tzadik Books, 2007.

———. *Arcana III: Musicians on Music.* New York: Tzadik Books, 2008.

Bibliography

Abrahams, Israel. *A Companion to the Authorized Prayer Book.* New York: Sepher-Hermon, 1966.
Appleton, Lewis. *Bibliography of Jewish Vocal Music.* New York: National Jewish Book Council, 1968.
Atkins, Harold, and Archie Newman, ed. *Beecham Stories: Anecdotes, Sayings and Impressions of Sir Thomas Beecham.* London: Robson, 1978.
Avenary, Hanoch. *Encounters of East and West in Music: Selected Writings.* Tel Aviv: Tel Aviv University Press, 1979.
Barzilai, Shmuel. *Chassidic Ecstasy in Music.* New York: Peter Lang, 2009.
Berlin, Adele. *Esther: JPS Bible Commentary.* Philadelphia: Jewish Publication Society, 2001.
Bernard, Andrew. *The Sound of Sacred Time: A Basic Music Theory Textbook to Teach the Jewish Prayer Modes.* Charlotte, NC: Temple Beth El, 2005.
Binder, Abraham W. "*V'shomru*: A Century of Musical Interpretations." p. 51–64 in Irene Heskes, ed., *Studies in Jewish Music: Collected Writings of A. W. Binder.* New York: Bloch, 1971.
Blackwell, Albert L. *The Sacred in Music.* Louisville, KY: Westminster John Knox, 1999.
Bohlman, Philip V. *"The Land Where Two Streams Flow": Music in the German-Jewish Community of Israel.* Urbana and Chicago: University of Illinois Press, 1989.
Bolinger, Dwight L. *The Symbolism of Music.* Yellow Springs, OH: Antioch Press, 1941.
Burns, George. *All My Best Friends.* New York: G. K. Hall, 1991.
Chang, Larry, ed. *Wisdom for the Soul: Five Millennia of Prescriptions for Spiritual Healing.* Washington, DC: Gnosophia, 2006.
Cobussen, Marcel. *Thresholds: Rethinking Spirituality Through Music.* Burlington, VT: Ashgate, 2008.
Cohen, A. Irma. *An Introduction to Jewish Music in Eight Illustrated Lectures.* New York: Bloch, 1923.
Cohen, Francis L. "Addir Hu." p. 186–188 in *The Jewish Encyclopedia.* New York: Funk and Wagnalls, 1901–1906.
_____. "Adon Olam." p. 205–206 in *Jewish Encyclopedia.* New York: Funk and Wagnalls, 1901–1906.

_____. "Choir." P. 41 in *Jewish Encyclopedia*, vol. 4. New York: Funk and Wagnalls, 1901–1906.

Cohen, Judah M. *The Making of a Reform Jewish Cantor: Musical Authority, Cultural Investment*. Bloomington: Indiana University Press, 2009.

Cook, Nicholas. *A Guide to Musical Analysis*. New York: Oxford University Press, 1987.

Copland, Aaron. *Music and Imagination*. Cambridge: Harvard University Press, 1953.

Crowdy, Denis. "Tribute Without Attribution: Kopikat, Covers and Copyright in Papua New Guinea." p. 229–240 in Shane Homan, ed., *Access All Eras: Tribute Bands and Global Pop Culture*. Berkshire: Open University Press, 2006.

Darwin, Charles. *The Descent of Man*. New York: D. Appleton and Co., 1871.

_____. *On the Origin of Species*. New York: D. Appleton and Co., 1864.

Davidson, Charles. *From Szatmar to the New World: Max Wohlberg, American Cantor*. New York: Jewish Theological Seminary, 2001.

Davis, Edwin, ed. *Great Thoughts on Great Truths*. New York: Ward, Lock, and Co., 1882.

Dawkins, Richard. "Good and Bad Reasons for Believing." p. 13–19 in Dale McGowan, ed., *Parenting Beyond Belief: On Raising Ethical Caring Kids Without Religion*. New York: Amacom, 2007.

Durkheim, Émile. *The Elementary Forms of Religious Life*. Trans. Carol Cossman. New York: Oxford University Press, 2001.

Edelman, Marsha Bryan. *A Bibliography of Jewish Music*. New York: The Hebrew Arts School, 1986.

Eisen, Arnold M. *Rethinking Modern Judaism: Ritual, Commandment, Community*. Chicago: University of Chicago Press, 1998.

Eisenstein, Judith K. *Heritage of Music: The Music of the Jewish People*. Wyncote, PA: Reconstructionist Press, 1981.

Elbogen, Ismar. *Jewish Liturgy: A Comprehensive History*. Trans. Raymond P. Scheindlin. Philadelphia: Jewish Publication Society, 1993.

Eliade, Mircea. *The Myth of the Eternal Return*. New York: Pantheon, 1954.

_____. *The Sacred and the Profane: The Nature of Religion*. New York: Harcourt, 1959.

Fishkoff, Sue. "Survey Indicates Jewish Singing Spurs Jewish Engagement." *Jewish Journal of Greater Los Angeles* 25:28 (2010): 27, 35.

Fisk, Josiah, ed. *Composers on Music: Eight Centuries of Writing*. Boston: Northeastern University Press, 1997.

Fleisher, Robert. *Twenty Israeli Composers: Voices of a Culture*. Detroit: Wayne State University Press, 1997.

Friedmann, Jonathan L., ed. *Quotations on Jewish Sacred Music*. Lanham, MD: Hamilton, 2011.

_____. *20th Century Synagogue Music: Essential Readings*. Woodland Hills, CA: Isaac Nathan, 2010.

Fromm, Herbert. *On Jewish Music: A Composer's View*. New York: Bloch, 1978.

Gerson-Kiwi, Edith. *Migrations and Mutations of the Music in East and West: Selected Writings*. Tel Aviv: Tel Aviv University Press, 1980.

Gioia, Ted. *Work Songs*. Durham, NC: Duke University Press, 2006.

Glantz, Jerry, ed. *Leib Glantz: The Man Who Spoke to God*. Tel Aviv: The Tel Aviv Institute for Jewish Liturgical Music, 2008.

Glantz, Leib. "The Cantor — A Unique Creation of Jewish Life." p. 368–371 in Jerry

Glantz, ed., *Leib Glantz: The Man Who Spoke to God*. Tel Aviv: Tel Aviv Institute for Jewish Liturgical Music, 2008.

———. "The Sin of '*Maoz Tzur.*'" p. 449–451 in Jerry Glantz, ed., *Leib Glantz: The Man Who Spoke to God*. Tel Aviv: Tel Aviv Institute of Jewish Liturgical Music, 2008.

Greenboym, Nathan. "Yerushalayim Shel Zahav Ke'shir Koddesh." *Mayim Midalav* (1993): 27–37.

Hadow, William Henry. *Studies in Modern Music: Hector Berlioz, Robert Schumann, Richard Wagner*. New York: Macmillan, 1893.

Harris, Samuel. *The Self-Revelation of God*. New York: Charles Scribner's Sons, 1886.

Hertz, Joseph H. *The Authorized Daily Prayer Book*. New York: Bloch, 1987.

Heschel, Abraham Joshua. *God in Search of Man: A Philosophy of Judaism*. New York: Farrar, Straus and Giroux, 1955.

———. *The Insecurity of Freedom*. New York: Macmillan, 1963.

———. "No Religion Is an Island." *Union Seminary Quarterly Review* 21:2 (1966): 117–134.

Heskes, Irene. "The Golden Age of Cantorial Artistry." p. 5–11 in Velvel Pasternak and Noah Schall, ed., *The Golden Age of Cantors: Musical Masterpieces of the Synagogue*. New York: Tara, 1991.

———. *Passport to Jewish Music: Its History, Traditions, and Culture*. New York: Tara, 1994.

Heskes, Irene, and Suzanne Bloch. *Ernest Bloch, Creative Spirit: A Source Book*. New York: Jewish Music Council of the Jewish Welfare Board, 1976.

Hoffman, Jeffrey. "Akdamut: History, Folklore, and Meaning." *Jewish Quarterly Review* 99:2 (2009): 161–183.

Holde, Arthur. *Jews in Music: From the Age of Enlightenment to the Present*. New York: Philosophical Library, 1959.

Idelsohn, Abraham Z. *Jewish Music in Its Historical Development*. New York: Henry Holt and Co., 1929.

———. *Thesaurus of Hebrew Oriental Melodies*. Lepzig: Friedrich Hofmeister, 1914–1933.

Imber, Naftali Herz. "The Music of the Psalms." p. 81–95 in Jonathan L. Friedmann, comp., *Music in Jewish Thought: Selected Writings, 1890–1920*. Jefferson, NC: McFarland & Company, 2009.

Isaacs, Ronald H. *Jewish Music: Its History, People, and Song*. Northvale, NJ: Jason Aronson, 1997.

Isaacson, Michael. *Jewish Music as Midrash: What Makes Music Jewish?* Los Angeles: Egg Cream Music, 2007.

Jacobson, Joshua R. *Chanting the Hebrew Bible: The Complete Guide to the Art of Cantillation*. Philadelphia: Jewish Publication Society, 2002.

Jacobson, Sam L. "The Music of the Jews." p. 29–33 in Jonathan L. Friedmann, comp., *Music in Jewish Thought: Selected Writings, 1890–1920*. Jefferson, NC: McFarland & Company, 2009.

Jassinowski, Pinchos. "Hazzanim and Hazzanut." p. 122–129 in Jonathan L. Friedmann, comp., *Music in Jewish Thought: Selected Writings, 1890–1920*. Jefferson, NC: McFarland & Company, 2009.

Kalib, Sholom. *The Musical Tradition of the Eastern European Synagogue*. Syracuse, NY: Syracuse University Press, 2002.

Katz, Ruth. *The Lachmann Problem: An Unsung Chapter in Comparative Musicology*. Jerusalem: Magnes, 2003.

Kung, Hans. *Art and the Question of Meaning.* New York: Crossroad, 1981.
Landman, Leo. *The Cantor: An Historical Perspective.* New York: Yeshiva University Press, 1972.
Leiser, Joseph. *American Judaism: A Historical Survey.* Westport, CT: Greenwood, 1979.
Levine, Joseph A. *Synagogue Song in America.* Crown Point, IN: White Cliffs, 1989.
Levitin, Daniel J. *The World in Six Songs: How the Musical Brain Created Human Nature.* New York: Dutton, 2008.
Lewandowski, Louis. *Kol Rinnah U'T' fillah.* Berlin, 1871.
Lewis, C. S. "On Church Music." *Journal of Synagogue Music* 8:1 (1978): 27–31.
Lifschitz, Chaim. "David Cohen." *Encyclopedia Judaica,* vol. 5 (2006): 13.
Loeffler, James Benjamin. *The Most Musical Nation: Jews and Culture in the Late Russian Empire.* New Haven, CT: Yale University Press, 2010.
Longfellow, Henry Wadsworth. *The Prose Works of Henry Wadsworth Longfellow.* London: David Bogue, 1851.
Lowenstein, Steven M. *The Jewish Cultural Tapestry: International Jewish Folk Traditions.* New York: Oxford University Press, 2000.
Matson, Albert. *Psalmodic Science vs. Psalmodic Sciolism.* San Diego, CA: Press of Frye and Smith, 1907.
Mendelsohn, Ezra, ed. *Modern Jews and Their Musical Agendas.* New York: Oxford University Press, 1993.
Mendelssohn-Bartholdy, Felix. *Selected Letters of Mendelssohn.* New York: S. Sonnenschein and Co., 1894.
Michelman, Henry D. "The Journey of a Hebrew Melody: Israel Goldfarb's *Shalom Aleichem.*" *The Synagogue Journal* (Dec. 2006): 14–20.
Mitchell, Deborah. *How to Live Well with Early Alzheimer's: A Complete Program for Enhancing Your Quality of Life.* New York: Macmillan, 2010.
Moddel, Philip. *Max Helfman: A Biographical Sketch.* Berkeley, CA: Judah L. Magnes, 1974.
Montagu, Jeremy. *Musical Instruments of the Bible.* Lanham, MD: Scarecrow Press, 2002.
Morrison, Richard. "Join a Choir and Stave Off the Onset of Old Age." *BBC Music Magazine* (June 2008): 23.
Newman, Harry. *Thirty-Four Years on the Bimah: Vignettes of a "Professional" Jew.* Bloomington, IN: AuthorHouse, 2007.
Nulman, Macy. *Concepts of Jewish Prayer and Music.* New York: Yeshiva University Press, 1985.
_____. *The Encyclopedia of Jewish Music.* Northvale, NJ: Jason Aronson, 1996.
_____. *The Encyclopedia of the Sayings of the Jewish People.* Northvale, NJ: Jason Aronson, 1997.
Opatoshu, Joseph. *In Polish Woods.* Philadelphia: Jewish Publication Society, 1921.
Orenstein, Walter. *The Cantor's Manual of Jewish Law.* Northvale, NJ: Jason Aronson, 1994.
Otto, Rudolf. *The Idea of the Holy.* London: Oxford University Press, 1923.
Pasternak, Velvel. *Beyond Hava Nagila.* Owing Mills, MD: Tara, 1999.
Pinson, DovBer. *Inner Rhythms: The Kabbalah of Music.* Northvale, NJ: Jason Aronson, 2000.
Pool, David de Sola. *The Ancient Melodies of the Liturgy of the Spanish and Portuguese Jews.* London: Wertheimer and Co., 1857.

_____. "The Music of the Synagogue." p. 18–25 in Jonathan L. Friedmann, ed., *20th Century Synagogue Music: Essential Readings.* Woodland Hills, CA: Isaac Nathan, 2010.
Richards, Stephen. "Music and Prayer in Reform Worship." *Journal of Synagogue Music* 9:1 (1979): 20–25.
Ringer, Alexander L. *Arnold Schoenberg: The Composer as Jew.* New York: Clarendon, 1990.
Robinson, Reuben T. "Congregational Singing." *The Congregational Review* (1868): 260–273.
Rogovoy, Seth. *The Essential Klezmer: A Music Lover's Guide to Jewish Roots and Soul Music, from the Old World to the Jazz Age to the Downtown Avant-Garde.* Chapel Hill, NC: Alonquin Books of Chapel Hill, 2000.
Routley, Erik. *The Church and Music: An Enquiry into the History, the Nature, and the Scope of Christian Judgment on Music.* London: Gerald Duckworth and Co., 1950.
Sachs, Henry Baruch. *Heine in America.* Philadelphia: University of Pennsylvania, 1916.
Sacks, Oliver. *Musicophilia: Tales of Music and the Brain.* New York: Vintage, 2008.
Saliers, Don E. *Music and Theology.* Nashville, TN: Abingdon Press, 2007.
Saminsky, Lazare. *Music of the Ghetto and the Bible.* New York: Bloch, 1934.
Schillebeeckx, Edward. *Jesus: An Experiment in Christology.* New York: Seabury, 1979.
Sendrey, Alfred. *Music in Ancient Israel.* New York: Philosophical Library, 1969.
Sharlin, William. "Trust the Process: My Life in Sacred Song." p. 97–136 in Jonathan L. Friedmann, ed., *Perspectives on Jewish Music: Secular and Sacred.* Lanham, MD: Lexington, 2009.
_____. "Why Can't a Woman Chant like a Man?" p. 93–97 in Jonathan L. Friedmann and Brad Stetson, eds., *Jewish Sacred Music and Jewish Identity: Continuity and Fragmentation.* St. Paul, MN: Paragon House, 2008.
Shiloah, Amnon. *Jewish Musical Traditions.* Detroit, MI: Wayne State University Press, 1995.
Silverman, Jerry. *The Undying Flame: Ballads and Songs of the Holocaust.* Syracuse, NY: Syracuse University Press, 2002.
Slobin, Mark. *Chosen Voices: The Story of the American Cantorate.* Urbana and Chicago: University of Illinois Press, 1989.
_____. "Learning the Lessons of Studying Jewish Music." *Judaism* 44:2 (1995): 220–225.
Soltes, Avraham. "A Lion to Sing His Will." p. 43–50 in Jerry Glantz, ed., *Leib Glantz: The Man Who Spoke to God.* Tel Aviv: Tel Aviv Institute of Jewish Liturgical Music, 2008.
Spencer, Herbert. *Education: Intellectual, Moral and Physical.* New York: D. Appleton and Co., 1864.
Staiman, Mordechai. *Niggun: Stories Behind the Chasidic Songs that Inspire Jews.* Northvale, NJ: Jason Aronson, 1994.
Strom, Yale. *Dave Tarras: The King of Klezmer.* Kfar Sava: OR-TAV, 2010.
Unterman, Alan. *The Jews: Their Religious Beliefs and Practices.* Sussex: Sussex Academic Press, 1996.
van Der Leeuw, Gerardus. *Sacred and Profane Beauty: The Holy in Art.* New York: Oxford University Press: 2006.
Vinaver, Chemjo. *Anthology of Hassidic Music.* Jerusalem: Jewish Music Centre, 1985.

_____. "Synagogue Music — Traditional." p. 39–46 in Jonathan L. Friedmann, ed., *20th Century Synagogue Music: Essential Readings*. Woodland Hills, CA: Isaac Nathan, 2010.

Weber, Max. *The Theory of Social and Economic Organization*. Ed. Talcott Parsons. New York: Simon and Schuster, 1997.

Weiss, Sam. "Ein Keloheinu." *Chazzanut Online* (2002). <http://www.chazzanut.com/articles/on-ein-keloheinu.html>

Weisser, Albert. *The Modern Renaissance of Jewish Music: Events and Figures, Eastern Europe and America*. New York: Bloch, 1954.

Werner, Eric. "The Tunes of the Haggadah." *Studies in Bibliography and Booklore* 7 (1965): 57–83.

_____. *A Voice Still Heard: The Sacred Songs of the Ashkenazic Jews*. University Park: Pennsylvania University Press, 1976.

Whitfield, Stephen J. *In Search of American Culture*. Hanover, MA: Brandeis University Press, 1999.

Wohlberg, Max. "The Hazzan as Spokesman of the Congregation." *Journal of Synagogue Music* 20, no. 2 (1990): 28–32.

Wuthnow, Robert. *Producing the Sacred: An Essay on Public Religion*. Urbana and Chicago: University of Illinois Press, 1994.

Yellen, Gigi. "Scales out of Shul." *Hadassah Magazine* 88:9 (2007): 50.

Index

Aaron 30
Abba Arika 139
Abraham 141
Abrahams, Israel 115
Absalom 114
Adam 114
Addir Hu 17, 118–119
Adler, Samuel 158
Adon Olam 18, 47, 84, 141–142, 158, 163
Adonai Malach 72, 73
Africa 18, 104
Agagite 135
Ahavah Rabbah 72–73, 116
Ahavat Olam 47
Akdamut 17, 121–123
Akiva 117
Al Ayelet ha-Shachar 162
Al Ginot Egoz 118
Al Hanisim 112
Al Shoshanim 162
Al Tashchet 162
Albuquerque 89
Aleinu 138–140, 158
Aleinu Gadol 124
"Aloha 'Oe" 142
Amalek 135
American Music Therapy Association 108
Amidah 111–112
Amsterdam 101
Ani Purim 131
Anker, Perryne 2
Aramaic 17, 22, 122–123, 129
Aristotle 137

Ark 66, 84, 130
Armstrong, Louis 36, 86
Asaph 114
Ashkenazi Judaism 8, 17, 39, 71, 72, 73, 100, 115, 117, 118, 119, 121, 124, 125–126, 133, 135, 139, 141, 143, 157
Asia 104
Augustine 79–80, 83–84
Authorized Daily Prayer Book 112
Avebury 19
Avinu Malkeinu 73, 129, 131
axis mundi 147–148

Baal Shem Tov 79, 129
Babylonia 45, 133, 139
Bach, Johann Sebastian 89
banquets 13
Bar'chu 18, 124
baseball 155–157
Bashanah Haba'ah 47–48
Beatles 142
Beckett, Samuel 131
Beethoven, Ludwig van 70–71, 89–90
Beimel, Jacob 5
Belafonte, Harry 144
Bell, Catherine 103
Belzer, Nissi 152
Berditchev 129, 152
Berlin 139
Berlin, Adele 136
Berlin, Irving 127
Bernstein, Leonard 57, 105
Bethel United Methodist Church 164
Bible 10–12, 13–14, 15, 18, 20, 47, 48, 62,

189

64–65, 66, 67, 74, 78, 83, 99, 108, 112, 114, 117, 120, 126, 130, 132, 136, 149, 165
Bim Bam Shabbat Shalom 110
bimah 100, 150, 152, 154, 155
Binder, A.W. 5, 113, 158
birchot ha-shachar 61
Blackwell, Albert 43
Bloch, Ernest 105
Blois 140
bluegrass 41
Bolinger, Dwight L. 42
bossa nova 41
Boulez, Pierre 73
Brahms, Johannes 43
Brazil 105
Broadway 57
Brooklyn 115
Brooks, Hershel 2
Bruch, Max 127–128
Buber, Martin 68
Bukharia 45
Bukovina 144
Burns, George 75
Byron, Don 128

Cahn, Meredith 2
Cain 11
camp music 27, 38, 39, 100
cantillation 31, 38, 120, 127
Cantors Assembly 26, 115
Carlebach, Shlomo 37
Catholicism 132
"Celebration" 127
Cello 89, 127
Chabad 81, 97
charisma 36–38
Charleston, South Carolina 164
chozeh 149
Christianity 3, 37, 39, 93, 139–140, 162, 163, 169
chukkat ha-goy 29
Church of Beethoven 89–90
clarinet 128
classical music 41
Cohen, David 73
Cohen, Francis L. 119, 141
Cohen, Idov 69–70
Confucius 86
Conservative Judaism 49, 104
Cook, Nicholas 72
Copland, Aaron 57, 76, 88
country 9, 90
Crowdy, Denis 55–56
Crusades 123, 124

Cuando El Rey Nimrod 37
cymbals 157

Dan 122
dance 48, 49, 77, 78, 80, 81, 85, 130–131, 132, 137, 138
Darwin, Annie 54
Darwin, Charles 53–54
Darwin, Emma 54
David 12, 48, 84, 108–109, 114, 121, 130, 157
Dawkins, Richard 6, 50–51
dementia 102
Derash 45–46
Deuteronomy 85, 130
devekut 85–86
Diaspora 44, 45, 50, 62, 104–105, 135
disco 47
Dixieland 92
Dodi Li 118
Donne, John 31
Dorian mode 72
Durkheim, Émile 101
Dylan, Bob 144

earworm 41
Eastern Orthodox 132
Eden 114
Egypt 14, 117, 118, 120, 130, 132, 133, 135
Ein Keloheinu 84, 142–144
Eisen, Arnold 97
Eisenmenger, Johann Andreas 139
Elbogen, Ismar 141
Eliade, Mircea 11–112, 148
Elisha 90
Elkanah 66
English 23, 32, 39, 48, 56, 129
Ephros, Gershon 163
Epstein, David W. 2
Erev Shel Shoshanim 37
Esperanto 23–24
Esther 134, 135, 136, 137
Etz Chayim Hi 43, 44
Europe 27, 33, 45, 71, 77, 79, 81, 93, 97, 104, 105, 116, 119, 124, 126, 140, 153, 158, 162
Exodus 12, 84, 113, 117, 118, 120, 135, 138
Ezekiel of Kuzmir 78

feast 65, 136, 157
festivals 12, 17, 40, 52, 100, 118, 119, 121, 123, 125, 126, 142
Fine, Irving 57
Finley, Mordecai 2

First Maccabees 132
flute 65, 70, 89, 128–130
folk music 37, 48, 92, 115, 116, 119, 121, 127, 130, 133, 142, 153
folk-rock 33, 39, 56, 57, 93, 103
Frailich, Jay 2
France 26, 81, 100, 124, 135, 139, 140
Frankfurt 158
Frankiel, Tamar 2
Freelander, Dan 39
Freudenthal, Julius 143
Friedman, Debbie 29, 37, 55–56
Friedmann, Elvia 2
From Jewish Folk Poetry 128
Fromm, Herbert 158
funeral 13, 164

Gabirol, Solomon Ibn 141
Genesis 11, 111
Geonic period 15, 151
Gereboff, Joel 2
Germany 10, 21, 26, 38, 45, 52, 94, 100, 105, 119, 122, 124, 125–126, 127, 133, 135, 139, 143–144, 158, 162
Gerovitsch, Eliezer 141–142, 163
Gershwin, George 127
Gioia, Ted 13
Glantz, Leib 62, 69–70, 133
God in Search of Man 87
Golden Age of *Hazzanut* 152, 153
Goldfarb, Israel 28, 115–116, 123
Goldfarb, Samuel 116
Gottlieb, Jack 57–58
Greeks 18, 72, 93, 131, 159
Green, William Scott 98
Greenboym, Natan 47
Gregorian chant 9
griots 18
grogger 134–135
"*Grosser Gott wir loben Dich*" 143
guitar 35, 39, 103, 105, 167
Gunkel, Herman 83
Gurney, Don 2

Ha-Chasid, Yehudah 31, 67
Hadar, Yosef 37
Haftarah 15
Haggadah 117, 119
halakha 49, 50, 78, 99–100, 101, 118, 150, 153
Halevi, Judah 107
Hallel 84, 119
hallelujah 83, 84
Haman 133, 134–135, 136

hamantaschen 12
Hannah 66
Hannover, Nathan 154
Hanukkah 17, 112, 131–134
harp 21, 75, 156, 157
Harris, Samuel 53
Hashkiveinu 43, 72, 138, 163
Hassidic 9
Hatikvah 48
Hava Nagila 116, 144–145
havurah 36
hazzan 71, 105, 149, 151–152, 154
Hebrew 18, 22–23, 31, 39, 44, 48, 57, 69, 78, 102, 104, 128, 142, 139, 144, 145, 149
Heine, Heinrich 20–22
Helfgot, Yitzchak Meir 152
Helfman, Max 43, 57, 72, 90–91, 163
Herodotus 93
Hershman, Mordecai 153
Heschel, Abraham Joshua 10, 16, 53–54, 87–88
Heschel, Sylvia 54
Heskes, Irene 5, 153
Hevenu Shalom Aleichem 48
hiddur mitzvah 16
High Holy Days 10, 16, 40, 52, 68, 100, 116, 123–125, 125–126, 129, 131, 140, 142, 155
Hinach Yafeh 118
Hinei Ma Tov 65, 110
Hineni 155
Hirsch, Nurit 28
Hirsch, Samson Raphael 158
Hodo Al Eretz 140
Hoffman, Abraham 122–123
Höller, Karl 89
Horowitz, Isaiah 107–108
hymn 26, 27, 29, 31, 33, 38, 39, 63, 67, 83–84, 105, 115, 118, 120, 122, 124, 132, 141, 143–144, 164, 165, 158, 169

"I Have a Little Dreydl" 132
The Idea of the Holy 59–61
Idelsohn, Abraham Z. 44, 45, 71, 125, 143, 145
Imber, Naftali Herz 89–90
India 103, 116
Institute for Music and Neurologic Function 102
instruments 13, 14, 48–50, 67–68, 75, 100, 114, 129, 133, 134, 157
Isaacson, Michael 2
Isaiah 20, 139
isomorphism 34–36

Israel 11, 14, 29, 48, 66, 79, 97, 104, 108, 110, 113, 117, 129, 135, 136, 155
Isserles, Moses 31
Italy 24, 135, 158
Ivdu et Hashem 78, 131

Jabal 11
Jacob of Orleans 140
Jacobs, Louis 98
Jacobson, Sam L. 153
Jassinowsky, Pinchos 69, 152
jazz 9, 57, 128
Jericho 139
Jerusalem 13, 17, 20, 29, 44, 62, 71, 114, 118, 133, 136, 144–145, 147, 151, 157, 159, 162
Jesus 139
The Jewish Daily Forward 109
Jewish Theological Seminary 115
Job 65, 159
Joshua 139
Josiah 14
Jubal 10–12
jubilus 79–80

Kabbalah 9, 77, 79
Kabbalat Shabbat 72
Kaddish 15
Kane Street Synagogue 115
kavvanah 66–67
Kedushah 22, 37
Kertzer, Morris 116
Kevodo Malei Olam 37
Ki Mitziyon 140
Kiddush 111, 123
kippah 12, 99
Klal Yisrael 104, 161
Klepper, Jeff 39
klezmer 23, 128
kohanim 50
Kol Nidrei 71, 100, 123, 124, 127–128
Kook, Abraham Isaac 73
Korachites 29–30
Kosmer, James K. 21
Kripper, Roni 2
Küng, Hans 95–96

Lam, Nathan 2
Lashon Kodesh 22
Latin America 104
Lazar, Matthew 161
Lecha Dodi 44, 141, 163
Leo Baeck Temple 44
Levi Yitzchok of Berditchev 129

Levine, Joseph A. 73
Levites 13–14, 84, 114, 149–151, 157, 159
Levitin, Daniel J. 64–65
Lewandowski, Louis 26, 158, 162, 163
Lewis, C.S. 63–64
liberal Judaism 8, 29, 31, 33, 35, 39, 42, 55, 58, 97, 99, 105, 151, 167, 168
Lichtenstein, Abraham J. 127
"A Literary Nightmare" 40
London 75, 101, 112
Longfellow, Henry Wadsworth 92
Lonzano, Menachem de 165
Lord Byron 127
Los Angeles 44
Lowenstein, Steven M. 104
lulav 17
Luther, Martin 133
Lutheran hymn 26, 143, 158
lyre 11, 108, 157

Ma Tovu 110, 112
Ma Yafeh HaYom 110
Maccabees 17, 132, 133
Macquarie University 55
Magein Avot 72, 73
Maharil 100, 125
Maimonides 15, 66, 157, 159
major mode 72
El Male Rachamim 123
Malkhuyyot 138, 140
Manchester 101
Mantua 158
Maoz Tzur 17, 112, 132–134
marches 11, 26
Mars 160
matbeah shel tefillah 42
Matisyahu 9
Matson, Albert 46
medieval period 10, 27, 52, 79, 119, 122, 123, 125, 126, 139, 142, 151, 157, 159
Megillah 135–137
Meir ben Isaac of Worms 122
Men of the Great Assembly 139
Mendelssohn, Felix 82–83
Mesopotamia 117
Messianic era 48, 71
Mexico City 23
mezuzah 22, 97
Mi Chamocha 17, 37, 85, 113, 119, 124, 133, 138
Mi Shebeirach 55, 75
Mi-Sinai tunes 17, 52, 100, 123, 124, 125–126, 140, 142
Mi Yimalel 132

Middle East 103, 126
midrash 16, 135–137
Midrash Esther 136
Milken Archive of Jewish Music 56
Miller, Benzion 148
minhag 98–100
minor mode 72
Mintz, Yocheved 2
minyan 15, 31, 47, 147
Miriam 12, 55, 121, 130, 138
Mirisch, Robert 2
Mishnah 22, 49, 157
Misnagdim 77–78
Mississippi 23
Mitchell, Joni 43
mitzvah 16, 54, 81, 87–88, 96–98, 131
Mitzvah Gedolah 131
Mizrahi 21, 126
Modzitz 78
Moldova 23
Montreal 101
Mordecai 135
Morocco 31, 45, 71, 141, 144
Morrison, Richard 75
Moses 12, 29, 30, 31, 32, 38, 52, 65, 100, 116, 120, 121, 124, 125–126, 138, 142, 159
Mount Sinai 28, 73, 116, 121, 124, 125–126, 142, 159
mourning 49, 65, 69
Mozart, Wolfgang Amadeus 89
music therapy 72–73, 74–75, 102, 108–109

Nachman of Breslov 68, 108, 111
"Napoleon's March" 81
National Federation of Temple Youth 39
Nebuchadnezzar 136
Neilah 81
Neolithic stones 19
Neusner, Jacob 98
New Age 93
New Mexico 89
New York 28, 57, 101, 158
New York Philharmonic 57
Newman, Harry 155–156
Nietzsche, Friedrich 65, 95
niggun 68, 79–80, 81, 82–83, 97–98, 110, 143, 145
Ninth Mass of the Virgin 140
Ninth of Av 136
nostalgia 43, 96–98
Nulman, Macy 110
Numbers 150

numinous 59–60
nusach ha-tefillah 6, 27, 32, 39–41, 101, 103, 104

obsessive-compulsive disorder 41
oneg Shabbat 35
Opatoshu, Joseph 149
organ 81, 84, 158, 164, 166
Orthodox Judaism 27, 38, 49, 93, 96, 97, 99, 103, 104, 116, 129, 132, 151, 158
Oseh Shalom 28, 48
Otto, Rudolf 59–61
Ovadia, Haim 2

pagoda 147
Paleolithic paintings 19
Palestrina, Giovanni 24–25
Papua New Guinea 55
Pardes 45–46
Passover 12, 17, 33, 117–119, 131, 140
Peninah 66
Persia 45, 135, 136
Peshat 45–46
pesukei d'zimra 61–62, 84
Pharaoh 12, 112, 120, 121
Pharisees 50
Philo of Alexandria 159
piano 53–54, 82, 167
Piar, Carlos R. 2
Poland 105, 115
Pool, David de Sola 101
Presley, Elvis 36
prophet 20, 37, 52, 66, 90, 148–149
Protestantism 53, 59, 127, 128, 158u
Prussia 139
Psalmodic Science vs. Psalmodic Sciolism 46
Psalms 1, 9, 29, 44, 62, 65, 67, 72, 75, 80, 83–84, 89, 112, 114, 130, 132, 149, 162, 165
Purim 131, 134–137
Pythagoras 159

rabbinic Judaism 9, 12, 15, 23, 45, 48–50, 51, 66, 68, 99, 114, 117, 135, 136, 150
ragtime 92
Rashi 49
Rebbe of Kossov 154–155
Reconstructionist Judaism 104
Red Sea 1, 13, 65, 113, 120, 121, 130, 138
Reform Judaism 38, 39, 93, 101, 103, 104, 143, 158, 162
reggae 9, 62
Remez 45–46

Renaissance 24, 62, 158
Renewal Judaism 31, 93, 103, 104
Rhapsody in Blue 128
Richards, Stephen 49–50
rikkud 85–86
Robinson, Reuben T. 166
Rochester, Kathleen 2
Rosenbaum, Samuel 5
Rosenblatt, Yossele 152, 153
Rosh Hashanah 17, 123, 124, 129, 136, 139
Rossi, Salamone 158
Rothblum, Moshe 43
Routley, Erik 169
Russia 23, 69, 81, 139, 141, 144

Sachs, Curt 127–128
Sacks, Oliver 41
Sadigora 143–144
Saliers, Don E. 69, 74, 164
Sambatyon 122
Samuel 66
Sanctus 140
Sartre, Jean-Paul 88
Saul 108–109
SCAN for Solo Flute 89
Schillebeeckx, Edward 28
Schnee, Elaine 2
Schoenberg, Arnold 25
Second Maccabees 132
Secular Humanist Judaism 104
Secunda, Sholom 5
seder 33, 117, 118
Sendrey, Alfred 11
Sephardic Judaism 9, 26, 37, 45, 71, 101, 117, 121, 126, 141
sermon 18, 35, 90–91, 156–157
Sha-arei Tziyon 154
Shabbat 12, 29, 37, 41–43, 44, 49, 50, 72, 87, 103, 107–111, 113, 114–115, 116, 118, 121
Shabbat Shalom 110
Shalom Aleichem 28, 48, 110, 115–116, 123
Sharlin, William 2, 44, 142, 154, 158
Shavuot 17, 118, 121–123, 131
Shearith Israel 158
Shekhinah 68
sheliach tzibbur 31, 148, 149, 153
Shema 43, 112, 140
Shemini Atzeret 130
Shiloh 66
shir koddesh 47–48
Shirah 121

Shnuer Zalman of Liadi 80, 81
shofar 70
shomer shabbos 97
Shostakovich, Dmitri 128
shtetl 153
Shulhan Arukh 31
Shuster, Diane Tickton 161
Sidney 55
Sim Shalom 48, 85, 163
Simchat Torah 130–131
Simeon bar Yochai
Sirota, Gershon 153
Slobin, Mark 101, 102, 105
"*So weiss ich eins*" 133
Sod 45–46
Sola, David Aaron de 121
Solomon 1, 65, 159
Song of Songs 65, 117–118
Song of the Sea 1, 12–13, 48, 112, 120–121
Souchay, Marc-André 82
Spain 105, 107, 141
Spencer, Herbert 32
Stetson, Brad 2
Stone, Jon R. 2
Stonehenge 19
Strom, Yale 23–24
Sufism 105
Sukkot 118
Sulzer, Salomon 43, 143, 158, 163
Sweden 23
Sweeney, Marvin A. 2
The Symbolism of Music 42
Syrian-Greeks 131

tallit 22
Talmud 1, 12, 15, 49, 68, 99, 109, 118, 125, 130, 132, 141, 153, 165
Taubman, Craig 25
tefillin 97
Temple (Jerusalem) 13, 14, 17, 20, 29, 30, 44, 49–50, 62, 105, 112, 117, 114, 118, 119, 132, 133, 136, 137, 139, 150–151, 159, 162
Ten Commandments 122
Tetragrammaton 114, 136
Texas 71
Thesaurus of Hebrew Oriental Melodies 45, 144, 145
Thirty-Four Years on the Bimah 153
timbrel 48, 65
Tomaino, Concetta M. 102
Torah 10–12, 13, 15, 16, 17, 22, 38, 85, 110, 118, 120, 121, 122, 130–131, 135, 136, 151, 159

totem pole 147
Tourette's syndrome 41
trumpet 70, 113, 120, 135, 159
Tubal-Cain 11
Tunisia 71
Twain, Mark 40
tzaddik 68, 77
tzitzit 97

Union Hymnal 158
University of London 75
Uriel 160

van der Leeuw, Gerardus 130
van Rooy, Herrie 2
Vayekhulu 11–112
Veshamru 43, 113–114
Veterans Administration 72
Vienna 140
Vilna Gaon 77, 141
Vinaver, Chemjo 26
violin 23, 70, 89
V'samachta B'chagecha 131

waltz 40, 81, 140
war 65
Weber, Max 37
wedding 13, 36, 49, 55, 117–118, 164
Weiss, Sam 143
Welch, Graham 75
Wells, Thornton 67–68

Werner, Eric 5, 119, 133, 140
White Christmas 128
Wissenschaft des Judentums 4
work songs 13–134
The World in Six Songs 64–65
World War II 72
Wurman, Felix 89
Wuthnow, Robert 35

"Yellow Submarine" 142
Yemen 45, 71, 94, 105, 144
Yerushalayim shel Zahav 48
Yiddish 23, 104, 122, 149
Yigdal 84
Yih'yu L'ratzon 85
Yism'chu 43, 85
Yisrael Meir Kagen 139
"YMCA" 127
Yom Kippur 17, 81, 85, 123, 124, 127–128, 129, 131, 136
Yom Tov 49
youth 33, 38, 39, 94, 96

Zamenhof, L.L. 23
Zamir Choral Foundation 160
Zeh Dodi 118
zemirot 108, 109
Zevi, Shabbatai 77
Zionism 89, 99, 104
Zochreinu 116
Zunz, Leopold 119

www.ingramcontent.com/pod-product-compliance
Lightning Source LLC
Chambersburg PA
CBHW032101300426
44116CB00007B/838